D0828570

Aspects of Bengali History and Society

Rachel Van M. Baumer
Editor

ASIAN STUDIES PROGRAM
UNIVERSITY OF HAWAII
THE UNIVERSITY PRESS OF HAWAII

Library of Congress Cataloging in Publication Data

Main entry under title:

Aspects of Bengali history and society.

  (Asian studies at Hawaii; no. 12)
  "Essays delivered by most of the guest speakers in a seminar on Bengal
convened in the spring of 1972 at the University of Hawaii."
  Includes bibliographical references and index.
  1. Bengal—Civilization—Addresses, essays, lectures.
2. Bengal—History—Addresses, essays, lectures.
I. Baumer, Rachel Van M., 1928–   ed. II. Series.
DS3.A2A82 no. 12 [DS485.B44]   915.4′14′03 73–90491
ISBN 0–8248–0318–3

Dedicated

to the memory of our colleagues whose lives and fruitful scholarship were cut off during the independence struggle in Bangladesh.

অবনতাবস্থায়ও বঙ্গমাতা রত্নপ্রসবিনী।

– বঙ্কিমচন্দ্র

Contents

Introduction

This volume presents essays delivered by most of the guest speakers in a seminar on Bengal convened in the spring of 1972 at the University of Hawaii. The seminar was organized by several South Asianists at the University of Hawaii out of their concern for the independence struggle in Bangladesh and for United States foreign policy toward the emerging nation and its friends. It was their view that the events leading up to and culminating in the war for independence could not be adequately understood unless a knowledge of social and political development over a period of several centuries in Bengal provided a basis for judgment. Their intention in the seminar was twofold: to provide students with a rigorous interdisciplinary study of Bengal that would result in new insights into its contemporary problems, and to provide a group of Bengal specialists with an opportunity to address themselves to certain aspects of history and society that they understand to be influential on current developments in Bengal.

The essays in this volume deal with three time units in the history of Bengal—the middle period, the nineteenth century, and the twentieth century.

The first essay, by Edward C. Dimock, Jr., describes his efforts to find sources of contemporary Hindu-Muslim antagonism in the medieval literature. Changes in family structure and social and world views in the late middle and early modern periods are the subject of Tapan Raychaudhuri's study. These two essays take a brief look at an earlier period in Bengali history and society.

The following four essays deal primarily with the nineteenth century, although Blair B. Kling's study covers the transitional period from the middle to the modern history of Bengal, as well. While Kling's contribution deals with practical and material aspects of upper-class Bengali life, the next three essays are concerned with intellectual debate and developing ideas in the scintillating decades of the Bengal renaissance. John N. Gray, a graduate student in the seminar, offers a critique of David Kopf's and my essays and goes on to develop a theory which would extend our work a step further. Readers will notice that these studies deal almost exclusively with the Hindu community in the nineteenth century, an imbalance which may seem to reflect lack of deep involvement on the part of the Muslim community in the social and intellectual ferment of the century. This dearth of Western scholarship concerned with the Bengali Muslims is a subject to which I shall return.

J. H. Broomfield and John R. McLane both concern themselves with aspects of the independence movement in the twentieth century and the phenomenon of communal politics. Nicolaas Luykx traces the evolvement of public policy on rural development in East Bengal, including the role played by American agencies in development projects.

The bibliographic essay by David Kopf is devoted entirely to publications by Bengal specialists in American universities. Sufficient time was not available to cover the vast literature on Bengal produced by scholars of many countries. In addition it seemed appropriate to this volume to discuss the work of American specialists, most of whom had been trained on United States government grants intended to provide the nation with resources of specialized knowledge of the various areas of the world, including Bengal.

Bringing together the work of nine authors in a single volume results in a certain amount of variety, most obviously in style. Scarcely less obvious in this volume are differences of spelling and use of diacritics in foreign words and names. Several years ago the Bengal Studies Group made a serious effort to standardize a system of transliteration for Bengali words; nevertheless, wide variations still exist in the methods of Bengal specialists. The problem with proper names is even greater. Some writers use a transliteration of the name as spelled in Bengali; others use anglicized spellings, many of which were used by the owners of the names themselves when writing in English. Given the extent of variation in these essays, it seemed best to let each author keep his own system rather than inflict the radical changes that would be necessary in some essays in order to employ a uniform method throughout the volume. The result of this decision is that a single name may appear in several versions if it appears in more than one contribution.

Finally, these essays, while dealing exclusively with Bengal, undoubtedly contain much that is of interest to other South Asianists and quite possibly will furnish materials for area specialists of other regions who are interested in comparative studies. Still it must be pointed out that a collection of essays is often less than what its planners would have hoped to present. Although this volume was never intended to be an introductory or comprehensive work on Bengal, it was expected to be more representative of the studies done in the various periods of Bengal's history. Unfortunately, three excellent essays, on society in ancient India, anthropology, and art history, were not submitted for publication. Larger problems have also provided obstacles to the fulfillment of our objectives. The singular lack of substantial material on the Bengali Muslim community in this volume reflects the limited amount of research done on that group by Bengal specialists in American universities. A few younger scholars have now begun to work in that area, thus undertaking to correct a major neglect of many years. Other areas of study similarly have not been approached by American scholars, or, in fact, by anyone else. The present work simply offers the views of a number of scholars on elements from their own areas of research influential on the contemporary history of Bengal. If, as a secondary result, research is stimulated in areas about which this publication is silent, it will have made our effort doubly worthwhile.

There is particular pleasure in writing this final paragraph of these introductory remarks, the paragraph traditionally reserved for acknowledgment of help received in the preparation of the volume. This work, like most others, could not have come into existence without a great deal of help from people whose names are not listed in the table of contents. Of fundamental help in both the planning and the execution of the seminar were Professors Harry Friedman and Burton Stein. Without the practical and intellectual contributions of these two colleagues at Hawaii, neither the seminar nor the volume would have been possible. The University of Hawaii and its Asian Studies Program joined together in providing all the funding for both the seminar and the publication, a noteworthy undertaking in this time of academic poverty. The support and recommendations of the Asian Studies Publications Committee, and the excellent clerical assistance of Machiko Tsuruya, have been directly responsible for placing this volume in your hands.

RACHEL VAN M. BAUMER
Honolulu

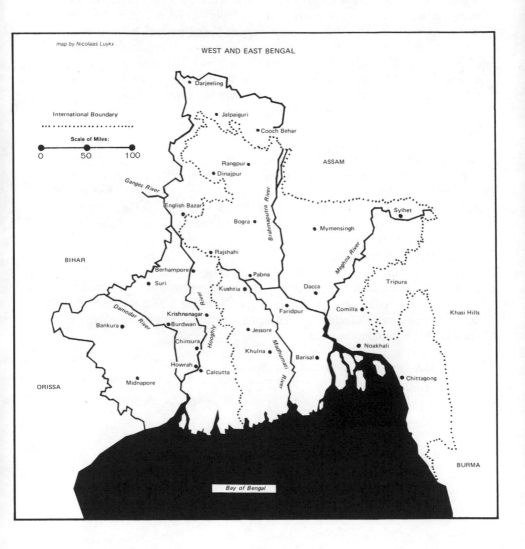

map by Nicolaas Luykx

WEST AND EAST BENGAL

International Boundary
• • • • • • • • • • • • • • • • • • •

Scale of Miles:

0   50   100

• Darjeeling

• Jalpaiguri

• Cooch Behar

ASSAM

Ganges River

• Rangpur
• Dinajpur

English Bazar

• Bogra

Brahmaputra River

• Sylhet

• Mymensingh

Meghna River

BIHAR

• Rajshahi

Berhampore
• Suri
Damodar River
• Bankura
Krishnanagar
• Burdwan
Chinsura
Howrah
• Calcutta
• Midnapore

• Pabna
• Kushtia

• Dacca

Tripura

Khasi Hills

• Faridpur

• Comilla

River

Hooghly

• Jessore

Khulna

Madhumati River

Barisal

• Noakhali

• Chittagong

ORISSA

BURMA

Bay of Bengal

Hinduism and Islam in Medieval Bengal

EDWARD C. DIMOCK, JR.
University of Chicago

The Hindu-Muslim riots in January 1964—those which, some may remember, were touched off by the theft of the Prophet's hair—are the only
ones I have ever seen but they made an indelible impression. The scenario
of the riots in Calcutta, if described, should sound familiar, for it would
be reminiscent of more recent scenes in Bangladesh.

After the Gurkhas had quieted the city, I went to Dacca. On a panel in
Washington not long ago, I heard the remark that communal riots have
been frequent in India, but rare in East Bengal and nonexistent in West
Pakistan. I do not know about West Pakistan, but Dacca in 1964 suggests
that such remarks stem from a common type of selective vision. The
government of India in 1964 sent a judicial commission to interview Hindu
refugees and find out what had happened. Here are two completely
random and typical excerpts from the report of that commission:

> On the night of January 3, 1964, a large mob attacked and set fire to Hindu
> houses in the village. People started running and they were chased. Quite a
> lot of persons got killed, others burnt to death. The mob was shouting
> with glee and also shouting the slogan "Jehad." Many women were
> abducted, ravished, and killed. [Case K 746, p. 61]

> During the looting many Hindus took refuge in the bazaar, which was
> attacked by a large gang of Muslims who started killing people including
> women and children indiscriminately. They snatched away suckling chil-
> dren from the arms of their mothers, killed them in one stroke as one breaks
> an egg, and threw them into the river. They also threw the dead and muti-
> lated bodies of older persons into the river. The water of the river turned
> red, the surface strewn with innumerable bodies. [Case DN 117, p. 141][1]

1

The report is a long one, and these interviews are in every way typical. In many cases the Muslims specified as committing the atrocities were Biharis (a general term for non-Bengalis); but this is not always specified. And if the stories from Bangladesh are true—that the murders of the day before Dacca fell, the killing of people from the university and elsewhere, were committed by right-wing Bengali Muslim extremists from the Al-Badr and Al-Shams groups—one is forced to wonder.

Political history was not my concern before 1964, nor has it been since. But the violence was of such a degree that it seemed to me that it could only have stemmed from hatred of many centuries duration. Yet in my reading of texts from the so-called medieval period (fifteenth to eighteenth centuries) I had found little indication of such deep-rooted antagonism. The sixteenth-century *Kavikaṅkan Caṇḍī*, of the keen-eyed and witty Mukundarām, accepts the fact of Hindus living side by side with Muslims with perfect equanimity. The writer seems to look upon the Muslims as simply another caste, somewhat varied in occupation. His description of the settlement of the new town of Gujarāta runs in part, in Ron Inden's translation, like this:

> [He] brought subjects of many castes [*jāti*] to the town. . . . Many Muslims settled there, receiving the hero's pan. He gave them the western quarter. . . . They rise at dawn, spread out their red-colored mats, and prostrate themselves five times. With Cholemānī garlands, they mutter prayers to the Pīr Pegambar and light evening lamps in the pīr's hall. Kinsmen, sitting in groups of ten to twenty, constantly deliberate on the Quran. . . . They do not abandon their ways; they wear tightly tied pājāmā and on their heads ten-striped caps. . . . Some marry according to Hindu usage. . . . Hindus who have become Muslims are called Garsāl. Those who become blind only at night, beg during the night.[2]

The last two lines are particularly interesting, as is the tone of respect that runs throughout. The last line is funny; the next to last means that Hindu converts are looked down upon, *garsāl* being a term of disrespect. This despite the fact that conversion is traditionally in Islam quite a legitimate way of gaining adherents to the faith. Recently, in a paper given at Chicago, T. N. Madan of Delhi University told the story of how, in Kashmir, that other "seam" of two cultures, he knew a Brahman who had converted to Islam out of loneliness and a desire to marry. Not only would no Muslim girl marry him, but he was ostracized by both cultures. To the meaning of life and accommodation in such cultural seams I shall return.

Nor was I able to find much evidence of a consistent religious antagonism between Hindus and Muslims in the great body of medieval Bengali literature, that of the Vaiṣṇavas. In these texts is found suggestion of an occasional campaign designed to destroy Hindu temples; Sanātana Gos-vāmin, who had been a high minister in the court of Husain Shah (1494–1525), left the service of the king because the king was about to embark upon a campaign in Orissa, in which temples would be destroyed. There are stories of how (though this takes place in northern India) an image of Kṛṣṇa had to be moved from place to place for fear that the Muslims would capture and defile it. There are stories of how Muslims would come to the houses of recalcitrant Hindu officials and sacrifice cattle in the Caṇḍī-maṇḍapa, thereby defiling it and its owner. And there are oc-casional *qāzi* who treat individual Vaiṣṇavas harshly: one such has the great disciple Haridāsa brutally whipped through twenty-two market-places because, although born in a Muslim family, Haridāsa refused to recite the Koran and iterate his faith in Islam. Here, though, it seems to be Haridāsa's apostasy rather than his Vaiṣṇavism that brought about this cruel treatment. There are other *qāzi* who speak the name of Kṛṣṇa and are thus saved; for, says Haridāsa, even if a Muslim uses the term *harām* ("defiled, unclean"), he is saved, that word having the name of Rāma embedded in it. And still other *qāzi* allow, extraordinarily, the *nagara-kīrtan*, the Vaiṣṇava street procession; this, from the attention given it in the texts, was an unusual concession. Cases of oppression and even antagonism seem to be random, and for every instance of hostility there is one in the other direction. Husain Shah may have destroyed temples in Orissa; but the *Caitanya-Caritāmṛta* text (II:25:184ff.) has this to say about his personal relations with Hindus:

> Subuddhi Rāya had been a ruler in Gauṛa, formerly, and Husain Shāh Sāyed was his servant. He gave him a commission, to excavate a tank; he made a mistake, and Rāya hit him with a whip. Afterwards, when Husain Shāh himself had become king of Gauṛa, he paid much respect to Subuddhi Rāya. His wife, seeing the marks of the whipping on his body, told the king to whip Subuddhi Rāya. But the king said: Rāya was my protector and was like a father. It is not proper that I should strike him. And his wife said: If you will not take his life, take his caste. And the king replied: If I take his caste, he will not live.[3]

There may have been cruel *qāzi*; but there were others in this high ad-ministrative post who respected their very real social ties with Hindus, based on village relationships. *Caitanya-Caritāmṛta* 1:17:140ff. tells us that one *qāzi*, speaking to Caitanya, said:

> You have come in anger; I remained hidden to pacify you. Now you have been pacified, and I have come to meet you. It is my good fortune that I have received such a guest as you. By village relationship Cakravartī [i.e., Caitanya's maternal grandfather] is my father's brother; village relation-ship is stronger than blood-ties. Nīlambara Cakravartī is your mother's

father, and so you are my nephew. A maternal uncle always endures the anger of his nephew, and a nephew does not take offense at his maternal uncle.

Even further, as I have tried to suggest elsewhere,[4] there were Muslim poets who wrote on Hindu themes: the beauty of the Ganges (Daraf Kahn, in Sanskrit) or the love between Rādhā and Kṛṣṇa. The following poem, though not the best that could be found, is not atypical:

> You do not know how to play the flute.
> You play it at the wrong times. You care nothing for me.
> When I am sitting with my elders,
> you call me with your flute. I could die of shame.
> You play it on the farther bank. I hear it here.
> I am an unlucky girl; I do not know how to swim.
>
> If you find the bamboo clump from which this flute was made,
> tear it up by the roots and throw it in the river!
>
> Cānd Qāzi says: I hear the flute, my life ebbs from me—
> I shall not live, unless I see my Hari.

Except for the signature line, it is a Vaiṣṇava song. Whether the poet was a Vaiṣṇava or whether he was simply substituting the names of Rādhā and Kṛṣṇa for the Sufi concepts of the soul and God is not known. Whichever the case, it is clear that there was no scorn, on the part of the Muslims who wrote these songs, at least, of the Vaiṣṇava form of Hinduism.

Nor is there scorn of Islam on the part of the Vaiṣṇavas. When, in the biographies, Caitanya is arguing with one Muslim or another, he treats his antagonist just as he treats the Vedāntins and other Hindus: he does not tell them that they are wrong, merely that they have misread and misinterpreted their own scriptures. In the *Caitanya-Caritāmṛta*, Caitanya argues in the following way (illustrating, perhaps less than in some other places, its author Kṛṣṇadāsa's interesting ideas of the Koran and Islamic theology).

Caitanya with four companions is on his way home from a pilgrimage to Vṛndāvana; they are in a forest, and he has fallen unconscious in a fit. The party is approached by some Muslim soldiers, Pathans, who accuse Caitanya's four companions of having poisoned him to rob him. Two of Caitanya's companions are from western India, and two are from Bengal. Indicative of the attitude of the Pathans toward Bengalis is the Muslim leader's remark: "You two are from the west and are good men; but these two Gauṛiyas [i.e., Bengalis] are rogues; and so they tremble" (II:18:162). II:18:177–188 reads:

> And among those mlecchas [i.e., Muslims] there was a most brave man; he
> wore black cloth, and people called him "pīr." His heart softened when he

saw Prabhu [i.e., Caitanya]. "Our own śāstras [i.e., the Koran] establish the qualityless Brahmā and preach nondualism." Prabhu refuted his arguments using those very śāstras. . . . Prabhu said: "In your śāstras the qualityless [God] is established; in your śāstras it says at the end that īśvara [God] is one, that his body is dark in color, and that he is full of all divine qualities. . . . From him are creation, establishment, and destruction, the equal refuge for worlds both gross and subtle; he is the best of all things, to be worshipped by all, and is the cause of causes. . . . Except for service of him, the worldly pain of the living creature does not pass away; love at his feet is the essence of the meaning of mankind. . . . None of your pandits understand your śāstras, and that among injunctions what is earlier and what is later, that which is later is stronger. Examine your own śāstras, and ascertain what has been written there at the end.

But as Joseph O'Connell points out in his doctoral dissertation "Social Implications of the Gaudiya Vaisnava Movement"[5]—and it should be noted that much of this essay owes a debt to that excellent study—by and large the Vaisnavas do not seem to single out the Muslims by religion. They treat them, as we have seen Mukundarām do, as a caste among many other castes, having odd customs of dress, but having a place, just as do Brahmans and Kayasthas, in a complex society. The terms *Muslim* or *Mussulman* are not used by Vaisnavas to single out this beard-bearing, cap-wearing group until texts of the late eighteenth and even nineteenth centuries *(Prema-vilāsa* and *Bhakta-mālā).*[6] Before these relatively late dates the terms used were secular: Muslims were called *mleccha*, which was not originally very complimentary, meaning something like "barbarian," and *yavana*, which is simply "foreigner" and is applied to Greeks as well as to Muslims. From the other point of view, the term *Hindu* is used sometimes by Muslims, and sometimes also by Hindus, but only when they are addressing Muslims. It must be remembered, however, that in the middle period it is quite possible that the term was not used to designate a religious community, as it is today, but a people inhabiting a geographically definable piece of territory. The term comes from the name of the Indus River and was used by the Greeks and later by other invaders from the west to designate the people of a strange new land. So it is far from certain that Muslims were using this term in a religious sense; the usage possibly denotes no more about religion than the terms *Bengali* or *Maharashtrian*: geography, language, and culture of which religion is but a part.

Hindus, when they are talking among themselves, speak of Vaisnavas and Śāktas, Brahmans and *purohit*. When they use the term *Hindu*, it is to reply to Muslims in categories the Muslims themselves use. The *Caitanya-Caritāmṛta*, interestingly, uses the term *Hindu-dharma*, which would suggest that Muslims saw a specifically Hindu way of looking at things, on a couple of occasions. In the passage where Caitanya is confronting the *qāzi* who has tried to stop the *nagara-kīrtan*, he says:

> You are the qāzi, and have power over hindu-dharma; but you do not use it. I do not understand this respect. [I:17:174]
>
> In the city the hindu-dharma grows greatly; nothing is heard except for the sound of the name of Hari. [I:17:193]

As O'Connell points out, in the first of these statements there is recognition of the potential power of repression that lies in the hands of the Muslims. But there is also recognition of the fact that it is not being used. To the Vaiṣṇavas, not only were the Muslims acceptable as one religious and social group among many, but their political dominance was also accepted, if with some trepidation. Vṛndāvana-dāsa in his *Caitanya-bhāgavata* uses the term *kālā-yavana* ("the *yavana* as death") and *mahātībrayavana* ("most cruel *yavana*").[7] But so long as this potential was not realized, the Vaiṣṇavas were content. Their real enemies were the Hindu *pasaṇḍī*, Brahmans antagonistic to Vaiṣṇavism who tried to bring about persecution by informing Husain Shah of the prophecy, Christian-like, that a revolt in Navadvīp, Caitanya's city, would rid the land of *yavana* rule. The Vaiṣṇavas did not go so far as the *Śunya-purāna*, a text of the cult of the god Dharma which rejoices in the Muslim conquest, seeing it as chastisement of proud Brahmans;[8] but neither, so long as there was no systematic persecution, did they attempt anything except coexistence.

If such mutual understanding and even sympathy were present in the seventeenth century, the contrast is at least impressive, with pictures of burning bustees and people being shot from rooftops as they fled the flames seemingly typical of the twentieth. O'Connell (p. 63) paraphrases Muin ud din Ahmad Khan's *History of the Fara'idi Movement in Bengal, 1818–1906* as follows:

> Even though the total Muslim population of Bengal probably was larger than elsewhere the population became polarized into antagonistic competing Hindu and Muslim communities only in the 20th century and then only after intensive efforts to pry Bengali Muslims loose from their Bengali cultural moorings.

If this is true, it will take a historian of British India to explain why. And if it is true, it will suggest further that Bengal in this as in other respects cannot be fully included in the generalizations made about India. Bernard Cohn, in conversation, tells of genuine Hindu-Muslim riots in Benares as early as 1809, with all the trappings thereof: temples desecrated by the slaughter of cattle, destruction of temples to build mosques, and so forth. And in the middle of the nineteenth century in Kerala there were riots, at first for economic reasons but later polarized along communal lines, the reports of which sound much like those taken in Calcutta in 1964. At this point it might be helpful to go back to the beginning.

Every region of the Indian subcontinent differs from every other region in a variety of ways, and each region varies in different ways from the two main classical traditions that otherwise unite them—the Sanskritic tradition and the Perso-Arabic tradition of Islam. It can be argued that Bengal differs more than most. In the first place, long before the coming of Islam, Bengal was recognized as far from the heartland of the Indo-Aryan people, in the upper Gangetic plain. Bengal was quite literally beyond the pale, and in early Sanskrit texts references to the place are invariably full of scorn. A Jaina text points out that Bengal is a perilous place in which to travel, being filled with barbarians who think nothing of murdering even monks.[9] Other texts say that Bengal is so impure that those who are ill-advised enough to go there must submit to ritual purification upon their return to God's country.[10] And there is the legend of the king Adisura, who wanted to perform an elaborate Vedic sacrifice but could not find any priests in Bengal with enough knowledge to do it; so he sent to the west for these priests, and they came and performed the sacrifice and were rewarded with lands on which they established hierarchical societies with themselves at the top.[11] And in Mogul times, generals were sent to Bengal as punishment,[12] for the place, as one of them succinctly put it, was a malarial swamp. Besides, the Bengalis were always revolting about one thing or another, and more often than not succeeding, because they knew the watery terrain and how to use it.

If the British had had any control over history, it is certain that they would not have established their capital at Calcutta. But history, with her incomparable sense of humor, had seen fit to have Job Charnock establish his trading post in those three little villages on the Hugli. The British did not much like Bengal, or the Bengalis either. If one scans the texts written by servants of the Company, or even Kipling, one cannot but be struck by phrases like "toadying, sly and deceitful, cowardly, pompous, slight of build and dark of skin" applied to the Bengalis. By contrast, the people of northwestern India were "tall, strong, and brave, eaters of beef, direct and truthful, courageous enemies and staunch friends." And so the native regiments of the British armies were made up of these people—Panjabis, Pathans, Baluchis, warlike peoples with qualities much like those the British considered their own. In *Black Watch* (1929), brave Muslim troops from the northwest frontier, fighting side by side with their red-coated comrades, save India for England during World War I, taking their place in the British military Hall of Fame beside the Fuzzy Wuzzy, as those first-class fightin' men hurl themselves forever against the British square.

Some have characterized the Bengalis as paranoid. But it is not paranoia if somebody really is after you. So many factors have had their effect: the geographical location of Bengal on the far eastern end of Indo-Aryan expansion so far as Hindus are concerned, cut off from the birthplace of Islam (and geography is significant in Islam, as the fact of the hajj attests) to the Muslims; the contempt of the British for lacking warlike qualities and of the Brahmans from other parts of India for eating fish and mispronouncing Sanskrit. These factors alone, contrasting with and stimulating a pride in intellect, in language and literature, have understandably made Bengalis feel apart. And, too, there is the Bengali pride in the motherland, shared by Hindus and Muslims alike. It is not insignificant that the anthem of Bangladesh, written by the non-Muslim Tagore, *Āmār sonār bāṅglā*, explicitly speaks of Bengal as mother. Nor is the poem written by the Muslim Nazrul Islam insignificant:

> We are two flowers on one stem [or, in a Bengali pun, at one nipple][13]—
> Hindu and Muslim—
> the Muslim the jewel of the eye, the Hindu the breath—
> that sky is one, where moon and sun swing, in the lap of the mother,
> one blood in the deeps of the heart, one the pull of that pounding pulse.[14]

Full-fledged Muslim invasions of Bengal began in the thirteenth century. There had been a trickle of Sufis, some gentle and some warlike, at earlier times; and the Muslims ruled the place, either from local courts in Bengal or from imperial courts in Delhi, until the defeat of Sirāj-ud-ullāh by the British at Plassey in 1757. When Islam came to India in the tenth century, it arrived with a religious book, a complete set of interpretations of that book, a set of laws, and a social structure relatively fixed. Because of this cultural cohesion, Peter Hardy argues, Islam was able to retain a kind of "cultural apartheid" vis-à-vis the Hindus. It is true, he admits, that the Muslim rulers of Delhi and elsewhere used Hindus in the administration of their vast empires and that Hindus sometimes reached positions of great power in these administrative networks. It is also true that Akbar was a student of Hindu among other scriptures, that Dara Shikoh, eldest son of Shah Jahan, was a profound and serious student of Hindu philosophy, and that syncretistic cults such as that of Kabir sought to blend the religious systems by seeking the best in both of them. But, Hardy would say, Akbar, Dara Shikoh, Abul Fazl, and the rest were exceptions, and Kabir came from, and spoke to, the lower cultural orders.[15]

In regard to Bengal, his argument would be harder to make. It is true that one stratum of Bengali Muslim society is the *ashrāf*—Muslims of the aristocracy who seek to preserve the cultural apartheid, looking to the west for their heritage and claiming descent from the lineally pure invaders, who in their turn were descended from those close to the Prophet. Some question the historicity of this claim; in an excellent thesis for the Australian National University, Ashim Roy characterizes the *ashrāf* as follows: "The upper strata of the Muslim society in Bengal had thus been organized into a distinct social entity on the basis of an amalgam of history and fiction welded onto the body of material power."[16]

Such people are more tied to their western lineage and to Islam than to the Bengali motherland. But there are other strata of Bengali Muslim society. There are village people who, together with their Hindu neighbors, visit, or used to visit, the same shrines, tombs of saints; there are cults shared by Hindu and Muslim, that called Satya-pīr by Muslims and Satyanārāyaṇa by Hindus, for example; there are Hindu festivals celebrated by Muslims, and vice versa; we shall see an example in a moment. And there is the stratum which is Bengali by birth and heritage, and proud of the fact, and which, unlike the village people, see distinctions between Hinduism and Islam and are Islamic in all their habits and beliefs. There may be some among these who, like the *ashrāf*, have contempt for those who make no distinctions and contempt for Hindus. But there are others who see Hindus as fellow Bengalis and fellow human beings, with a right to their own beliefs. They are like the Kashmiri Muslim merchant whose advertising calendar shows the gods of the Hindu pantheon.

The second and third of these three strata have another thing in common—the Bengali language—and it is here that the cultural apartheid between the *ashrāf* and other Muslims in Bengal is most obvious. Let me quote Ashim Roy again:

> Thus in their thought, ideas, and even their language the ashrāf remained, or at least posed to remain, alien to their coreligionists in Bengal, and looked down upon the Muslim masses because they thought themselves nearer to Islam, as they were closer to the Arabic and Persian languages, literature, and culture, which according to them were permeated with Islamic values, while the Bengali language and literature, subjected to the influence of the Hindus, was steeped in idolatry.[17]

Roy quotes Yaqinuddin Ahmad, writing in the *Moslem Chronicle* in 1896: "The Muhammadans of Bengal had leaders who tried their utmost to belong to the northwest. They talked Hindustani, imitated Delhi or Lucknow manners, but in spite of that they were Bengalis."[18] And Ni'am ud din, in *Zudbat ul masa'il* in 1873: "The accomplished men of [Bengal] do not take themselves to Bengali books for the poor quality of the language, not worth listening to. . . . They do not like their children to read them; rather, it is forbidden by many."[19] One cannot take pride in one's language and literature, if one is a Bengali, and be a Muslim. An instructive letter appeared anonymously in the *Moslem Chronicle in* 1895:

Several heathen customs have crept into the society and [innovations in Islamic custom] and [belief in local deities] are practiced with impunity every day by thousands of so-called Mussulmans in their feasts and festivals. There are places where widow-marriage is looked upon with hatred. . . . In every district of Bengal there are benighted places where people profess a corrupt form of Islam . . . they even openly worship Hindu gods and goddesses. Nearly all of the people of [Nadiya district] have Hindu names; their manners and customs are those of Hindus; they celebrate the pujas; they have caste distinctions too. We are choked with inward shame and mortification by witnessing a scene, which we did the other day in Taltola. . . . It was the day of Sripancami puja when we saw troops of Muhammadan lads, children of lower-class people and reading in Hindu patsalas, carrying small flags and chanting heathen ditties in praise of Ma Sarasvati.[20]

If the Bengali *ashrāf* felt this way, how much more so Muslims from the untainted West? For the attitude is that no matter how pure their personal Islamic beliefs and practices, all Bengalis, excepting perhaps the *ashrāf*, have been stained by Hinduism. To become contemporary for a moment, it was reported in the *New York Times* for 13 May 1971 that a Pakistani army major, asked about the army's attack on Dacca University, replied: "We have to consider that an entire generation of students has been lost, because of the laxity and permissiveness of parents. You hear of alcohol drinking and raping going on at the university—things unheard of in a Muslim society." The mention of rape is particularly ironic: but then Bengali Muslim girls are not Muslims.

There are millions of Bengalis, however, who call themselves Muslim; where did they all come from? They are not all *ashrāf*, nor do they all claim to be. O'Connell calculates on the basis of some figures in Abdul Karim's *Social History of the Muslims in Bengal* that in 1650 there were in Bengal 8.6 million Hindus and 4.1 million Muslims. At that time, the Muslims had been in Bengal over three hundred years. Although I have not stopped to calculate it, the original invaders, who probably did not number over a few tens of thousands, would have had to multiply at a prodigious rate. The obvious theory is that most Bengali Muslims became Muslims through large-scale conversions. The question of course is this: If conversions there were, how did they come about and who was converted?

There may have been large-scale forcible conversions. And there are examples of how Hindus lost caste—Subuddhi Rāya, who did finally lose his caste at the insistence of Husain Shah's wife, is an example—by being forced to eat, perhaps, forbidden food and, no longer accepted by the Hindu community, became Muslims. But the case of Subuddhi Rāya is instructive, though no one knows how typical: while some Brahmans told him that he might as well kill himself, others prescribed the simplest possible *prayascitta* (ritual purification): the taking of the name of God. And Mirza Nathan in his history tells of a severe reprimand given a Muslim official for forcibly converting a Hindu. There were such conversions, then, but seemingly not on a vast enough scale to answer the question. Another argument is that lower-caste Hindus and noncaste people, and Buddhists who, everybody seems to feel, were running about the place in numbers, found social and religious satisfaction in Islam, which did not discriminate so rigidly. These, the argument goes, converted voluntarily. All these arguments have some merit; as is often pointed out, not only is it difficult to tell by physical features most Bengali Muslims from most Bengali Hindus, but many Muslims perform the same services as their Hindu neighbors: both are fishermen, both are weavers, both are cultivators, and the like. There were probably high-caste converts too, attracted especially by the warmth of Sufi Islam; Sanātana Gosvāmin, minister to Husain Shah and later a favorite of Caitanya, seems to have been of a Brahman family, but became a *dārveś*, a Sufi.

It is perhaps unfair to conclude with a series of questions I cannot answer. As to what it all means to Bangladesh: rivers of communal blood have flowed in Bengal and may yet flow. And in Bangladesh the term *communal* takes on a new dimension: there are Hindus who are Hindu and Bengali, Muslims who are Muslim and Bengali, and Muslims who are Muslim but not, psychologically at least, Bengali. The last have hunted the first two, and may be hunted in their turn. Hindus have been hunted by some of the second and most of the third, and may be again. But history has shown too that Bengalis of all communities have lived together, if not always in tranquillity, drawn together, as Nazrul would have it, by the common blood of their common mother. That common blood has soaked the soil of the new nation. One keeps one's fingers crossed and hopes that, as Abul Fazl, minister to the Great Mogul, said, "the thorn of strife and hatred be caused to bloom into a garden of peace."

NOTES

1. *Recent Exodus of Minorities from East Pakistan and Disturbances in India;* a report to the Indian Commission of Jurists by its Committee of Inquiry (New Delhi: Indian Commission of Jurists, 1965).

2. Mukundarām, *Kavi-kaṅkaṇ-caṇḍi,* eds. S. K. Bandyopadhyāy and V. P. Chaudhuri (Calcutta, 1958), pp. 343, 344.

3. Kṛṣṇadās Kavirāj, *Caitanya-Caritāmṛta,* ed. Rādhāgovinda Nāth, 6 vols. (Calcutta, 1949–1950).

4. "Muslim Vaisnava Poets of Bengal," in *Bengal: Regional Identity;* ed. David

Kopf (East Lansing: Michigan State University, 1969).

5.   Unpublished; Harvard, 1970.

6.   I have been told that the terms are so used in texts from Sylhet and Mymensingh as early as the sixteenth century; I have been unable to verify this.

7.   Vṛndāvana-dās, *Caitanya-bhāgavata* (Calcutta, 1952), II:389.

8.   S. B. Dasgupta, *Obscure Religious Cults*, 2nd ed. (Calcutta, 1962), p. 265.

9.   Acaranga Sutra 1.8.3; see W. Norman Brown, "The Place of Bengal in South Asian Studies," in *Bengal East and West*, ed. Alexander Lipski (East Lansing: Michigan State University, 1969), p. 6.

10. R. C. Majumdar, ed., *History of Bengal*, vol. I (Dacca, 1943), p. 8.

11. For a complete discussion and bibliography, see Ronald B. Inden, "Marriage and Rank in Bengali Culture: A Social History of Brahmans and Kayasthas in Middle Period Bengal" (unpublished Ph.D. diss., University of Chicago, 1972), pp. 36–41.

12. See Jadunath Sarkar, *History of Arangzib* (London, 1920), IV:51, 374.

13. *eka bṛnte.*

14. *Nazrul-racanabali*, Vol. II, p. 189, poem 82. Dacca: Kendriya Bangla Unnayan Board, 1970.

15. "Islam in Medieval India," in *Sources of Indian Tradition*, eds. T. de Bary, et al. (New York: Columbia University Press, 1958), p. 370.

16. "Islam in The Environment of Medieval Bengal," 1970, p. 33.

17. Ibid., p. 43.

18. Ibid., p. 44.

19. Ibid., p. 44.

20. Ibid., p. 38.

Norms of Family Life and Personal Morality among the Bengali Hindu Elite, 1600–1850

TAPAN RAYCHAUDHURI
Oxford University

Until at least the latter half of the eighteenth century, our chief sources of information for Bengali social values are the literary and religious texts besides a meager amount of biographical data contained in these very texts. The caste histories and the chronologically uncertain traditions preserved in the district histories written in the nineteenth and twentieth centuries marginally supplement this information. Most of these works are written by the members of the upper castes with traditions of literary education and reflect their values. Even when they write of other orders of society, they present an outsider's image of a different social group and unconsciously interpolate their own values; often the incongruities are obvious; more often the authenticity of the portrait cannot be checked. In the nineteenth century, especially the latter part, descriptions of social groups without any literary traditions become more abundant, but the paucity of evidence for the earlier period precludes any comparison with former conditions or the discussion of any trends over time. A study of social norms in Bengal for the period under discussion has hence to be concerned with the "upper stratum"—"upper" in terms of social status more than anything else—who have been described somewhat loosely as the "elite" for the purposes of this study. This stratum, of course, was not homogeneous, but the sources do indicate a basic uniformity of norms and a limited range of diversities. The differences between the Hindu and the Muslim elites—determined by differences in social organization and religious ideology—were more basic. Such a comparison has not been attempted here, partly to keep the essay within reasonable limits. Finally, the time period covered here is really less awe-inspiring than it seems. The continuity of relevant values is considerable, and even if the starting point of this study were pushed back by two more centuries it would not have made a great difference. The time limits refer simply to the broad chronology of the sources used. The significant changes are concentrated in the last half century and, to some extent, in the last one hundred years of the period.

A striking fact about Bengal's social life before the mid-eighteenth century is the relative absence of the joint family. Although our information on this point is by no means exhaustive, it is too extensive to be explained away as mere coincidence. Several writers of *panchali* in the seventeenth century—Mukundaram, Ruparam, Kshemananda—have left behind some autobiographical data. The life stories of the Vaishnava hagiographers are known, and we have a number of biographies of Chaitanya and his followers. The typical family in nearly all these cases is nuclear and rather small. The heroes and heroines of the medieval ballads are also portrayed as belonging to small nuclear families. The one major exception is to be found in the legend of the merchant Chand, who had seven grown-up sons living with him.

The norms associated with the nuclear family were necessarily different from those of a joint family. Negatively, there was a lack of concern with duties to a wide range of uncles, grand-uncles, cousins, and the like, and family obligations referred typically to one's immediate blood relations. The reverence due to the *jñāti* or the kinship group—especially the latter's right to sit in judgment on one's conduct—was recognized.[1] But the total involvement with the larger kinship group—in terms of one's associations, affections, and family duties—appears to be a later development.

There is only one feature of the joint family one can trace back to the seventeenth-century literature. The aged parents apparently continued to live with the grown-up and married son unless they preferred to live in retirement after a while in the holy city of Benares. In such cases, however, the father became an honored guest rather than the head of the family, although in the domestic setup the daughter-in-law was expected to submit respectfully to the mother-in-law's instructions.[2] The principle that the aged parents were not to interfere with the decisions of their grown-up sons in such households was recognized even in the late eighteenth century, though it was deemphasized if not consciously abandoned later on. The household of Umapati Tarkasiddhanta, great-grandfather of Iswarchandra Vidyasagar, as described by the latter, is an instance in point: "Tarkashiddhanta was very old by now; hence, the affairs of the family were under the control of his son, Ramsundar Vidyabhushan. Therefore, the latter was the real master and his wife the real mistress. According to the custom of the land, Tarkasiddhanta and his wife were mere figureheads; their writ did not run in any sphere."[3] This withdrawal of the older generation from positions of real authority in the family probably stemmed from the basically nuclear character of the family, though the custom persisted even after the joint family had become a marked feature of social life.

By the latter part of the eighteenth century, the joint family was very much an established fact of upper-caste Bengali society. The family annals contained in the district histories and the biographies of the nineteenth-century literary lions compiled by B. N. Banerji confirm this fact. If the seventeenth-century poets were scions of nuclear families, their most famous eighteenth-century counterpart, Bharatchandra, broke away from a family dominated by unfriendly brothers.[4] Vidyasagar's great-grandfathers—both on his mother's and on his father's side—were the heads of large joint families.[5]

Vidyasagar thus described an ideal joint family in the latter years of the eighteenth century, spelling out the contemporary norms:

> On Vidyavagish's death, his eldest son Radhamohan Vidyabhushan be-came the head of the family, the second, Ramdhan Nyayrathna, began to teach in his father's college [Chatushpathi], the third Guruprasad and the fourth Bisweswar Mukherji began to earn their livings in Calcutta. The four brothers lived together in a joint family ["shared a common kitchen]" all their lives; everyone handed over his earnings to the eldest. The eldest was just and equitable in his conduct, as far as was humanly possible. His care and affection for his brothers' families exceeded, if anything, those for his own family. In fine, under his authority nobody had any reason for anger or displeasure. . . . All the four [brothers] were equally worthy and full of goodwill; hence, no one ever found them in mutual dispute or misunderstanding. Leave aside their own families, they never treated differently even their sisters, sisters' daughters and sisters' grandchildren.[6]

The preeminent claims of one's extended family on one's affections were taken for granted by the upper-caste Bengali in the early decades of the nineteenth century. One of the first autobiographies written in Bengali —that of Kartikeyachandra Ray, dewan of the Nadia Raj—repeatedly expresses such sentiments. The author thus described the happy life of his early youth: "All the twelve months in the year I spent at home; I could [thus] see my elders, I was surrounded by my relations, the most desired objects of life." His ancestors who worked for the Nadia Raj had two houses, one near the palace where they lived with their relations "in pleasures and entertainments" and another in a neighboring village for their immediate families. "Therefore, either in their family affairs or

psychologically, they experienced no inconvenience or unhappiness."
He further explains that formerly aristocratic families preferred to live
where their relations could live with them when necessary. The attachment to one's extended family was reinforced by regular instruction in
one's genealogy in all its aspects. The earlier generations knew the genealogy of one's neighbors belonging to other castes as well. A deficiency in
such knowledge was considered a matter for shame. These good practices,
the dewan writing in the latter half of the nineteenth century regretted,
had fallen into disuse. The poignancy of the loss is thus expressed:

> If I do not know the name of my great-grandfather and my kin also does
> not know the name of his great-grandfather, then how should one know
> that they are the same person? Consider, through our ignorance, nothing
> could be known about our close relationship and the joy that could have
> been derived [from the knowledge] or the mutual services we could have
> rendered would not materialize.[7]

In the same vein, while he accepts as entirely natural the friendship of
his cousin (his father's sister's son), he humbly wonders how people
unrelated to him became his close friends.

The tensions within the joint families reflected a conflict of values
traceable largely to the changing economic milieu. An early instance of
an individual opting out of a joint family is that of the eighteenth-century
poet Bharatchandra. Son of an improverished zamindar, Bharat wanted
to follow scholarly pursuits and learned Sanskrit, much to the chagrin of
his elder brothers who saw no possibility of restoring the family fortunes
through such useless knowledge. Bharat left home to make his career.
After some wanderings he eventually became the court poet of Raja
Krishnachandra and set up his separate establishment, refusing to return
to his family.[8] The economic opportunity which the poet found and the
circumstances of the ruin of his ancestral fortune—an armed attack on
their property by the Burdwan maharani—were not atypical of the earlier
centuries. The atypical fact of a zamindar's son trying to make a career
of service and learning Persian for that purpose is, however, not unrelated
with the opportunities in commerce and services, which undoubtedly
increased in the eighteenth century. Significantly enough, Bharat's patron
was the dewan to the French government at Chandernagore and his host
was the dewan to the Dutch at Chinsura. It was only the insight of his
patron which prevented Bharat from following in his footsteps. So long
as the traditional means of livelihood provided a family income to be
shared by all concerned, the only threat to the norms and continuity of
the joint family could arise from a clash of personalities, which tend to be
muted in nonindividualistic societies. The new economic opportunities

created an accent on individual aspirations and, eventually, an inequality of income which undermined the norms of fraternal harmony. This process, witnessed by Kartikeyachandra Ray and Vidyasagar[9] among many others early in the nineteenth century, has slowly worked toward the dissolution of the system.

It would, however, be incorrect to suggest that there was a total revolution in values affecting family life in the late eighteenth or early nineteenth century. The old norms showed in fact a remarkable capacity for survival. The ritual purity of the extended family, as the prime determinant of the family's status, had long been a major preoccupation of the upper-caste Bengali Hindu.[10] When *kulīn* polygamy turned ritual purity of one's *kula* into a lucrative source of income in the course of the eighteenth century, its maintenance and projection were naturally even more emphasized than before. Besides, the reformist assault on orthodox prejudices led to a reinforcement rather than a weakening of older values so far as a large section of the Bengali caste Hindus were concerned. Even individuals influenced by Brahmoism and critical of the *kulīn* preoccupation with ritual purity to the exclusion of all else saw some justification in the orthodox practice of inquiring into the prospective bride's family background as far back as four generations on the ground of the heritability of negative traits.[11] That the inquiry was concerned mainly with ritual purity, especially from the point of view of the matrimonial alliances contracted by the girl's forebears, was apparently overlooked in this argument.

In any society, marriage is one of the major institutions around which the norms of interpersonal relationship tend to crystallize. The peculiar ambivalence of Bengali society with regard to the question of polygamy reveals a conflict of values—between a preference for ritual excellence and a desire for psychological security and domestic peace. Polygamy appears in medieval Bengali literature as an accepted, but exceptional, fact of life. Few medieval Bengali personalities of whose lives we have any knowledge were either polygamous themselves or came from polygamous homes. The same pattern is reflected in the lives of the fictional characters. Marriage to polygamous husbands was considered a great calamity by the bride as well as by her mother.[12] Polygamous homes were described as the abode of continuous quarrels, enough to drive away benign deities.[13] But all such humane considerations were counterbalanced by the status dividends of giving one's daughter in marriage to a ritually pure *kulīn* and, presumably, the expectation of benefits in the hereafter from such an act of religious merit. For reasons not quite clear, *kulīn* polygamy increased enormously during the eighteenth century; yet even during this period and later the majority of *kulīn* must have remained monogamous. The family histories of well-known *kulīn* personalities contain few instances of polygamy. Besides, demographic factors surely acted as a check on this aberration: if some *kulīn* rejoiced in hundreds of wives, most of their fellows would have to be satisfied with one each, the supply of high-caste women being subject to some natural limits. The pathetic fate of *kulīn* women, doomed either to dishonorable spinster-hood in their brothers' households or to a nominal marriage which per-mitted them to meet their husbands only once a year, was described in Bengali literature from the first novel in the language[14] down to the days of Saratchandra.[15] Yet the inhuman system persisted well into the twen-tieth century. Even kindhearted and sensitive men, fully aware of the misery it implied, gave their daughters in marriage to polygamous *kulīn* husbands.[16] In the first half of the nineteenth century, among the caste Hindus the only social group that broke away from this practice com-pletely—under the influence of humanistic and puritanical social ideologies of the West—was the Brahmos.[17]

Another institution which persisted from medieval times well into the twentieth century was that of child marriage. Toward the closing years of the sixteenth century, Mukundaram wrote:

> Blessed is the girl given in marriage at the age of seven. . . . If at the age of nine a daughter is given according to proper rites to a bridegroom, the water offered by her son ensures a place in heaven [for the grandfather]. . . . At the age of twelve, a girl attains puberty and is no longer afraid of men. . . . If on seeing a handsome man, the [unmarried] daughter feels the stirrings of desire, the father will suffer in hell.[18]

Both before Mukundaram and after, the image of the child bride appears repeatedly in medieval Bengali literature. In fact, the "English-educated" youth of the early nineteenth century sought to discover a romantic di-mension in this institution. Kartikeyachandra Ray, married at the age of fifteen, later observed:

> No doubt, the system of child marriage has many faults; but it offers a happiness which courtship [Western style] cannot.. . . . For, at the time of courtship, even if the lover and the beloved may be deeply enamoured, sometimes through accidents their engagements break up. Hence the happiness of courtship is not comparable to that of the first phase in our marriage.[19]

Even among the Brahmos, the age of marriage was pushed up by only a few years; for girls, it hardly ever exceeded fourteen.

As I have discussed elsewhere,[20] the institution of child marriage was linked to the normative requirements of absolute chastity and devotion to one's husband expected of all married women. The literary conventions of the period repeatedly emphasize the good wife's unqualified devotion to her husband—the Radha-Krishna legend and the opposite convention of wives lamenting their fate on seeing a handsome hero notwithstanding. That the wife's love for her husband was necessarily more intense than the husband's attachment to her was a generally accepted image of marital relations. To quote Bharatchandra: "Can the husband's feelings for his wife compare with a woman's desire for her husband? A woman longs for her husband's body, as is evident from her burning herself to death with her dead husband. Consider, when the wife dies, a man forgets her and takes another wife."[21] The belief that a husband's love is the panacea for all ills to a woman is continually emphasized in the literary and biographical works of the nineteenth and early twentieth centuries as well.

Within the limits of such innocent faith, the norms permitted a frankly voluptuous attitude to marriage—a frankness which got shrouded in the sentimental verbiage of Indian "Victoriana" by the middle years of the nineteenth century. Mukundaram writing in the late sixteenth century thus describes his enamored hero: "Having heard from people of Khullana, the merchant's heart was afflicted by the darts of desire ["lust"]. He discussed [the matter] with Jamai Pandit and told him, 'Save me by arranging the marriage.'[22] Thus Bharatchandra even more explicitly: "A woman's life is in love-making. Who can survive without it? Fie on the life of she who lives without this essence of life."[23] And thus a nineteenth-century worthy reminiscing on his married bliss: "To our wives, we were their sole treasure. . . . Whatever their unhappiness at home . . . they forgot it all when they saw their husbands. . . . If saddened by any family circumstances, they lost their sorrow on seeing their husbands, just as darkness is dispelled when the sun rises, and like mariners of old they had their eyes fixed on their [only true] star, the husband."[24]

Kulīn polygamy pushed into the background certain older norms of marital relationship. The literary conventions down to the days of Bharatchandra emphasize the feminine expectation that the husband should be a good provider.[25] A married woman living with her parents or a man dependent on his in-laws was the object of contempt and pity.[26] The kulīn polygamist, however, made a profession of marriage, and no social stigma attached to his living entirely off his year-round visits to in-laws' houses where his numerous wives lived permanently. Even the kulīn not given to such excesses grew up in the expectation of being provided for by their in-laws and often had no other means of livelihood.[27] By virtue of the ritual purity of their genealogy alone, such pedigreed stud bulls were much sought after.

The nineteenth-century Bengali reformers' preoccupation with the condition of women—the debates and agitations over widow burning, widow marriage, women's education, and the age of marriage—probably

makes sense in the context of a degradation in the position of women.
Widow burning, for instance, definitely increased in the nineteenth century.[28] Nowhere in the literature before the mid-eighteenth century are
women represented as objects of contempt or pity. A bigamous husband
is shown as extremely anxious to soothe the elder wife's feelings not only
in Mukundaram but even in Bharatchandra.[29] The fate of the *kulīn* grass
widow portrayed in *Ālāler gharer dulāl*[30] has no parallel in earlier literature. That this degradation had become part of the accepted norm is clear
from the well-known conservative resistance to all attempts at reform,
often blatant, at times sheltering behind shamefaced sophistry. Western
education, and especially education of women, brought about a slow
change in attitude.[31] Yet in the first half of the nineteenth century such
change was confined to a small segment of caste Hindu society—mainly
the Brahmos and the "reformed" Hindus.[32]

An important outcome of the change in values was an increased freedom
of social contact between men and women. Outside the circles of reform,
men's contact with women unrelated to them long consisted only in visits
to prostitutes or brief encounters with the young women of the neighborhood who came to visit the new bridegroom. Women could enjoy the
pleasures of conversing only with the new bridegroom either in their own
family or in the family of relatives in the neighborhood. Even such contact
was unlikely except with one's own husband or one's husband's sister's
husband. "Their joy knew no bounds when they met a good-natured,
simple-hearted and sweet-spoken bridegroom. . . . Whatever accomplishments they had, they sought to display before him. In all this," we are
assured, "neither the girls nor the young women ever had any impure
feelings in their hearts. Later, writes Ray, "when several of us, friends,
began to meet one another's wives, we and our wives were deeply grati-
fied."[33]

The shift in attitudes toward women had its counterpart in the growing
discrimination between male and female children on the part of the
parents. The literary record before the rise of *kulīn* polygamy shows that
the birth of a daughter was less welcome than that of a son but was by no
means considered a calamity.[34] As *kulīn* polygamy turned the daughter's
marriage into a serious financial liability, there was a corresponding
decline in the value of daughters in parental eyes. Kartikeyachandra Ray
records a pathetic incident in which *kulīn* parents virtually allowed their
little daughter to die while fussing over their not-so-sick son.[35] The married
or widowed *kulīn* girls lived in their brother's or father's house almost as
menials, though there were occasional exceptions to this pattern.[36]

A different type of change in parental attitude toward sons was determined by new economic opportunities. In the traditional Bengali society

a son was expected to inherit his father's estate or follow his father's profession without any special effort to achieve excellence. The scholar or poet seeking fame was perhaps an exception to this pattern, and an ambitious scholar might even want his son to achieve great academic distinction. The notion that a man might aspire after such wealth and status beyond his birth appears to have been rare. The education given to a child conformed to this status-oriented pattern of expectation. A Brahmin scholar's son acquired knowledge of Sanskrit; others learned Bengali and Persian, which would be useful in securing clerical jobs. The experience of the companies' compradors, however, set in motion a new pattern of expectation. Education, especially knowledge of English, came to be regarded as a passport to wealth through jobs with the various agencies of government or at least in the city of Calcutta. Someone like Vidyasagar's father might still desire a Sanskritic education for his son in tune with the scholarly tradition of his family, but in general the emphasis had definitely shifted to job-oriented education likely to lead to wealth and a new status. The quaint custom of subjecting the prospective bride-groom to a written test of his knowledge of the useful languages was evidence of this new concern.[37] As a determinant of status, wealth had gained an altogether new importance and made possible a divergence in the values of family life as between the rich and the poor. Seeking marriage alliance with rich families never appears to have been by itself an object of ambition with the genteel Bengali Hindu until the latter half of the eighteenth century.[38] The spoiled son of the rich family repeatedly parodied in the nineteenth-century novels was a newcomer in Bengali literature, a product of the new cult of money.

The traditional morality of the Bengali upper castes had two distinct but interrelated dimensions. The dharma of one's *jāti* had a hard core of ritualism and, beyond a point, personal ethics was not distinguishable from ritual correctness. But even the caste duties were particular applications of some generally accepted ethical norms—notions of universal morality summed up in the expression *śīl* (right conduct). For the upper castes, Brahmins in particular, *śīl* consisted in righteousness, humility, generosity, self-restraint, love of scholarship, knowledge of the scriptures, and devotion to the gods, Brahmins, and the guru.[39] A nineteenth-century writer describes the virtues of earlier generations in similar terms: "Devotion to gods and one's parents, affection for brothers and sisters, filial attachment, love for one's neighbors, hospitality, charity, forgiveness— to such great virtues they were deeply attached." Elsewhere the same writer eulogizes a relation who lived by the traditional norms as a person who never turned away a suitor for charity, never desired any woman but his wife, was kind to people who had harmed him, totally honest, always in control of his temper, and stoically unmoved by suffering.[40] Vidyasagar's grandfather, another embodiment of traditional virtues, is described by the savant as a man of independent spirit who never hesitated to speak out his mind and scorned to speak to ill-behaved men, even though they were scholarly, rich, and powerful. His anger had no outward expression. He preferred not to depend on anybody. "He took only one meal a day, was a vegetarian, clean in his conduct and careful in the performance of his daily duties. Hence everyone pointed him out as a living saint."[41]

The nineteenth-century Bengali humanists were acutely aware of the blind spots in the traditional norms. Lying, bribery, and sensual indulgence were apparently considered only minor vices by the older generations around the turn of the century.[42] It seems likely, however, that there was some ambivalence in these respects and also some fluctuation over time. The distinction between bribes and perquisites was rather blurred to the medieval mind in India as elsewhere, and there was nothing special about Bengali upper-caste attitudes in this regard. Nepotism was considered a blameless and natural behavior, if not actually a virtue, even by the nineteenth-century humanists in Bengal.[43] In the traditional system of values, the notions of public morality were indeed dim. Administrative oppression was calmly accepted as a divine visitation in retribution for people's sins.[44] But at least some literary references of the eighteenth century imply disapproval of oppressive officials.[45] And, again, one passage in Bharatchandra has a curiously nineteenth-century flavor in its scorn for masculine self-indulgence: "Even if a woman suffers the pangs of desire for 12 years, she should not cohabit with a lecherous man. What sort of a woman is she who kisses a man that has kissed another woman? Even one who touches a person who has a stomach for the leftovers from other people's plates is herself defiled."[46] This is not the conventional idiom of the *khaṇḍita nāyikā*, the heroine crossed in love of Vaishnava poetry.

However, to the rising generation of the 1820s a certain laxity of sexual morals, some proneness to lying, and a weakness for easy money were vices commonly associated with the older generation. The ethical message they derived from their Western education implied a rejection of these vices and a desire to imitate "English ways."[47]

The results were not always fortunate. Drinking, formerly associated with religious rituals and practiced generally in moderation and quietly at night, became respectable as a part of "English ways." If the wild youth of commercial Calcutta rejoiced in smoking opium, the sophisticated Hindu College students took to drinking in earnest. Rajnarayan Basu recalls in his memoirs his honest but unsuccessful attempts to follow his father's advice—to drink only in moderation. The excesses of Young Bengal which went much further were a deliberate rejection of all traditional norms.[48]

Although the oldest profession in the world was surely not brought to Bengal by the British rulers, the economic and administrative changes of the late eighteenth century provided it with a market probably unprecedented in its scale. The growth of the new administrative centers fostered colonies of clerks, lawyers, and the like—grass widowers all, who left their families back in their village homes according to the custom of the times. Many of them found solace in the company of concubines recruited from the fast expanding red light districts. Even the more inhibited regularly visited the "huts," which became centers for social gathering. "Especially on the festive days, there was hardly space enough for people there. Just as on the Puja nights people go around to look at the images [of the deity], so on the night of Bijaya men went around to have a look at the prostitutes."[49]

The puritanical creed of Brahmoism sternly rejected such laxities and put forward a new ideal of personal morality. Barada Babu, a character in the first Bengali novel, is one of the best-known embodiments of the new puritan ethic. Barada Babu "was continually engaged in discourses about God from his boyhood days. Hence his sufferings did not worry him." A poor man, he spent his youth in study and meditation. He had none of the false pride of the English-educated. He was gentle and polite, dutiful to his family and relations, charitable to the poor, performed good deeds in secret, and "would never take to unrighteousness even if it cost him his life." He performed only such acts as were dear to God and avoided all that was not dear to Him. Discipline, meditation, analysis of self, and continuous study of the works of worthy men enabled him to find out what the Lord desired. He did not spend his time in frivolity. His devotion was evident from the tears that flowed every morning when he prayed. "Through such practices has his soul become pure and calm."[50]

Besides the morality of the Brahmo patriarch a new humane sensibility gradually emerged, giving a fresh dimension to personal ethics. Kartikeyachandra Ray, who lived a blameless life despite many temptations, recalls in his old age the love a fallen woman had offered him and he could not accept:

> I used to think this singer's body is impure, her heart is impure, but her love is not impure. If a flower grows in some foul spot, does the flower become foul as well? If one enjoys the love of a dog, why should one not be happy when a human being loves you? I felt both happy and sad about her love. . . . How tragic is the fate of women. We despise the man guilty

of adultery, but do not feel defiled if we sit or converse with him. But when a woman is adulterous, we feel defiled even if we look at her.[51]

A passionate skepticism and a melancholy awareness of the human condition eventually provided the basis for a very different personal morality in Bengali elite culture. The sentimental reminiscences of a suburban babu quoted above anticipated the tortured individualistic groping of a later age toward norms which required no external sanction.

NOTES

1. See, for instance, Mukundaram Chakravarti, *Chaṇḍimaṅgala*, ed. Abina-schandhra Mukherji (Calcutta, B.S. 1344), p. 224: "If one's kins are wrath, even the celestial bird Garuda would lose his wings." Again: "The king takes one's wealth, the judge takes one's life, the kin takes one's Jati [i.e., ostracizes)." [B.S. = *Bāṅglā sāl, year of the Bengali calendar.*]

2. The life of the hunter Dharmaketu and his wife Nidaya after their son's marriage is described in such terms in the *Chaṇḍimaṅgala*, pp. 59–60.

3. *Vidyasagar-charit* in Works of Vidyasagar (*Vidyasagar-rachaṇāsambhar)*, ed. P. Bisi, 4th ed. (Calcutta, B.S. 1371), p. 323.

4. Biographical sketch of the poet by Iswar Gupta (dated 1855), reproduced in the introduction to *Bharatchandra-granthāvalī*, ed. B. Banerji and S. Das (Calcutta, B.S. 1369), pp. 25, 28, 31.

5. *Vidyasagar-rachaṇāmbhar,* pp. 322, 329f.

6. Ibid., pp. 330, 331.

7. *Dewan Kartikeyachandra Rayer Jivancharit* (Calcutta, B.S. 1363), pp. 4f., 44, 68, 104, 105, 114–15.

8. Biographical sketch of Bharatchandra (see note 4 above), pp. 25–31.

9. Kartikeyachandra Ray, op. cit., p. 29; Vidyasagar, op. cit., p. 331.

10. For a detailed discussion, see my *Bengal under Akbar and Jahangir* (Delhi, 1969), pp. 6–8.

11. Kartikeyachandra Ray, op. cit., pp. 37–38.

12. *Chaṇḍimaṅgala*, p. 145.

13. *Bharatchandra-granthāvalī*, p. 149: "The four co-wives continuously quarrelled. . . . [The goddess] Annada was annoyed by these quarrels. . . . The goddess shows kindness where there is love. She does not abide where there is quarrel."

14. Tekchand Thakur, *Ālāler gharer dulāl,* eds. B. Banerji and S. Das (Calcutta, B.S. 1362), pp. 23–25.

15. See his *Bāmuner Meye.*

16. See Kartikeyachandra Ray, op. cit., p. 31.

17. See Rajnarayan Basu, *Ātmācharit*, 3rd ed. (Calcutta, 1953) and Sibnath Sastri, *Rāmtanu Lā iṛi O Tatkālin Baṅgasamāj.*

18. Mukundaram, op. cit., p. 143.

19. Kartikeyachandra Ray, op. cit., pp. 66–67.

20. Raychaudhuri, op. cit., Introduction, pp. 10f.

21. Bharatchandra, op. cit., p. 51.

22. Ray, op. cit., p. 142.

23. Op. cit., p. 256. *Bharatchandra-granthāvalī*, p. 256.
24. Kartikeyachandra Ray, op. cit., p. 66.
25. Bharatchandra, op. cit., p. 67: "He who has no food at home should better be dead. How can he aspire after pleasures?"
26. Raychaudhuri, op. cit., Introduction; also Mukundaram, *Chaṇḍimaṅgala*.
27. See, for instance, K. Ray, op. cit., p. 31.
28. N. K. Sinha in the *Annual Report of the Regional Records Survey Committee, West Bengal*, 1959.
29. See for instance, the story of Dhanapati and Lahana in *Kavikankan Chaṇḍi* and that of the bigamous Bhavananda in *Annadāmaṅgal*.
30. Tekchand Thakur, op. cit., pp. 25–26.
31. See Binay Ghosh, *Samvādpatre Bānglār Samējchitra*, vol. I (Calcutta, 1962), pp. 163f., 184, 216, 304, 308, 310.
32. Sibnath Sastri, op. cit.
33. Ray, op. cit., pp. 35–36.
34. Raychaudhuri, op. cit., Introduction.
35. Kartikeyachandra Ray, op. cit., pp. 77, 84.
36. *Ālāler gharer dulāl*, pp. 25–26; Vidyasagar, op. cit., pp. 323, 330.
37. Ray, op. cit., p. 22; Vidyasagar, op. cit., pp. 328, 341; Brajendranath Bandyopadhyay, *Sahitya-sādhak Charitmālā, Bhabānicharan Bandyopadhyay*, p. 8.
38. *Ālāler gharer dulāl*, pp. 45–46.
39. Raychaudhuri, op. cit., Introduction.
40. Ray, op. cit., pp. 110, 112.
41. Vidyasagar, op. cit., pp. 330, 331.
42. Ray, op. cit., p. 16.
43. Ibid. p., 249.
44. See Mukundaram's autobiographical sketch, op. cit.; see also Kshemananda, quoted in Sukumar Sen, *Bāṅglā Sāntityer Itihās*, vol. I.
45. Bharatchandra, op. cit., p., 242.
46. Ibid., p. 233.
47. Ray, op. cit., pp. 16, 41.
48. Ibid., p. 97f.; Rajnarayan Basu, *Ātmājibanī;* Sibnath Sastri, op. cit.
49. Ray, op. cit., p. 128f.
50. *Ālāler gharer dulāl*, pp. 27f., 54f.
51. Ray, op. cit., pp. 126–127.

Economic Foundations of the Bengal Renaissance

BLAIR B. KLING
University of Illinois

Most historians of the Italian Renaissance have assumed the existence of a high correlation between commercial vitality and cultural renaissance. Robert S. Lopez, however, has warned against accepting any simplistic cause-and-effect relationship between economics and art, and he observes that "intellectual development must be traced primarily to intellectual roots."[1] On the other hand, he writes, the content, themes, and fashions of art are a function of the morale of the creative artist and cannot help being affected by his total environment, including the economic condition of his society.[2] In the Bengal renaissance there was a perceptible change in literary themes between the early and latter nineteenth century, and without going any further than the unobjectionable generalization offered by Lopez, one may be able to associate these changes with changing economic conditions in Bengal.

The dominant literary theme of the first half of the nineteenth century, expressed by such diverse writers as Rammohun Roy, Bhabanicharan Bannerji,[3] and the radical students of Young Bengal, was Indo-British collaboration. They wrote in a period of economic cooperation between the races, a time of embryonic industrialization in Lower Bengal when the area was technologically advanced and when the mercantile community, composed of both races, was attempting to establish independent economic institutions.

After mid-century, Bengali attitudes changed. David Kopf has referred to the growing xenophobia and cultural nationalism of the latter nineteenth century, and Warren Gunderson has noted that "by the 1870s . . . new cultural patterns were emerging which were more assertive and more aggressively national. . . . In the new age new men appeared on the stage who were much more skeptical about the value of cooperation with the British."[4] The period of nationalism and xenophobia in literature corresponded with a period in which Calcutta had become an economic dependency of Great Britain and locked into the imperial economic system. Furthermore, the Bengali merchant was no longer a partner in the modern sector of the Calcutta business world but subordinate to both British and western-Indian merchant communities.

One result of Calcutta's economic backwardness was a shortage of employment opportunities for the growing number of Western-educated Bengalis. But this problem was not manifest until the 1880s, and the earliest expressions of economic nationalism in Bengal antedate by at least a decade economic stress among the *bhadralok*.[5] In 1869 Chandranath Bose, and in 1873 Bholanath Chandra, called for protective tariffs to encourage the development of indigenous factory industries. Bholanath, in particular, urged the Indians to establish their own banks, corporations, mills, and factories, and he denounced those of his countrymen who preferred foreign goods to indigenous manufactures.[6] These early expressions of nationalist economic doctrines were inspired not by personal economic hardship but by the poverty of the masses and disappointment with the government for its failure to encourage economic development. The decade of the 1850s was a transitional period that marked both the beginning of purposeful economic imperialism and the end of over 150 years of Bengali-British business collaboration.

The modern Bengali business class, in fact, owes its origin to British commercial activity. When Europeans began trading in Bengal in the sixteenth century, the traditional Bengali merchant castes had been displaced by traders from north India who had captured the lucrative foreign trade in Bengali silk and cotton textiles. It was from these outsiders— Marwaris, Pathans, Kashmiris, and others—and not from Bengalis that the British seized the trade of Bengal in the eighteenth century. Greater resources and the use of the *dastak* enabled the British to outbid the merchants of north India for the products of Bengal. In addition, wherever possible the British bypassed the middlemen and gathered handloom weavers and silk winders into compounds under their own control. They also diverted the extensive coastal trade between Bengal and Gujarat from the boats of independent Indian merchants to their own ships and changed the direction of the flourishing trade between these provinces to a separate trade of each with the Far East.[7]

As they drove the north Indian traders from Bengal, the British developed in Calcutta a new Bengali merchant class. In the late seventeenth century, when they first came to the site of Calcutta, the British found a few villages of Setts and Basaks, lower-caste Bengali weavers who had learned while dealing with the Portuguese in the previous century to combine trade with weaving. Under British rule many Setts and Basaks amassed fortunes as brokers and *dadni* merchants.[8] Other Bengali communities quickly became aware of commercial opportunities under British auspices and migrated to Calcutta. By 1763, along with those of Setts and Basaks, the names of Kayasthas and Baniks appear on lists of investment agents of the East India Company, and after Plassey, Brahmin names were added.[9]

By the end of the eighteenth century Calcutta had moved far ahead of the older trading and administrative cities of Bengal in population and in wealth. Among its citizenry was a new Indian elite composed of banians, dewans, and pundits associated with the British in trade, government, and educational institutions. They were drawn from a variety of Bengali Hindu castes. What they had in common were ambitious ancestors who had come to the city in search of wealth. The new elite invested their money in both modern and traditional activities. To establish status in Bengali society, they built temples and ghats, supported Brahmin priests, threw great feasts, and performed expensive *shraddha*. But they also built new mansions and furnished them with Western imports. In their productive investments they joined with Europeans in commerce, shipping, and land development. On their own they purchased zamindaris and urban real estate.

In addition to Bengalis Calcutta attracted a large cosmopolitan population from all parts of India and Asia. A new wave of north Indian business communities, primarily Marwaris, settled in Calcutta to work as shroffs (moneychangers) and *kothiwal* (merchant bankers) in the Burrah bazaar. During the nineteenth century they complemented the international commercial system by advancing money to agency houses that imported British textiles and acted as middlemen for the distribution of British imports to northwestern India. Until the Opium War they also speculated heavily in opium.[10] But unlike the Bengalis they usually remained outside British commercial institutions and maintained their traditional upcountry networks along with their traditional "bania" way of life.

The British carried on their international trade through a group of firms known as agency houses. Formed in the late eighteenth century by enterprising men who left the Company service to try their hand in private trade, these houses represented the sector of the economy oriented toward international markets. They used the money of their constituents, civil and military servants of the Company, to finance the import-export trade, especially the country trade, and to produce indigo and other agricultural products for export. By the 1820s competition had forced them to expand their activities. They built and operated ships, served as bill brokers, formed banks and insurance companies, and lent their support to ventures in mining, manufacturing, and plantation industries.[11] The number of agency houses steadily increased over the years. In 1790 there were fifteen; in 1828, twenty-seven; in 1835, sixty-one; and by 1846, ninety-three.[12] Of these only half a dozen at any one time were great houses; the majority were limited in their activities and operated with small sums of capital.

Bengali capitalists known as banians were directly associated with the Calcutta agency houses and provided money for the international export trade. In the eighteenth century the banian was valued for his knowledge of internal markets and sources of supply. As the British learned more about India, his value declined; but after the free-trade charter of 1813 and the influx of a new set of adventurers from Britain who came with little capital of their own, the banian again became important, now as a source of finance. His importance continued to grow after the crash of 1830–1833, which frightened off the capital that had been provided by the British nonmercantile community. By the 1840s Europeans were employed "as agents of native capital,"[13] and one writer complained that the new banians had "assumed airs which their more wealthy predecessors had never taken on themselves; they treated their European connections not only with contemptuous disregard, but often with much insolence. The Hindoo star was in the ascendant, and these men made the most of it."[14] In the mid-1850s capital from Britain began to move increasingly into India and the banian, who now lost much of his financial power, was demoted or discarded altogether.

In their heyday the banians also joined in the development of Calcutta's commercial infrastructure, including insurance companies, a docking company, banking, warehousing, a chamber of commerce, and commercial newspapers. After 1834, British and Indian merchants invested together in a number of joint-stock companies engaged in steam tugging, coal mining, indigo manufacturing, tea planting, river steamboat services, and railroad building. In these enterprises Indians held, on the average, one-fourth to one-third of the shares.[15]

Finally, Indians also joined in the development of modern power-operated residentiary industries that competed for capital with export industries and counterbalanced the colonial export economy. For the time, it appeared that Calcutta was on the threshold of a small-scale industrial revolution. In 1844 J. H. Stocqueler, a Calcutta journalist, noted that "on approaching Calcutta, the smoking chimneys of steam engines are now seen in every direction, on either side of the river, presenting the gratifying appearance of a seat of numerous extensive manufactories, vying with many British cities."[16] In the first half of the nineteenth century, when the application of steam power was the measure of a nation's industrial standing, India led all other colonies and dependencies of Great Britain in the use of steam power,[17] Bengal saw its first steam engine in 1818, and by 1845 there were 150 engines generating six thousand horsepower in use in the Presidency. A few of these had been locally produced by British engineer-technicians, but almost all the rest were imported from Britain. Half the engines were used in sugar refineries, docks, collieries, flour and rice mills, and paper factories; the remainder saw service in sea and river steamers, tugs, and pleasure boats.[18]

In the Calcutta area the largest single industrial complex was located at Fort Gloster, fifteen miles south of Calcutta. The complex included a factory for making cotton twist, a rum distillery, an iron foundry, an oilseed mill, and a paper mill, all worked by five steam engines.[19] The cotton mill, set up in 1817, was the oldest in India.[20] In 1833 the mill, worked by two engines of fifty horsepower each, produced a large quantity of cotton twist which, according to a contemporary report, "was daily rising in the estimation of the natives and . . . the labour of men initiated in the art of weaving is now almost double of what was performed at the commencement of the undertaking."[21] After Fergusson and Company, its owner, went bankrupt in 1833, the Fort Gloster complex was purchased by a joint-stock company most of whose shareholders were old India hands resident in England. But at least one Bengali, Dwarkanath Tagore, and possibly others, were major shareholders. By 1840 the mill was producing 700,000 pounds of yarn annually, the lower numbers of which sold in Calcutta better than imported yarn and the larger numbers on a par with imports. The labor force, with the exception of the European superintendent, was recruited from Orissa and Bengal, paid by the task, and worked eleven hours a day.[22]

Before the middle of the nineteenth century manufacturing activity had spread northward along the right bank of the Hughli River into the suburbs of Hughli, Howrah, Sibpur, and Sulkea, called by one writer "the Southwark of Calcutta."[23] Included were sugar factories, rum distilleries, cotton screws, a biscuit factory, flour mills, a mustard oil mill, and a paper factory. In and near Calcutta itself were a number of steam-operated iron foundries; Jessop and Company, established in the eighteenth century, repaired steamboats, manufactured tools and simple machinery, and in 1825 offered to build a railway from Calcutta to Diamond Harbor.[24] The government itself operated the most extensive foundry. From a modern plant opened in 1834 at Cossipore, four miles north of Calcutta, the foundry supplied brass ordnance to the whole of India. The court of directors had sent out twelve boring and turning lathes, some lighter lathes, and two small steam engines to power the works. Adjacent to the foundry was a casting and smelting house with cupola blast furnaces for smelting iron and large reverberatory furnaces for smelting gun metal.[25]

A large, docile, and talented labor force was available to operate the factories and mills. The leading employer was the Government Steam Department, which hired Indian and Eurasian labor as mechanics, shipwrights, millwrights, plumbers, and boilermakers. Elsewhere in the city skilled workmen, recruited from Hindu artisan castes and from the Chinese community, worked as carpenters, painters, blacksmiths, locksmiths, and jewelers, some under European master craftsmen. Workmen were hired in gangs under contract with a chief *mistry*, an Indian master craftsman who received the wages from the entire gang and distributed them as he wished.[26] Although there were mixed reports on the quality of Indian labor, those employed in the mint were said to handle the machinery, including the steam engine, with facility.[27] Similarly, the workmen at the Fort Gloster cotton mill were considered experts in their machinery duties.[28]

In terms of the total production of Bengal this industrial activity was probably not of great significance. Its importance, instead, must have been in its effect on the intellectual and moral climate of the city, in awakening a pride of citizenship. Calcutta appeared to be moving inexorably toward industrialization, and a sense of progress pervaded the city. Indian participation in the modern sector of the economy was on an upward trend, and the Bengali elite must have participated in the prevailing pride of citizenship and sense of progress.

An important factor was the encouragement given by the government. Before the mid-nineteenth century the government of India supported economic development, including industrialization, even when it conflicted with home interests. The governors general—Bentinck, Auckland, Ellenborough, and Hardinge—were expected to balance the budget and remit the home charges in the face of rising expenses and the prevailing poverty of the peasantry. The obvious answer was to find new sources of revenue. Lord Bentinck's minute favoring European colonization aroused opposition from the manufacturing interests of Britain, who "saw in colonization the spectre of a second Lancashire on the bank of the Ganges, which could beat the original with cheap Indian labour and raw material."[29] But evidently Bentinck anticipated no conflict between British and Indian economic interests. After leaving office he testified that he had supported steam communication with India on grounds that it would facilitate the education of Indian students in England, from which they would return with technological knowledge, the key to progress in India. It would also facilitate the influx of British businessmen, who had done much for

Indian economic development. And along with plantation industries he unabashedly cited with approval the Gloster mills, the iron foundries, and the coal mines, all of which competed with British products.[30]

Lord Auckland (1836–1842) was even stronger in his conviction that India must industrialize. He favored both the revival of Heath's modern steel mill in Madras and cast-iron manufacturing among the primitive hill tribes of Assam. Auckland directed the Cossipore foundry to supply the government's needs for suspension bridges and iron boats and instructed the Coal Committee to expand its activities to locating the best ores and fluxes available in India as the foundation for a local steel industry. He promoted experiments for the improvement of cotton, the processing of hemp, the manufacture of pottery and porcelain, and the growing of nutmeg, pepper plants, and cochineal insects. Moreover he looked forward to the development of Assam, "a country of vast promise," by the application of both European and Indian capital.[31]

His successors, Ellenborough (1842–1844) and Hardinge (1844–1848), were too involved in military affairs to devote time to internal development, but their sentiments were not essentially different from those of Bentinck and Auckland. In 1828, as president of the Board of Control, Ellenborough had encouraged, in the face of strong opposition from the private trade interests in the Court of Directors, a policy of import substitution to save the Indian government money.[32] As governor general he strove to develop public works and establish experimental cotton farms but was thwarted because of a shortage of funds.[33] Hardinge encouraged the early planning of railway building. "Our rule," he wrote Hobhouse on the subject of railways, "has been distinguished by building large Prisons; and the contrast with the Mogul Emperors, in the respect of public works, is not to our advantage."[34] At a ceremony awarding prizes to college students in Calcutta for their recitation of Shakespeare, he concluded his address "by giving his hearers a practical account of the magic powers of steam and electricity."[35]

Among the British publicists of the period, some were willing to admit that India possessed an industrial potential and others were not. George W. Johnson, an attorney who spent three years in Calcutta in the early 1840s, minced no words on the subject:

> Doubtless, it is of high importance for the increase of India's wealth to improve her cotton growth, and to establish extensively on her soil the cultivation of the tea-plant, but these are only some of the first steps towards the desired object. . . . It is now shown that the mineral wealth of India fits her for a higher destiny; and that she, like America, may be at first agricultural, but gradually may become, also, a manufacturing country.[36]

A Madras civil servant named Everett, after a visit to Fort Gloster, predicted that abundant raw cotton and cheap labor would enable the local textile mill to supply "a great part, if not the whole, of the Eastern world, to the exclusion of the European manufacture." He deplored British opposition to the export of cotton mill machinery and asked whether "the manufactures of Bengal have not as good a claim to the protection of the sovereign as those of Lancashire. . . . But India," he concluded, "has never yet been regarded as part of the empire. It goes by the unhappy name of colony, a place . . . made expressly to be plundered by the Mother-country."[37]

On the other hand, far more influential publicists such as Robert M. Martin and John Crawfurd, who were trying to promote British investment in India, stressed the enormous potential of India as an importer of British capital. To allay the fears of British industrialists and exporters, they emphasized the potential of India as a producer of raw cotton and plantation products. Crawfurd considered that any "attempt to introduce the complex manufactures of Europe into India [would be] a signal commercial blunder."[38] In the same vein R. M. Martin wrote of the ideal relationship of mother country and colony: "*the one* [Britain] teeming with a hardy, industrious and ingenious population, two-thirds of whom are engaged in manipulating and vending the produce of more genial climes . . . *the other* [India] rich to overflowing with bounty with which nature has enriched the earth, and peculiarly so in those agricultural products necessary to the manufactures, comforts and luxuries of the more civilized nation."[39] His racial arrogance turned to doubt by 1860, when he became aware of the industrial potential of the Indian textile industry that had developed in Bombay. "Even the present generation," he warned, "may witness the Lancashire manufacturer beaten by his Hindu competitor."[40]

Indians, noting the effects of both machine-made imports and Fort Gloster yarn on the rural weavers and spinners, were at first less certain of the efficacy of industrialization.[41] A Hindu traveler who visited Fort Gloster mill in 1830 reported that the local people considered industrialization a mixed blessing. As consumers they benefited from cheaper cloth; but some, who had learned from English friends about the results of the industrial revolution in cities like Glasgow and Manchester, were fearful of the long-term effects of industrialization on human life.[42] Other westernized intelligentsia lumped commerce and industry together and called on the youth of the country to turn from the study of English literature to such practical subjects as science and commerce.[43] Gradually, however, Indian writers recognized the importance of industrial development. An editorial written in 1847, probably by Iswar Chundra Gupta, lamented the closing down of the Calcutta Mechanics Institute because of a lack of public interest and noted that industry and technical skills were essential for a nation's progress.[44]

The issue may never have occurred to the leading entrepreneur of the day, Dwarkanath Tagore. He saw immediate profit in the production of staples and plantation products, and though he may have believed that India would eventually produce its own steam engines and iron and steel, he was content for the time to import superior British engines at reasonable prices. Dwarkanath cast his lot with the free traders and joined in their attack upon the restrictive policies of the East India Company. He believed the end of the Company's business operations would stimulate the import of British capital and skill, hasten the economic development of India, and lead to the rise of a strong, independent, and reform-minded Indian middle class. It was natural for an enlightened and politically astute Indian like Tagore to associate himself with the party of progress in Britain. But he closed his eyes to the full implications of a movement grounded in the concept of an industrialized England supported by agricultural colonies. It was, in fact, free-trade imperialism that would frustrate the industrial development that he and his British partners were to promote with such vigor in the 1830s and 1840s.[45]

Indian attitudes carried over from business into politics, and by the fourth decade of the nineteenth century the Indian elite of Calcutta considered themselves potential partners with the British not only in commerce and industry but also in citizenship. Rammohun and Dwarkanath traveled to England to visit the capital city of an empire they considered their own,[46] and one reason they wanted the end of Company rule was that they preferred to be subjects of the crown rather than of a mere trading company. Admittedly, British rule in India was looked upon as far from perfect, and the intelligentsia were outspoken in their criticism. But they felt that improvement would come in time, and they could point to many signs of progress achieved thus far under British rule—battles won for a free press and jury trial, colleges founded, law and order established, economic opportunities opened. Most important, the British were the bearers of a new culture of science and technology in which alone lay any hope for transforming India.[47]

While Indians were developing a loyalty to the empire, among the Calcutta British a group was emerging that could be called an "Indian interest." It was composed of the partners of the major agency houses with heavy investments in mofussil industries such as indigo. One of the first expressions of a "Calcutta" as opposed to a "metropolitan" interest was the attempt of the Calcutta community to promote steam communication with Britain. The struggle lasted from 1823 to 1840 and was finally lost when the British-based Peninsular and Oriental Line obtained a government charter.[48] The Calcuttans also opposed any competition from British-domiciled banking with their own Union Bank and succeeded until 1853 in keeping an imperial bank out of India.[48] Again, the Calcutta board of directors of the Assam Tea Company battled against the London board for control over local operations, though the latter represented over ninety percent of the capital. Eventually they too lost to London.[50] Finally, the local interest groups united in 1846 in a life and death struggle against Manchester-supported houses to prevent the abolition of the "hypothecation system." Under this system, which existed until 1850, the government of India advanced money to Calcutta export houses hypothecated to the shipment of indigo and other staples, advances made by the government in order to remit funds to England to pay its home charges.[51]

Thus, until the mid-nineteenth century the leading indigenous merchants were gaining in strength and anticipating a larger share in the operation of the economy if not the administration itself. At the same time a sector of the Calcutta British mercantile community was increasingly identifying its interests with India and holding the line against metropolitan control over the economy of the country. Together they were building a local, independent economic structure that formed the basis for a vigorous interracial social and cultural life.

But their promising achievements were destined to fail. Even in the heyday of local enterprise powerful currents were undermining the foundations of Calcutta's economy. One basic problem was the huge remittance pressures that distorted the foreign trade of Bengal. From 1817 to 1840 the annual volume of Calcutta's commodity exports averaged twice its imports—rupees $2\frac{1}{2}$ crores of imports against rupees 5 crores of exports. In the 1840s both imports and exports increased to almost double their previous value. Calcutta's large merchandise export surplus formed part of a total export of capital from India that exceeded imports by £5 to £6 million annually. Of this amount, £3.5 million was remitted on behalf of the East India Company, primarily to meet its home charges, and the balance represented remittances by private British subjects. The unilateral transfer of funds had severe repercussions on the economy of Bengal. When commodity exports failed to meet remittance demands, bullion was exported and, in the absence of a paper currency, this resulted in a contraction of the money supply and lower prices. Because the land revenue demand was constant, many zamindars could not meet their taxes. The most acute instance of this problem occurred during the commercial crisis of 1830–1833 when landed estates, sold in default of taxes, glutted the market. Another effect of the transfer problem was to encourage the diversion of capital from other sectors of the economy into export industries; this situation resulted in an imbalanced economic structure.[52]

In Bengal the export industry that received the bulk of investment was indigo. Demand for the blue dye was rising in Britain, and Bengal had the natural endowments to produce the finest indigo in the world. In the 1820s, to pay for the increasing importation of British yarn and textiles, indigo production expanded greatly. From Dacca to Delhi over one million acres were put under indigo, producing annually a crop valued at £2 to £3 million. But indigo production and export created more problems for the houses than it solved. The market for indigo fluctuated with European trade cycles and the supply varied with the Indian monsoon. Indigo production rose not in response to any real demand in Britain but in response to the need for an item for remittance. Even if the trade had been "spontaneous" rather than "induced," indigo would have presented problems. Seed had to be distributed and advances given to cultivators two years before the indigo was to be marketed in Britain. Its suitability for remittance purposes forced up its price in Calcutta independently of its price in London, resulting in overproduction and a glut on the London market. As often as not indigo planters, capitalized by the agency houses of Calcutta, went bankrupt. In these cases the entire investment was lost because the fields in which indigo was cultivated belonged to Indian zamindars while the expensive processing equipment was useless unless worked.[53]

By the mid-1820s, with so much of their capital tied up in indigo production, the agency houses began to experience a number of difficulties. In 1825 a commercial slump in England depressed the demand for indigo; to compensate for lower prices, still more indigo was produced and exported, leading to a further glut on the market. A number of agency house partners sold off their enormous Indian assets and retired home. Between 1830 and 1833 the entire edifice crumbled and the old houses, some of which had been in existence from the beginning of the century, failed.[54]

In 1834 a new commercial structure replaced the old. It lasted until the commercial crisis of 1847. One group of the new houses, which can be called "export houses," specialized in indigo production; a second group, which can be called "import houses," specialized in importing cotton textiles on consignment from British manufacturers.[55] Many of the import houses formed by British manufacturers specifically to serve as agents for the sale and distribution of yarn and textiles, had no independent resources. They remitted their funds to their British suppliers by advancing money on or purchasing indigo, further encouraging speculation in that overburdened commodity.[56]

This situation left the export houses to provide the bulk of local investment capital. Some of them invested not only in indigo, silk, and sugar production but also in mines, steamboats, and other local industries. Partners of export houses were heavily represented on the boards of directors of the Union Bank and of the joint-stock companies; they belonged to the group of British and Indians concerned with preserving local control; they tried to raise capital for these undertakings locally and were the entrepreneurs among the merchants of Calcutta. In their statements and activities can be glimpsed the first dim urges toward economic self-determination in India.[57]

Each set of houses developed its own sources of supply and its own marketing system. Import houses developed internal markets; but, because of their dependence on their British correspondents, they were not in a position to invest in local manufactures to supply these markets. Export houses invested their capital in the production of goods for markets abroad, and the economic structure of Bengal was bifurcated into two separate channels.

Conversely, in Bombay the same house was likely to combine an import with an export trade. Typical of Bombay merchants was the Parsi Cowasji Davar, the father of Bombay's modern textile industry. He was "involved in the export and financing of raw cotton and the import of cotton textiles. . . . It was inevitable that the notion of importing machinery and starting a textile mill would strike Davar or one of his contemporaries."[58]

Because of an international commercial crisis in 1847 the entire group of export houses and the Union Bank which they controlled crashed. The crisis had been touched off in Britain by the railroad mania and a precipitous fall in the price of rail stocks. It disrupted the commercial life of Britain and led to the bankruptcy of houses shipping colonial products from all parts of the world. In Calcutta the houses that had tried to build an independent capital position on the quicksand of indigo were hurt the most. The Union Bank had behaved as if indigo factories were sound capital assets that could be redeemed if loans against them were defaulted. Its directors closed their eyes to the truth that the expensive indigo establishments were worthless unless the price of indigo on the European market held the line.[59]

The crash of 1847 led to a readjustment in business thinking to correspond with the reality of Calcutta's economic situation. The businessmen of Calcutta could not build an independent economy on the basis of a colonial product that was inelastic both in its production and in its demand. In the absence of a manufacturing industry catering at least in part to an indigenous market, Bengal was doomed to a dependent colonial position. After the crash the merchants accepted their fate and Calcutta become a typical parasitic city in a colonial setting, a nerve center for colonial exploitation rather than a generator of economic growth.[60] Until the end of the nineteenth century its only important new industry was jute processing, an enclave industry with almost no internal market or backward linkages that would have stimulated the development of ancillary industries in Bengal.[61]

Until the middle of the nineteenth century Calcutta had been a center of industrial progress and advanced technology. This milieu, however small a part of the total economy, contributed to the exhilaration of social and cultural life in the city. But it was Bengal's unhappy fate to be the major provider of export staples, the strong demand for which was artificially stimulated by the remittance needs of the government and the British business community. Those of the business elite who identified themselves with local interests tried valiantly to overcome this skewed development, but the demand factors were too strong and their own capital resources too weak. Their attempt ended in the crash of 1847 and they succumbed to the subjugation of their economy of imperial requirements.

Once interrupted the momentum of industrial development in Bengal was not resumed until the twentieth century. Government policy after mid-century contributed to the decline in the rate of development of new industries. The government was obligated to develop India into a producer of raw materials and semifinished products that would feed into British industry. It facilitated this policy through fiscal means, particularly by refusing to establish protective tariffs. In addition, as the largest single consumer of manufactured goods, the government discriminated against indigenous manufacturers in its stores-purchasing policy.[62]

Related to the decline in the rate of technological progress was a deterioration in the position of the Bengali businessman in the advanced sector of the economy. Underlying this was an increased racial bias and social discrimination against Bengalis by both private and official Britishers.[63] Technological advance and industrialization leveled off until the end of the nineteenth century, and the inferior status of Calcutta's economy influenced the cultural and social life in the latter nineteenth century. In 1839 the *Bombay Gazette* had noted with envy:

> We are one good century behind Calcutta in matters of improvement, speculation, and so forth. We have here no public scheming and projecting, no active open system of public spiritedness, no companies forming, no societies emerging. All with us is as yet unwelded and unamalgamated. We hold counsel in a system of wrapt up secrecy and shrewdness in all our dealings with one another. Our monied people have a taste for solitude

and abstraction, and can seldom be made to meet, or subscribe, except on the departure of some Governor. . . . In Calcutta we observe a totally different spirit. There we do recognize something like community of feeling and a combined idiosyncrasy; societies, meetings, projections follow in quick succession, and a current of healthy sympathy and sentiment seems to pervade the monied mass. Instead of maintaining the lonely icicled state of magnificence in which we exist, the thaw of social harmony has produced a permeative process of coalescence, which is spreading in every direction, and resolving into one community both Europeans and Natives.[64]

In the next half century the positions of the two cities were reversed and, as the races drifted apart, the "renaissance" was infected with the virus of cultural chauvinism.

NOTES

1.   Robert S. Lopez, "Hard Times and Investment in Culture," in *The Renaissance*, eds. Wallace K. Ferguson et al. (New York: Holt, Rinehart & Winston, 1962), p. 43.
2.   Ibid., p. 44.
3.   David Kopf, *British Orientalism and the Bengal Renaissance* (Berkeley: University of California Press, 1969), pp. 208–213.
4.   Warren Gunderson, "The Self-Image and World-View of the Bengali Intelligentsia as Found in the Writings of the Mid-Nineteenth Century, 1830–1870," in *Bengal Literature and History*, ed. Edward C. Dimock (East Lansing: Asian Studies Center, Michigan State University, 1967), p. 146.
5.   John Broomfield, *Elite Conflict in a Plural Society* (Berkeley: University of California Press, 1968), pp. 32–33.
6.   Bimanbehari Majumdar, *History of Political Thought from Rammohun to Dayananda (1821–84)* (Calcutta, 1934), I:276–283.
7.   N. K. Sinha, *Economic History of Bengal from Plassey to the Permanent Settlement*, 2 vols. (Calcutta, 1956–1962), I:99ff.; Sukumar Bhattacharya, *The East India Company and the Economy of Bengal from 1704 to 1740* (London, 1954), p. 187; and Holden Furber, *John Company at Work* (Cambridge, Mass. Harvard University Press, 1948), pp. 162–163.
8.   Benoy Ghose, "Some Old Family-Founders in 18th Century Calcutta," *Bengal Past and Present*, vol. 79, part I, ser. no. 147 (January–June 1960).
9.   N. K. Sinha, op. cit., p. 93; and S. Bhattacharya, op. cit., p. 188.
10.   Kissen Mohun Mullick, *Brief History of Bengal Commerce from the Year 1814 to 1870* (Calcutta, 1871), pp. 16–21.
11.   S. B. Singh, *European Agency Houses in Bengal (1783–1833)* (Calcutta, 1966), pp. 1–35.
12.   See *Bengal and Agra Annual Registers* for years cited.
13.   George Campbell, *Modern India* (London, 1852), p. 204.
14.   John Capper, *The Three Presidencies of India* (London, 1853), pp. 381–382.
15.   Radhe Shyam Rungta, *The Rise of Business Corporations in India, 1851–1900* (Cambridge: Cambridge University Press, 1970), pp. 19–25, 274.

16. J. H. Stocqueler, *Handbook of India*, 2nd. ed. (London, 1845), p. 348.
17. G. A. Prinsep, *An Account of Steam Vessels and of Proceedings Connected with Steam Navigation in British India* (Calcutta, 1830), p. 1.
18. *Friend of India*, 27 November 1845.
19. Great Britain, H. C., *Parliamentary Papers*, 1840, vol. 8, Select Committee on East India Produce. Testimony of Henry Gouger, pp. 116–123.
20. Daniel Buchanan, *The Development of Capitalist Enterprise in India* (New York: Macmillan, 1934), p. 128.
21. *Asiatic Journal*, n. s., vol. 13 (January 1834), p. 6.
22. *Parliamentary Papers* (see note 19 above). For holdings of Dwarkanath Tagore see *Bengal Hurkaru*, 22 May 1848; for value of a share, see *Bengal Hurkaru*, 27 March 1852.
23. "Notes on the Right Bank of the Hoogly," *Calcutta Review*, vol. 6 (July–December 1845), p. 481.
24. Bengal Revenue Proceedings, 12 May (18) 1825 and 9 June (12–19) 1825.
25. H. A. Young, *The East India Company's Arsenals and Manufactories* (Oxford, 1937), pp. 142–143; and Stocqueler, op. cit., pp. 341ff.
26. Henry T. Bernstein, *Steamboats on the Ganges* (Calcutta, 1960), pp. 143–153.
27. George W. Johnson, *The Stranger in India; or, Three Years in Calcutta*, 2 vols. (London, 1843), I:54.
28. *Parliamentary Papers* (see note 19 above).
29. Quoted in Amales Tripathi, *Trade and Finance in the Bengal Presidency 1793–1833* (Calcutta, 1956), p. 228.
30. Great Britain, H. C., *Parliamentary Papers*, 1837, vol. 7, pp. 186ff.
31. British Museum add. mss. 37689, Auckland Private Letterbook I, letter dated 5 August 1836; ibid. 7 Jan. 1837 and 37693. Private Letterbook V, 5 July 1838; ibid. 37711, Auckland's Minute Books, minute on Cossipore Foundry, 2 June 1839, pp. 124–127; ibid. 37698, Private Letterbook X, 19 April 1840.
32. C. H. Philips, *The East India Company, 1784–1834* (Manchester, 1940), pp. 262–263.
33. Albert H. Imlah, *Lord Ellenborough* (Cambridge, Mass.: Harvard University Press, 1939), pp. 176ff.
34. Broughton Papers, India Office Home Misc. 853, letter from Hardinge to Hobhouse, 3 January 1847, p. 303.
35. Viscounte Hardinge, *Viscounte Hardinge and the Advance of British Dominion into the Punjab*. Rulers of India Series (Oxford, 1891), p. 64.
36. Johnson, op. cit., II:218–219.
37. I. Everett, *Observations on India by a Resident There of Many Years* (London, 1853), p. 58.
38. John Crawfurd, *A Sketch of the Commercial Resources and Monetary and Mercantile System of British India (1837)*, reprinted in *The Economic Development of India under the East India Company, 1814–58*, ed. K. N. Chaudhuri (Cambridge: Cambirdge University Press, 1971), pp. 226–227.
39. R. M. Martin, *History of the British Colonies*, 5 vols. (London, 1834), I:205.
40. Quoted in Morris D. Morris, *The Emergence of an Industrial Labor Force in India* (Berkeley: University of California Press,), p. 25.
41. *Reformer*, 13 April 1835, reprinted in *Asiatic Journal*, n. s., vol. 18 (October 1835), p. 92.
42. Quoted from *Banga Doot* in *Samachar Darpan*, 8 May 1830 in *Sambadpatrey Sekaler Katha 1818–1840*, ed. Brajendra Nath Bandopadhyaya, 2 vols. (Calcutta, 1949–1950, II:326.

43. *Reformer*, 18 March 1833.

44. *Sambad Prabhakar*, 8 June 1847 in *Samayek-Patre Banglar Samaj-Chitra 1840–1905*, ed. Benoy Ghosh, 3 vols. (Calcutta, 1963), I:50.

45. See speech by Dwarkanath Tagore of 18 June 1836 reprinted in Kissory Chand Mittra, *Memoir of Dwarkanath Tagore* (Calcutta, 1870), pp. 53–57. on "free-trade imperialism" see Bernard Semmel, *The Rise of Free Trade Imperialism* (Cambridge: Cambridge University Press, 1970).

46. On Rammohun Roy's self-identity as a British subject see Sophia Dobson Collet, *The Life and Letters of Raja Rammohun Roy*, 3rd. ed. (Calcutta, 1962), p. 334.

47. Speech by Tagore quoted in *Raja Rammohun Roy and Progressive Movements in India*, ed. J. K. Majumdar (Calcutta, 1941), pp. 438–439.

48. Daniel Thorner, *Investment in Empire* (Philadelphia: University of Pennsylvania Press, 1950), pp. 22–39.

49. *Bengal Hurkaru*, 11 November 1836, 25 February 1837, 17 April 1837; and Charles Northcote Cooke, *Rise, Progress and Present Condition of Banking in India* (Calcutta, 1863), pp. 345–347. Also, B. M. add. ms. 37705, Auckland Private Letterbook XVII, Auckland to Hobhouse, 22 April 1841.

50. H. A. Antrobus, *A History of the Assam Company*, 1839–1953 (Edinburgh, 1957), pp. 72–80, 137.

51. Financial Letter from India and Bengal with enclosures, 1846, vol. 93, app. 1 and 2; and *Parliamentary Papers*, vol. 8, 1847–1848, pp. 107ff.

52. K. N. Chaudhuri, op. cit., pp. 17–45.

53. Benoy Chowdhury, *Growth of Commercial Agriculture in Bengal (1757–1900)*, vol. 1 (Calcutta, 1964), pp. 83ff.; and Blair B. Kling, *The Blue Mutiny* (Philadelphia: University of Pennsylvania Press, 1966, pp. 15ff.

54. Amales Tripathi, op. cit., pp. 211ff.

55. The division between "import" and "export" houses was not absolute, but indicated the primary direction of their business. Contemporary observers such as John Crawfurd and John Marshman (author of "Commercial Morality and Commercial Prospects in Bengal," *Calcutta Review* vol. 9, 1848, pp. 163–189) do not make the distinction. But an analysis of the petitions for and against the continuation of the hypothecation system (see note 51 above) indicates that those firms who opposed the system were usually connected with Manchester exporters while those who favored the system were connected with London indigo, sugar, and silk import houses.

56. John Crawfurd, op. cit. pp. 284–287.

57. See, for example, *Bengal and Agra Directory and Annual Register for 1847*. Names of directors of various joint-stock companies correlate with names of partners of export houses, that is, houses favoring continuance of the hypothecation system. Statements expressing local interests are found in a speech by William Prinsep, a partner of Dwarkanath Tagore, in *Calcutta Monthly Journal*, May 1839, p. 250, and in the resolution of the Calcutta merchants to establish a steamship company between Calcutta and Europe with headquarters in Calcutta. See H. L. Hoskins, *British Routes to India* (Philadelphia, 1928; reprint ed., New York: Octagon, 1966, p. 249n.

58. Morris, op. cit., p. 24.

59. Cooke, op. cit., pp. 179ff.

60. A class of colonial cities described in T. G. McGee, *The Southeast Asian City* (N. Y.: Prager, 1967), pp. 55ff.

61. Morris D. Morris suggests that Bengali capital turned to rural marketing,

small-scale rural industry, and agriculture after mid-century because it was more profitable than investment in modern factories, and that these forms of activity are not less "modern." Granting this possibility, rural entrepreneurship would have contributed little to the élan of the Calcutta intelligentsia. See his "Values as an Obstacle to Economic Growth in South Asia: An Historical Survey," *Journal of Economic History*, vol. 27, no. 4 (December 1967), pp. 600ff.

62.   Amiya Kumar Bagchi, *Private Investment in India, 1900–1939* (Cambridge, 1972), pp. 43–47; Sunil Kumar Sen, *Studies in Industrial Policy and Development of India* (Calcutta, 1964).

63.   Bagchi, op. cit., pp. 150–156, 165ff; Robert I. Crane, "Technical Education and Economic Development in India before World War I," in *Education and Economic Development*, eds. C. A. Anderson and M. J. Bowman (Chicago: Aldine, 1965).

64.   Quoted in *Bengal Hurkaru*, 22 October 1839.

The Universal Man and the Yellow Dog:
The Orientalist Legacy and the Problem of
Brahmo Identity in the Bengal Renaissance

DAVID KOPF
University of Minnesota

The most important fact of the present age is that all the different races of the world have come close together. And again we are confronted with two alternatives. The problem is whether the different groups of peoples shall go on fighting with one another or find out some true basis of reconciliation and mutual help; whether it will be interminable competition or cooperation.

Rabindranath Tagore, Nationalism

When God finished making the world
He had a few stinking scraps of mud left over
   and used it to make a yellow dog
(And when they hate any race or nation they
   name that race or nation in place
   of the yellow dog).

Carl Sandburg, The People Yes

I. THE ORIENTALIST CONTRIBUTION TO THE BENGAL RENAISSANCE

This essay is in part an interpretation of the Bengal renaissance and in part an analysis of cultural identity among Bengali intellectuals struggling to maintain their outgoing universalism against the rising tide of militant and aggressive nationalism. The outgoing universalism of Rabindranath Tagore, which is relatively well known among Western scholars, was perhaps the single most significant idea to emerge from the Bengal renaissance. This renaissance—of which Tagore is often held to be both the finest and the final expression—occurred largely in the nineteenth and early twentieth centuries and was characterized by a remarkable creative outburst of literary, artistic, and ideological achievements.

Universalism, so characteristic of the renaissance spirit and thought, was an intellectual outgrowth of East-West contact in Calcutta. At that time the city was a dynamic pivot for acculturating India's most progressive intelligentsia to modernizing impulses from western Europe. The Brahmo Samaj (Society for the Worship of the One True God) was perhaps the most representative institutional expression of the Bengal renaissance. This movement, made up for the most part of a Western-educated professional elite dissatisfied with the shortcomings of their own society and culture vis-à-vis the West, sought to modernize their religious and social traditions.

The birth of a modernizing intelligentsia in Bengal is a subject I have treated in *British Orientalism and the Bengal Renaissance*. From my point of view, the renaissance was the child of eighteenth-century cosmopolitanism and pragmatic British policy (derived from Warren Hastings)[1] built around the need for an acculturated civil-service class of Englishmen (trained at the College of Fort William from 1800).[2] Calcutta, chosen as capital of British India in 1772, provided the ideal environment. Spurred on by a class of British officials known as Orientalists[3] sympathetically engaged in a scholarly reconstruction of the Hindu past, a newly formed intelligentsia selectively reinterpreted their heritage and strove to reshape their culture in the new image.[4]

Rationalism, cosmopolitanism, and dynamic classicism were the three key intellectual values transmitted by British Orientalists to the Bengali intelligentsia while functioning as windows to the West. These characteristic components, derived from the Age of Enlightenment in Europe, were universal rather than parochial in tenor. Rationalism pertained to the search for "constant and universal principles" of human nature.[5] Cosmopolitanism was based on the ideal of tolerance and understanding between all peoples and cultures.

Dynamic classicism is more subtle and requires some elaboration. Classicism in general may be defined as looking back through history to what one envisions as a classical age of one's culture, an age when one's distant ancestors seemed to have the right answers to the eternal questions of politics, society, and religion. This age was the real or imagined moment of truth for that culture. The implication to Afro-Asian intellectuals undergoing the same experience is that between the golden age and their own age lies a long, dark period of cultural stagnation. In the mind of such an intellectual awakened to a sense of inferiority as a result of his defensive encounter with the modern West, there arises the question invariably: How does one end the dark age and give one's culture a new lease on life?

The intelligentsia can solve this problem in a number of ways. They can try to disavow their heritage and history completely and succumb to some Western style of life. This is not an easy solution unless one moves physically from one's point of origin to a utopia across the seas. America was founded this way. The opposite of westernization is "static classicism," the attempt to make one's culture vital and strong again by reviving the purely ancient ideals and traditions without interference from Western influences. This is another impossible solution because the past is dead and buried. There is no way of revitalizing a decadent culture except by borrowing heavily from progressive cultures of the West. This is the root cause of "ambivalent modernization," which is in its more negative aspect a form of militant nationalism often bordering on fascism. Communalism in India and Pakistan, as well as aspects of black nationalism in the United States today, reflect both the dilemma and the dangerous consequences of this position.

The dynamic classicist stands somewhere in the middle—between the westernizer who renounces his culture in order to save it and the nativist who romanticizes it for the same purpose. The dynamic classicist argues that golden age models are to be used not to shape the present in the image of the past but to rediscover guidelines in one's classical heritage appropriate to a society in transition. Unlike the static classicist he uses history to justify accepting modern values from the West. But he makes a sharp distinction between adopting modern values from the West and westernization.

II. The Challenge of Macaulayism and the Origins of Modern Nationalism in Bengal

In the 1830s the antithesis to Orientalist cultural policy appeared in Bengal as Macaulayism, named after Thomas Babington Macaulay, author of the famous Education Minute of 1835.[6] Macaulayism represented both an alternative to Orientalism as a modernizing program for India and an alternative to universalism as an ideology for modern man.

Hans Kohn, an authority on nationalism in the West, places the rise of nationalism "as a general European movement in the nineteenth century" and refers to Macaulay as a chief participant in the movement.[7] "Nationalism," Kohn writes, "made the divisions of mankind more pronounced and spread the antagonistic aspirations to wider multitudes . . . than ever before." It also produced a "cultural tension which invested the national struggles with the halo of a semi-religious crusade."[8] When Macaulay wrote that the English "have become the greatest and most highly civilized people ever the world saw"[9] he was evidently expressing a chauvinism (however seemingly true to Victorians) that was in sharp contrast to what Kohn calls "the rationalism of the eighteenth century with its emphasis on the common sense of civilization."[10]

Rationalism—the belief in unity over diversity—now gave way to romanticism, the belief that each culture had a special genius which made it intrinsically different from its neighbor. Cosmopolitanism—the belief in humanity over nation—succumbed to nationalism, the contrary belief in the supremacy of national character and sovereignty. Dynamic classicism—the reinterpretation of tradition in the light of contemporary values from the West—now surrendered to dynamic futurism, the repudiation of all history and tradition. As Macaulay himself aptly put it, "Words, and more words, and nothing but words had been all the fruit of all the most renowned sages of sixty generations."[11]

Macaulay was, like his counterparts in continental Europe—including Hegel—a well-intentioned liberal optimist of the early nineteenth century, and it is historically unfair to accuse him of deliberately unleasing the yellow dog of national and racial hatred. Nevertheless, in Bengal of the 1830s, Macaulayism did have the immediate psychological effect of doing precisely that by polarizing the loyalties of the intelligentsia into two opposite camps.[12] The Calcutta cultural mediator who for decades had responded favorably to the culture of the British Orientalist (who was himself favorably impressed with Indian culture) now faced a different view: that all patterns of reform were an integral part of Western civilization and that all Asian civilizations were almost by definition static and decadent. (Macaulay had seriously advised Asians to dress like Englishmen, eat like Englishmen, speak like Englishmen, and act like Englishmen, as their only valid passport to modernity.)[13]

The intelligentsia in Calcutta therefore confronted a crisis in identity. The westernizers, called Young Bengal, followed Macaulayism and temporarily set themselves adrift in a cultural limbo between their own heritage, which they naturally rejected, and that of England, the utopia across the seas, which they understood only imperfectly and to which they could never really belong.[14] The older men, those who had worked with British Orientalists and were dynamic classicists for most of their adult lives,[15] turned defensive and nativist in their sudden zealous appreciation of Hinduism.[16] They formed an organization called the Dharma Sabha (Society in Defense of the Hindu Socio-Ethical Religious Order), which historically has the importance of being India's first modern nationalist movement.[17] Macaulayism, unwittingly perhaps, had unleashed the yellow dog of militant Hindu nationalism in Bengal.

III. TRINITARIAN ETHNOCENTRISM AND UNITARIAN UNIVERSALISM IN THE BENGALI SETTING: THE CASE OF RAMMOHUN ROY

The renaissance which owed its genesis to outgoing universalism seemed to be facing its first real crisis as a generation of intellectuals defected from modernism and turned to ingrown nationalism and xenophobia.

Looking back, however, the Dharma Sabha movement was never more than a yellow puppy of hatred for the English rather than a large ferocious dog for the simple reason that the government never implemented Macaulay's radical program of secular westernization. As it turned out, not secular Macaulayism but the religious variety proved far more formidable a threat to the universalist spirit of the renaissance. Represented by missionaries like the Presbyterian Alexander Duff and converts like Krishna Mohun Bannerji, the gospel of religious Macaulayism denied the validity of all things Indian and based its program on the ethnocentric proposition that Christianity was an integral part of European civilization.[18]

It was at this point that the Brahmo Samaj began to play its crucial role in the history of the Bengal renaissance. Under the patronage of the powerful Tagore family of Jorosanko, and under Debendranath Tagore's leadership in the 1840s, the Brahmo Samaj with its subsidiary Tattvabodhini Sabha became the most popular organization for the increasing number of Western-educated intelligentsia.[19] Within a single decade after 1843, Debendranath had endowed the movement with a structure (the Brahmo *mandir* or church), had evolved an ideology (the Brahmo Dharma), and had provided an identity (the Brahmo covenant).[20]

The Protestant missionaries, far more interested than the government in reshaping men's minds, began a campaign in competition with Brahmos to win over the Western-educated whose training, mentality, and new style of life had alienated them intellectually and psychologically from their countrymen. Whereas the government only anglicized Bengalis sufficiently to make subordinate officials and clerks out of them, the missionaries were anxious to transform total personalities to save souls for Christ. Moreover, since missionaries in those days were ethnocentric and elitist in sympathy, they worked mostly in cities and mostly with the Western-educated through the medium of English.

The missionaries did begin to make inroads with the intelligentsia, converting members of some of the best families.[21] The Brahmo Samaj met the challenge and provided what they hoped would prove an indigenous alternative to Europeanized Christianity. They offered the Western-educated a reformed Indian religion—Vedantism—which they argued was free of superstition and priestly tyranny. At the same time, Brahmos claimed to offer an ethical system based on Hindu scriptures but reflecting the identical sentiments of the Sermon on the Mount. Finally, Brahmos suggested a way of life within the framework of a classical Hindu social order which they said was as accommodating to this-worldly asceticism as was Protestantism.

The origins of Brahmo reformation ideology, upon which Debendranath and his associates constructed a system, date back to the domestication of modern Unitarianism in Bengal by a remarkable intellect named Rammohun Roy (1772–1833). The Bengali version of Unitarianism was from its infancy a far more complex phenomenon than the Western variety in that the problems faced by a Rammohun were always magnified by the perspective of cross-cultural contact. Unlike William Channing in America or Lant Carpenter in England, who sought simply to convince their own countrymen to liberalize their religion and care for the under-privileged among them, Rammohun was continually challenged by the questions Europeans invariably raised: Do you improve the lot of Hindus from within the system or must you undermine it by assimilating to a foreign system? As for the specific content of religious Unitarianism, Rammohun was confronted by such central questions as whether India should follow Christ (however denuded of later excrescences) or whether India should follow some Christlike figure in her own tradition who seemingly represented the same principles.

Rammohun's sympathies, as those of a leading pioneer of the reforma-tion, are quite apparent in the way he adapted Christian Unitarianism to Indian circumstances. To be sure, Rammohun's *Precepts of Jesus*, which constituted his side of a theological debate with a Baptist missionary named Joshua Marshman, was so thoroughly Unitarian in a European sense and so sophisticated in theological erudition and subtlety that one could easily be misled about the author's identity.[22] Indeed, one has only to compare the *Precepts* by Rammohun (1820) with a tract by Lant Car-penter (also 1820) entitled *An Examination of the Charges Made against Unitarians and Unitarianism* to understand the remarkable ideological kinship between the Bengali intellectual and Western Unitarians.[23]

One could certainly hypothesize that the *Precepts* was largely an ex-tension of the debate in the West between Unitarianism and orthodox Christianity. Rammohun's primary concern was to maintain the unity of God against all the false ideas and techniques devised by man to adulterate the purity of monotheistic faith. Thus he repudiated all myths, mysteries, miracles, and images which made a mockery of the unity of the God-head.[24] Rammohun here resembles the familiar liberal and rationalist Unitarian upholding the historic ethical Christ and rejecting vicarious atonement, the Trinity, and other "fabricated fables."[25] Rammohun's view that justice and mercy were more acceptable to God than sacrifice was equally Unitarian in spirit, as was his scriptural reliance on the "Synoptic Gospels with the emphasis on Jesus's teachings rather than the Gospel of St. John with its meditation of Jesus."[26]

Shortly after the debate, Rammohun and a former Baptist named William Adam formed the Calcutta Unitarian Committee.[27] By 1823, Adam, Rammohun and Dwarkanath Tagore (father of Debendranath) seem also to have established a Unitarian Press in north Calcutta.[28] In that same year, Rammohun under the pseudonym of Ram Doss found himself in another debate, this time with an orthodox Christian named Tytler, conducted for the most part in the local press. Remarks by Tytler make it evident that Rammohun was considered by Europeans to have been a Unitarian—a term of disrepute to the orthodox. But the debate was mere theological conflict as in the case of Marshman. Faced with narrow, bigoted attacks on Hinduism in particular and Asians in general by a member of the ruling foreign elite, Rammohun was forced into a defensively nationalist position. But because Rammohun was a modernizer and not a revivalist, he faced his opponent as an Orientalist would a westernizer.

This stance is elucidated well in Rammohun's "Reply to Certain Queries Directed against the Vedanta," printed in the *Brahmmunical Magazine* on 15 November 1823. Tytler had accused Rammohun of reading into the Vedanta the sublime message of Christ.[29] Since only the Christian Scriptures were revealed, he claimed, Rammohun's interpretation was a fraud. In reply, Rammohun with his customary analytical approach proceeded to prove that the message of the Vedanta not only contained the unity of God but did so in a way superior to the Judeo-Christian Bible. Unlike the Bible, the Vedanta did not attempt to categorize the attributes of the Almighty—a gesture which Rammohun found both anthropomorphic and futile.[30] That Rammohun was now using Unitarianism in an Indian way was evidenced by his attack on the Trinity. He argued that whereas Christianity required a blood sacrifice to expiate the sins of man, the Vedanta taught that the "only means of attaining victory over sin is sincere repentance and solemn meditation."[31] In the following quotation it appears as if the Bengali reformer had made a kind of cultural transference from the synoptic Gospels to Sankaracharya: "The sin which mankind contracts against God by the practice of wickedness is believed by us to be expiated by these penances, and not as supposed by the Querist, by the blood of a son of man or son of God, who never participated in our transgressions."[32]

Equally interesting was Rammohun's use of the comparative religious approach, which constituted another marked difference between himself and his Western Unitarian counterparts. Whereas a Channing or a Tuckerman maneuvered primarily in one religious tradition and aimed to reform it, Rammohun was challenged by the need to reconcile at least two major faiths. In the process he was compelled to think comparatively; and as a result his vision sharpened, leaving a narrow sectarian view of the universe behind. He could, for example, in the same reply to Tytler, rebuff his opponent for attacking popular Hinduism by pointing to comparable malpractices in popular Christianity: "A Hindoo would also be justified in taking as a standard of Christianity the system of religion which almost universally prevailed in Europe previous to the 15th century . . . and which is still followed by the majority of Christians with all its idols, crucifixes, saints, miracles, pecuniary absolutions from sin, trinity, transubstantiation, relics, holy water, and other idolatrous machinery."[33]

Rammohun could argue that in the same way the authentic Christian tradition was submerged and corrupted, so the authentic Hindu tradition was likewise submerged and corrupted. He willingly admitted that "our holy Vedanta and our ancient religion [have] been disregarded by the generality of moderns."[34] This comparativist approach, coupled with a modernist outlook, placed the Hindu reformation movement on an Orientalist foundation from which indigenous traditions could be defended at the same time they were modified according to progressive values in contemporary Western societies. Though the foundation was a precarious one it saved the Hindu reformation repeatedly from the snare of militant nationalism.

IV. RELIGIOUS MACAULYISM AND BRAHMO RESPONSE: RAJNARIAN
BASU AS GRANDFATHER OF INDIAN NATIONALISM

In the 1840s these writings by Rammohun were collected and reprinted as ammunition in the ideological struggle for the minds of Calcutta's Western-educated. Several of the missionary adversaries—men like Duff, Dyson, and Long—were keen intellects who were familiar with Rammohun's position and were inventive enough to find ways of countering it. In two areas particularly were the missionaries able to hit the Brahmos where they were weakest: on their historical presentation based on a virtually nonexistent historiographic tradition among the Hindus;[35] and on the lack of a systematic Brahmo theology.[36] On the other hand, following the lead of Rammohun, Brahmo intellectuals such as Rajnarian Basu and Akshoy Kumar Dutt were equally gifted and could turn every missionary argument into a boomerang aimed at similar inconsistencies and irrationalities—plus the presence of historically unverifiable events within Christianity.[37] These debates, because they were carried on at the highest level and because there was a good deal of soul-searching involved, are valuable today as a pioneering attempt at comparative religion.

One argument raised frequently by missionaries like Duff and by converts like K. M. Bannerji was that in the whole of the so-called Vedic tradition there was no notion of a personal god analogous to Jehovah.[38] Missionaries contended that even in the Upanishads the concept of God was so abstract as to be without analogy.[39] This was the monotheistic-monistic issue in the debate. Duff's concept of the ancient god of the Hindus was of a being who, "unencumbered by the cares of empire or the functions of a superintending providence, effectuates no good, inflicts no evil, suffers no pain, experiences no emotion; his beatitude is represented as consisting in a languid, monotonous and uninterrupted sleep—a sleep so very deep as never to be disturbed by the visitation of a dream."[40]

The Brahmo reply in *Vedantic Doctrines Vindicated* suggests the fiery and skilled debater Rajnarian Basu (1826–1899), who had acquired the skill at Hare's School, developed it in subsequent encounters with Christians, and brought it to perfection as a nationalist critic of Keshub Sen's universalism. In this tract of 1845, which was his first recorded encounter with the missionaries, he took a phrase like "cares of empire" and asked Duff whether God was a king or an emperor.[41] Rajnarian made capital of this ill-chosen expression, charging that the Christian god was more an oriental despot than a merciful Father.

Rajnarian's second point was directed at Duff's depiction of the Upanishadic Brahma as a god who "effectuates no good and inflicts no evil."[42] What kind of God is this, he replied, "who is author of evil?" How can we possibly ascribe "the indiscriminate murder of millions" through "religious fanaticism or political hostility" to "our immaculate Creator?"[43]

The third point seems reminiscent of Rammohun Roy's debate with Tytler in 1823—which was reprinted in 1845, the same year that Rajnarian published his tract. Rajnarian took Duff to task for characterizing God as a being which "suffers pain and experiences emotion." He accused Duff of "rushing headlong into the hideous errors of a reckless anthropomorphism."[44] "Can there be a worse doctrine than that which denudes and degrades God by bringing the Almighty Creator to the level of a man?"[45]

The Brahmos' ideological defense of Vedantism was certainly an important factor in stopping the advance of Christianity among the intelligentsia but, remarkably, such was accomplished without resorting to yellow-dog fanaticism. Besides ideology, the Brahmos, if they were convincing enough, held a certain advantage among their fellow alienated intellectuals: their reinterpretation of Hinduism, if accepted ultimately in place of popular Hinduism, would bridge the gap between themselves and the mass of their countrymen. The Macaulay-like missionaries, on the other hand, rigidly persisted in Europeanizing their converts with the inevitable result that each and every Indian Christian underwent excommunication and denationalization.

More significant still, perhaps, is the fact that the Brahmos retained, with modifications, the outgoing universalism of their founder Rammohun Roy and therefore saved the Bengal renaissance.[46] Throughout long years of ideological struggle with the missionaries they retained a firm distinction between orthodox Christian Trinitarians, who were their adversaries, and liberal Christian Unitarians, who were among their closest friends. Instead of hating Westerners indiscriminately (the yellow dog attitude), they maintained a steady intellectual and personal contact—through exchange of books and correspondence—with American and British Unitarians.[47] Emerson, Channing, Theodore Parker, Martineau, and others were as well known among Bengali Brahmos as they were among their own Unitarian followers.[48] The universalist doctrine of Unitarianism was itself a strong link in the chain which kept the yellow dog in check.

But it was very difficult, if not impossible, to retain the unqualified cosmopolitanism of Rammohun Roy while at the same time battling foreign missionaries who ridiculed and repudiated the foundation of Hindu tradition. To continually remind one that he was a descendant of an inferior heritage without any relevance in the contemporary world was tantamount to waving a red flag before the bull. Tormented minds, or mercenary ones, willingly submitted; but Brahmos of the mid-century with greater idealism and integrity resisted, challenged, and refuted the foreign missionaries. Thus despite their universalism the Brahmos were also nationalist by virtue of their defense of Hinduism.

But there was already present an even stronger, almost defiant nationalism in Rajnarian's *Vedantic Doctrines Vindicated.* It lies in the point-by-point defense of a Hindu tradition against the pretensions of religious revelation and superiority by an alien faith. If in Rammohun's writings cultural nationalism never went beyond the point of proving that Hinduism was equal to Christianity, in Rajnarian's earliest polemical tracts there is already the germ of a more aggressive attitude: that Hinduism is superior to Christianity. Of course, by Hinduism Rajnarian the Brahmo did not mean the accepted popular form but the reformed Hindu variety based on the classical Vedantic tradition:

> The Vedanta, while it utterly rejects and condemns such degrading notions of the deity, conveys to our minds a far loftier, a more adequate, consistent, and ennobling idea of His attributes, by prescribing His worship as the Supreme Regulator of this boundless universe and as the glorious and beneficent originator of all earthly good.[49]

If, however, in this kind of religious encounter, superiority depended on the validity of one's defense of Vedanta or Bible as being a revealed source, then Brahmo nationalism of this early period was never dogmatic but tempered by a cosmopolitan outlook. After years of soul-searching on the part of Debendranath Tagore and other Brahmos, the issue was dropped and in 1850 a momentous decision was reached: revelation for any scriptural source, Hindu or otherwise, was denied.[50] Rajnarian, who in the meantime was sharpening his wit in defense of classical Hindu superiority, accepted this decision against the Vedanta as the word of God with great reluctance.

V. ANTINATIONALIST REACTION: THE BRAHMO UNIVERSALISM OF KESHUB CHANDRA SEN

The positive side of this combination of outgoing universalism and defense of culture was, as implied, that it kept the mind free of yellow dog hatred. This was precisely what distinguished the Brahmo freedom fighter from his militant Hindu counterpart in the twentieth century. Termed "creative nationalism" by one such Brahmo, the attitude was simply one of trying to keep the freedom struggle separate from a hatred of Englishmen or a hatred of Europeans generally.[51] But on the negative side, the introduction of nationalism per se, creative or not, seemed to have a divisive effect on the Brahmo intellectuals. In the first place, many Brahmos, imbued with the Rammohun legacy of the universal man and universal religion, saw nationalism as a dangerous departure from true Brahmo doctrine. For them, Brahmoism was neither Hindu nor Christian but the quest to end sectarianism by establishing a true universal church and religion. In the second place, nationalism, so Brahmo intellectuals argued, had the tendency of glorifying a culture and thus concealing its defects and weaknesses. The result, they warned, would be to dampen the enthusiasm of Brahmos for social reform and cripple the Samaj as a modernizing movement.

In the 1860s it was becoming obvious that nationalism had cracked Brahmo unity. The Brahmos under Debendranath suddenly found themselves an old guard defending the charge of social inaction which the younger people associated with the movement's gradual drift back into the Hindu fold. Like an old guard, Debendranath's group rested on their laurels. Had they not arrested Christianity? Had they not refined Brahmo ideology? Had they not carried rationalism in religion to its ultimate in 1850 when they rejected all scripture as revealed and left each individual free to interpret truth according to the light of reason and intuition?[52]

By 1865, the issue of social reform had reached crisis proportion within Brahmo ranks. The younger generation under the leadership of Keshub Chandra Sen (1838–1884) insisted that the ministry be open to qualified members of all castes; that Brahmos who were Brahmans by caste renounce their sacred thread (symbol of caste inequality); that all the Brahmos openly and unequivocally declare themselves against the caste system; and that the Samaj publicly launch a vigorous campaign against *kulīn* polygamy and child marriage while promoting widow remarriage, intercaste marriage, and female improvement through education.[53] The underlying issue was national identity. Debendranath argued that such radical proposals at this time would alienate Hindus and tear down all the progress Brahmos had made in convincing Hindus to accept Brahmoism as reformed Hinduism.[54] This was the natural position of a man who had for twenty years defended the Hindu traditions against missionaries.

On 5 May 1866 Keshub Sen gave what was probably his most important, most popular, and most misquoted lecture, at Medical College Hall, Calcutta. This controversial talk greatly perturbed Debendranath and his friends because they believed Keshub had sold out to the missionaries and had publicly adopted the alien faith. Even the title created misunderstanding between older and younger Brahmos: "Jesus Christ: Europe and Asia."[55] On the surface, as many missionaries and Debendranath himself interpreted it, the lecture constituted a defense of Christ's teachings and early Christian dogma. Ignored for the most part was Keshub's careful distinction between "Christ's message of universal harmony"[56] and the institutional Christianity of the nineteenth century with its Europeanized, sectarian, and "muscular" view of Christ.[57] Also missed was his sophisticated challenge to British cultural imperialism not as a militant but as a creative nationalist who attacked foreign imposition without hating all persons and things foreign. The lecture was also an essay on comparative religion which, when saturated with Keshub's own spirit of universal Unitarianism, expressed an objective and scientific attitude remarkable for the times he lived in.

Keshub's Jesus, whom P. C. Mazumdar later popularized as the "Oriental Christ," was inspired by God to offer to "humanity, groaning under a deadly malady and on the verge of death, a remedy to save it."[58] Christ's remedy, a gift from the East to the West, was ethical and spiritual as characteristic of Asian religions.[59] The passage which shocked Debendranath as much as it pleased the missionaries was Keshub's apparent acceptance of the crucifixion. What Keshub accepted, as should be clear from the following quotation, was the ethical value of the symbol:

> He laid down his life that God might be glorified. I have always regarded the cross as a beautiful emblem of self-sacrifice into the glory of God . . . on which is calculated to quicken the hither feelings and aspirations of the heart, and to purify the soul . . . and I believe there is not a heart, how callous and hard, soever it may be, that can look with cool indifference at that grand and significant symbol.[60]

Most effective was Keshub's contrast between the noble self-sacrificing Christ of the Orient and the missionaries of Christ sent out from churches in the West to India. It is curious that such anti-imperialistic passages completely escaped the notice of Adi Brahmos and others who were quick to point to Keshub's surrender to westernized Christianity. After reporting that since the early part of the century only 154,000 converts had

been won over to Christ in South Asia, and that 519 missionaries representing 32 societies with an annual combined budget of £250,000 were
combing the subcontinent for potential candidates to the new faith,
Keshub asked why they had accomplished so little. The reason, he believed, was that many of the missionaries not only "hate the natives with
their whole heart but seem to take pleasure in doing so." Said Keshub:

> They regard the natives as one of the vilest nations on earth hopelessly im-
> mersed in all the vices which can degrade humanity. . . . They think it
> mean to associate with native ideas and tastes, native customs and man-
> ners, which seem to them odious and contemptible; while native character
> is considered to represent the lowest type of lying and wickedness.[61]

But Keshub's response was not that of the militant Hindu nationalist in
a blind defense of his own heritage. Like Akshoy Kumar Dutt, Keshub
Chandra Sen placed universalism above national character. It is again
curious how the following passage, so clear and unmistakable, has been
ignored by those who have presented the reformer as an unqualified
Christian apologist. Said Keshub:

> The fact is, human nature is the same everywhere—in all latitudes and
> climes, but circumstances modify it, and religion and usages mould it in
> different forms. Educate the native mind, and you will find it susceptible of
> as much improvement and elevation as that of the European.[62]

Indeed Keshub was one of the first Bengalis to refer to cultural stereo-
types, which he termed "caricatures."[63] It was not "national character"
which kept the Indian nation in darkness but circumstances. The trouble
is, he said, "that we are a subject race and have been for centuries."[64] In
such passionate terms we find the same indignant mood against imperialism in Vivekananda later on. But in contrast to Vivekananda, Keshub in
1866 attacked the excesses of imperialism in the name of the exalted image
of the true Christ:

> Christ . . . do Europeans follow him? I regard Europeans in India as
> missionaries of Christ and I have a right to demand they should always
> remember and act up to his high responsibilities. . . . But I find pseudo
> Christians with reckless conduct. . . . Yea their muscular Christianity has
> led many a native to identify the religion of Jesus with the power and
> privilege of inflicting blows and kicks with impunity. Had it not been for
> them, the name of Jesus . . . would have been ten times more glorified.[65]

It may be difficult to see how a detached comparative religious attitude
could possibly emerge from Keshub's angry mood, but it did. His underlying belief in unity over diversity made the comparative approach possible. In fact, though a theist and not a deist, Keshub in 1866 reminds one of

Akshoy Kumar Dutt in the way he was groping for the universal principles of religion. Even Keshub's identification with Christ may be misleading. There are a few revealing passages in the talk which suggest that it was not Christ as such that was crucial but what he represented universally in history: "It is my firm conviction that his teachings find a response in the universal consciousness of humanity, and are no more European than Asiatic, and that in his ethics there is neither Greek nor Jew, circumcision nor uncircumcision, barbarian, Scythian, bound or free."[66]

VI. Keshub's Schism of 1866 and Adi Samaj Reaction: The Nationalist Ideology of Dwijendranath Tagore and the Hindu Mela

At a general meeting of Brahmos on 15 November 1866 the formal break between generations finally occurred. The birth of the Brahmo Samaj of India at that meeting was anticlimactic, but the resolutions passed by the Keshubites and subsequent debates sharply define the increasingly vital issue of nationalism and universalism between the two camps. One resolution should be singled out in this regard—the one proposed by the Vaishnava Brahmo, Bijoy Krishna Goswami, on behalf of the Keshubites. It read: "Men and women of every nation and caste who believe in the fundamental doctrines of Brahmo Dharma shall be eligible as members of the Brahmo Samaj of India."[67]

Actually, Bijoy Krishna was not referring to Debendranath's book *Brahmo Dharma*, which had served as a bible for the Adi Samaj and which had neatly developed Brahmoism as the reformed Hinduism. Quite the contrary, Bijoy Krishna promptly called for a new "compilation of theistic texts to be taken from all the Scriptures of the world."[68] It was in reply to Bijoy Krishna that Nabagopal Mitra, personal friend of the Tagores and ardent Adi Brahmo nationalist, raised his voice. This was the same Nabagopal Mitra whose many subsequent activities of a patriotic nature would earn him the title "National Mitra." He argued at the meeting that "if there was truth sufficient near home, why should we go abroad? There was all the truth which we require in the Hindu scriptures and we need not therefore borrow anything from other scriptures."[69]

This mild statement hardly represented either Nabagopal Mitra's style of belittling universalists or the harsh Adi Brahmo treatment inflicted upon Keshub Chandra after the schism. The rupture had caused a second major crisis of the Bengal renaissance. The impact on the older generation of Brahmos was disastrous; Keshub became an object of hostility reminiscent of Macaulay's image in an earlier generation. The Adi Samaj turned into a snarling yellow dog of nationalist arrogance. Rajnarian Basu was perhaps earliest in his response with *Prospectus to Start a Society for the*

Promotion of National Feeling Among the Educated Natives of Bengal in April 1866.[70]

Though the association was soon replaced by the more ambitious Tagore-supported Hindu Mela, the prospectus was a powerfully worded document in defiance of Keshub's universalism. Rajnarian was unimpressed by Keshub's desire to look abroad for inspiration. More important to Basu was the realization of Bengal's degradation. How shameful, for example, that "Hindu youth" had not only "severed themselves from Hindu society but had renounced even the Hindu name."[71] A program of regenerating Hindu youth was therefore necessary, one which included physical training to "restore the manliness of Bengali youth" and their long-lost "military prowess"; the establishment of a school in Hindu music with the "composition of songs for moral, patriotic and martial enthusiasm"; the founding of a school for Hindu medicine to revive "our own medical sciences"; and the encouragement of "Indian antiquities" to illuminate the "glory of ancient India."[72]

Along with the program of general Sanskritic revival, Rajnarian offered proposals for building up contemporary Bengal as a society and culture. He was most adamant about cultivating the Bengali language. "We must learn to communicate in our language," he wrote. Do the English communicate with one another in French or German? He recommended that Bengali boys learn Bengali before English in school. He urged giving up English food, dress, and even dramatic entertainment for the Bengali variety.[73]

The *National Paper,* which Debendranath commissioned Nabagopal Mitra to edit in 1865, proved from 1867 onward to be the most effective means of propagating Hindu Brahmo nationalism against Keshubite universalism among the Western-educated in Bengal. The articles which graced the newspaper during its first years of existence, mostly written by Dwijendranath Tagore, were brilliant expositions in defense of both the Adi Samaj and the national culture. Dwijendranath, who was among the most defiant of all Indian patriots from the Bengali middle class, couched his nationalism in the Orientalist ideological heritage. Thus he accepted modernization but argued that the true modernizer had first to identify with his culture and then work within to revitalize it.

As a philosopher by inclination rather than by profession, Dwijendranath was one of Keshub Chandra's most formidable intellectual opponents. In contrast to his younger brother Rabindranath, who underwent prolonged identity crises and continually shifted between universalism and nationalism, Dwijendranath remained steadfastly nationalist—even much later in life when he debated his brother in support of Gandhi's noncooperation movement. As early as 1867, Dwijendranath was convinced that the only way the Adi Samaj could survive Keshub's schism was to identify itself closer than ever with the Hindu Samaj. If Keshub could command the loyalty of the progressive theistic youth on the grounds of universalism, the Adi Brahmos could command the support of the theists in the much greater Hindu society—to which at long last they would emerge as leaders.

The assumption behind Dwijendranath's nationalist ideology was the familiar notion that the westernizing model was a dead end to nation-building and modernism in India. In an article of 25 September 1867 called "European Model" he blasted those misguided progressives who "have mistaken views of progressive civilization."[74] These people have sold themselves to "an exotic civilization" as if "there were only one civilization in the world, viz. English civilization."[75] The more sensible alternative would be to work within that which was "genuine and national in the manners, customs, and habits of this country."[76] Certainly, he argued, "English civilization deserves our esteem" but only because it is the natural offshoot of the energies of the English nation and of no other people. Thus argued Dwijendranath:

> Each nation holds a distinct nationality and for so holding it is the more entitled to the appellation of a civilized nation. . . . But our countrymen rush madly to their own degradation by acting under the supposition that to imitate English civilization . . . is synonymous with making progress . . . and instead of making national institutions the bases of all progress, import a foreign air in all actions and reform.[77]

Dwijendranath continued his exploration of the problem and later added that a well-intentioned foreign import could, under certain circumstances, "destroy the inner vitality and integrity of our native character."[78] In an earlier article on "Hinduism is not Hostile to Brahmoism" he sought to define progress in terms of national identity. He discovered it to mean "what is harmonious in the fusion of past and present standards of a culture."[79] Progress was assuredly not the substitution of something foreign for something national but the "consolidation of institutions defunct as well as those fast growing up" for the benefit of a given culture.[80]

It was in the very depths of the psychology of cultural encounter under colonialism that Dwijendranath waxed most eloquent in his defense of nationalism. An article on "Nationality and Universality" was aimed specifically at Keshub. "That the Hindoos and the Europeans should have everything in common is no doubt a desirable end," he began, but before that, "we must have a footing of equality with the Europeans."[81] "Under present circumstance," he warned, "an adoption of European habits would be like wearing a badge of slavery."[82] In a later article on much the

same subject, Dwijendranath made a striking comparison between anglicized Bengalis and American Negroes:

> With all our present inferiority and infirmities we are little better respected
> by the world than the Christian negro of North America who speaks Eng-
> lish, dresses himself with the jacket and pantaloon, and whose habits of life
> in fact are mostly borrowed from the European settlers there. And why so?
> Simply because his civilization is nothing more than an image of European
> manners and habits, and he is no more like the true European than the
> monkey in the red-coat riding on the she-goat is like a human being. By
> means of mere imitation we can be just so much like the Europeans as
> slaves are like their masters.[83]

As evidenced in Keshub's own paper the *Indian Mirror*, which he had
managed to acquire after his break with Debendranath, these attacks did
not go unnoticed. But far more significant than the exchange of ideas in
debate were Keshub's innovations as charismatic hero of the younger
generation of theistic progressives.

In the early years Keshub championed reformism and universalism
without much apparent inconsistency. Bijoy Krishna's proposal in the
meeting of 15 November 1866 for a compilation of scriptures from all the
religious sources led to the publication of the *Sloka Sangraho*, first used in
Brahmo services, and then borrowed and adapted by Unitarians for their
own services abroad.[84] The opening of the Keshubite *mandir* on 22 August
1869 boldly proclaimed the universalism and reformist intent of the newly
formed Brahmo Samaj of India. Keshub's declaration of principles was
obviously derived from Rammohun Roy's tenets in the trust deed to the
first Brahmo church, established in 1829. "This building," Keshub declared, "is established with the object of paying reverence to all truths that
exist in the world . . . that all quarrel, all misunderstanding, all pride of
caste may be destroyed, and all brotherly feeling may be perpetuated."[85]
No idols were to be worshipped and no scripture was to be considered
infallible. Furthermore:

> No sect shall be vilified, ridiculed, or hated. No prayer, hymn, sermon, or
> discourse to be delivered or used here shall countenance or encourage any
> manner of idolatry, sectarianism or sin. Divine service shall be conducted
> here in such a spirit and manner as may enable men and women, irrespec-
> tive of distinctions of caste, color, and condition, to unite in one family,
> eschew all manner of error and sin, and advance in wisdom, faith and
> righteousness.[86]

Even the architecture of the *mandir* reflected Keshub's universalism.
It was a blend of a Hindu temple, Christian church, and Muslim mosque.[87]
In 1870, when an expanded edition of the *Sloka Sangraho* was published

for the congregation, the motto beautifully inscribed on the title page was "The Wide Universe was the Temple of God."[88]

The Tagore family responded to Keshub's universalism by beautifying and popularizing their yearly national festival which came later to be known as the Hindu Mela. Started in April 1867 by the combined efforts of Rajnarian Basu, Dwijendranath Tagore, and Nabagopal Mitra, it aimed at carrying out the principles articulated in Rajnarian's prospectus. Actually, by supporting local industry, it went even farther than Rajnarian had anticipated and may in this sense be looked upon as the precursor of the Swadeshi movement of the early 1900s.[89] Fervent nationalist poems and songs were composed for the occasion, and wrestling matches were arranged between Bengali and Punjabi students with the hope that the former would defeat the latter—if and when they did, as in 1868, the fact was well publicized. There were also exhibitions of every sort testifying to the abilities of Hindus in general but Bengali Hindus in particular.

In 1869, the year of Keshub's new *mandir*, the Tagores invested more money and talent in the festival, enlarging the program and drawing more people. The management was pleased to report that seven thousand people had attended the Hindu Mela that year.[90] Three themes were promoted in songs, poems, and speeches: "progress, unity, and self-reliance."[91] Progress to the Adi Brahmo backers of the Hindu Mela meant progress of Hindus, whereas unity meant burying regional and caste differences for the sake of Hindu unity and self-reliance meant the promotion of entrepreneurship among Bengali Hindu youths principally.

The Hindu Mela, although it did help the Adi Samaj stay alive by giving it a share in the leadership of Calcutta Hindu society, did not affect Keshub or his career. On the contrary, in the early 1870s the silver-tongued reformer was riding the crest of his popularity and success. His universalism seemed to endear him to all. An American Unitarian missionary named Charles Dall was made a member of the Keshubite community by signing the Brahmo covenant and was given every opportunity to spread Unitarian literature and ideas among Brahmos in Bengal and elsewhere in South Asia.[92] Dall predicted that Keshub's brand of Brahmoism would ultimately triumph in India as an indigenous form of Christian Unitarianism.[93] In 1866 Lant Carpenter's daughter Mary had come to India to promote social work, and while in Bengal it was to the younger Brahmos that she appealed directly for assistance. Her close friend was Monomohun Ghose, an active member of the Keshubite organization whom she called the "Bengali Unitarian." Her first visitor upon arriving in Calcutta was Keshub Chandra, whom she viewed at the time as the truest follower of her father's friend, Rammohun Roy.[94]

VII. IDENTITY, COMMUNITY, AND THE BRAHMO MARRIAGE ACT OF 1872

The problem of national identity was no mere ideological issue between Adi Brahmos and Keshubites but had serious practical implications as well. The difficulty may be traced back to the 1850s when Debendranath stated that "we Brahmos are situated amidst a community which views us with no friendly feelings" since we ourselves attack "their Puranic and tantric systems."[95] He went on to point out that Brahmos have little in common with anglicized "secularists" and with other "denationalized" sorts such as members of the Christian community. He characterized the Brahmo attitude to these persons as one of "practical hostility." Thus he concluded that the Brahmo community was in a delicate position between apologists of the Hindu status quo and apologists of a Western way of life. And he predicted that Brahmos would continue to have a hard time of it "so long as our numbers are so small, our resources so limited, and our enemies so powerful as they now are."[96]

When the new *mandir* opened, Keshub initiated twenty-one young men into what he tried to make them believe was not simply a religion or ideology or a social gospel but a full-fledged community. Three things were painfully obvious to Keshub at the time. First, that most of the young converts were excommunicated from their caste and ostracized from their families. Second, the reason why they had been cut off from Hindu society was that they were anusthanic Brahmos—Brahmos who practiced what they preached. These two factors together added up to the third realization: that his Brahmo community was already de facto separated from the Hindu *samaj* but lacked de jure recognition of their existence. Even the Christian families were protected legally as to inheritance and the validity of their marriages.

In fact a year before the Keshubite *mandir* was completed and the new community came into being officially, the advocate general of India ruled that Brahmo marriages which conformed neither to Muslim nor to Hindu rites "were invalid and the offspring of them were to be considered illegitimate."[97] Since their marriages departed so little from Hindu rites, Adi Brahmos had no problem. But the Keshubites found themselves in the lamentable position of being penalized by a Western government for adopting Western-inspired reform measures. Keshub had no recourse but to pressure the government to give legal recognition to the Brahmo marriage and family—a formidable task when it is considered how tiny a minority the new Brahmo community constituted as against any organized opposition by the vast majority of Hindus.

Between 1869 and 1872 the controversy over the proposed Brahmo Marriage Act was so violently abusive and so interlaced with other issues that it led to a final and irrevocable split between the Adi Brahmos and the Keshubites. Before then there was a kind of verbal truce between Keshub and Debendranath,[98] but after 1870 Debendranath withdrew from Brahmo affairs to Santineketan, leaving the presidency of the organization in the hands of his more militant successor, Rajnarian Basu. Rajnarian, Dwijendranath, and Jyotirindranath (another elder brother of Rabindranath Tagore) lashed out against the Marriage Act proposals from the pulpit of the church, from editorials in the *National Paper* and *Tattvabodhini Patrika,* and from the podium at public meetings. They hoped to stir up fear of the act's consequences among the Hindu *samaj.*

What appears to have disturbed the Adi Brahmos most of all was the familiar nationalist concern about estrangement from Hindu society. Most of their articles, speeches, and editorials led to the conclusion—by no means an unfounded one—that it would arrest the course of "healthy and spontaneous reformation" by legally defining the "Brahmos as a body distinct from the general body of Hindus." Said Rajnarian in an official memorial against the Marriage Act proposal on 12 April 1871: "The Brahmos now in fact form an integral part of Hindu Society. The law will dissociate the former from the latter—a contingency to be highly dreaded as it will injure the course of religious reformation in India."[99]

In the quest for identity, the Keshubites were now increasingly compelled to admit that Rajnarian was right in his conclusion but wrong in his gloomy prediction of the law's consequences. During the latter stage of the controversy P. C. Mazumdar, on behalf of Keshub, wrote a revealing article on the problem of identity in an effort to arrive at a new perspective. The question he posed was this: Who in fact were the Brahmos? Were they Christians as the Adi Samaj suggested? "How can we be Christians?" he asked. Said Mazumdar, "We do not believe in the divinity of Christ nor in the infallibility of the Bible, nor in miracles, nor in prophecies, nor in sacraments." Nor are Brahmos Muslims. Are Brahmos Hindus? Mazumdar's answer; "Yes, nationally and socially we are. The Brahmos take pride in calling themselves Hindus so far as the name of their country goes, so far as their ancestry and the society of their countrymen among them whom they love are concerned."[100]

But then Mazumdar went on to declare that in ideology, ethics, and social practice "we Brahmos are not Hindus."[101] Brahmos do not accept the Vedas and Puranas as infallible nor do they believe in "the sacred wisdom of the Rishis," nor do they accept the "incarnations of Vishnu." To round off his argument, Mazumdar said that "if again by Hinduism is meant idolatry, caste . . . incantations and all the false superstitions, then we are certainly not Hindus."[102]

The intensity of expression surrounding the controversy only magnified the seemingly insoluble problem of Brahmo identity. Keshub's own reasoning throughout was based on the proposition that so long as Brahmos practiced their tenets no wrongs would result. There was nothing in Brahmoism which would produce denationalizing tendencies. The Marriage Act would have the effect of enabling Brahmos to practice what they preached. Moreover it was the Adi Brahmo Samaj that was treading a dangerous path because it was sacrificing the Brahmo program for the sake of national identity. More and more, however, Keshub found himself arguing the universalist position that Brahmos were neither Hindu nor Christian but the pioneer community for a syncretic religion which represented the best features of the existing universal faiths.[103]

No theory could erase the fact that on 19 March 1872, when the Brahmo Marriage Act was enacted by the government, those Brahmos who adhered to it discovered themselves legally divorced from Hindu society. The fact was momentarily overshadowed by jubilant progressives all over India who hailed Keshub as a miracle worker. They pointed not to the provision on Brahmo identity but to the provisions allowing for such reforms as intercaste and widow marriage or prohibiting such social evils as child marriage and polygamy. Keshub had struggled and won against enormous odds. By means of memorials, letters, visits to bureaucrats in Simla, and by publicized consultations with doctors as to the proper marital age for young adults, Keshub had convinced Lord Lawrence to sign into law an act of social reform.

The only difficulty was in the wording of Sir Henry Maine, who wrote the act. The reforms applied to "those marrying parties who declared that they did not profess the Hindu, Mohammedan, Christian, Parsee, Buddhist, Sikh, or Jainna religion. "[104] Thus at the stroke of a pen, in the eyes of the government, Brahmoism was no longer reformed Hinduism but a distinct religious community with a distinct legal identity.

VIII. BRAHMO UNIVERSALISM BETWEEN CULTURAL IMPERIALISM AND MILITANT NATIONALISM: THE FAILURE OF KESHUB SEN'S NEW DISPENSATION

Thus Keshub was certainly not the Christ-lover or simplistic anglophile his critics have made him out to be. These same critics, rather inconsistently, also accuse him of Vaishnava emotionalism which prompted him to introduce the *kirtan* and processions as a regular Brahmo practice.[105] Keshub was an ardent universalist or cosmopolitan who in the 1870s drove his immediate disciples into an intensive study of all major religions from primary sources in their original languages.[106] Not only Christianity was studied as an alien religion but Buddhism, Zoroastrianism, Judaism, and Islam as well. The first Bengali translation of the Koran was a product of this research.[107] Then Keshub held seminars on comparative religion; from available accounts no single religion was held as revealed or superior to the others.[108] The purpose of all this: to ascertain the underlying unity of all religions.

So long as Keshub combined universalism with social activism as a modernizer, he maintained the loyalty of the progressive wing of the intelligentsia. This he managed to do until the middle of the decade. In 1878 he lost the progressives and younger people with the formation of the Sadharan Brahmo Samaj just as Debendranath had done twelve years earlier. In part, Keshub was victim of historical circumstances which dashed his program to pieces; and in part, he was victim of his uncontrollable obsession with the development of a true universal religion.[109]

The alarming increase of British yellow dog racism and cultural imperialism ultimately made a mockery of Brahmo universalism.[110] In the first place, there was a sharp rise of the educated unemployed who could not find suitable jobs.[111] The British were rightly blamed for their misfortune. Secondly, gifted Bengalis were discriminated against openly by Britishers who resented "niggers" in high positions.[112] Thirdly, the nonofficial British community blocked every effort to give Indian magistrates the power to judge cases involving whites as well as nonwhites. In short, the historical atmosphere suddenly made Keshub's universalism ludicrously inappropriate if not downright unpatriotic.

At a time when Indian cultural nationalism was rapidly becoming politicized, Keshub publicized his continuing loyalty to Queen Victoria, a gesture which must have seemed offensive to the younger radicals.[113] In this regard, it should be pointed out that the leaders of the Sadharan Brahmos who broke with Keshub in 1878 were the very same people who led the Indian Association, precursor of the Indian National Congress.[114] Ananda Mohun Bose in particular—who was among the twenty-one young men to proclaim publicly his adherence to anusthanic Brahmoism under Keshub's leadership at the *mandir* in 1869, and who rebelled against Keshub to found the Sadharan Samaj less than ten years later—proved to be the prime mover, organizer, and financier of the Indian Association.[115] Indeed it was Bose who employed Surendranath Bannerji after the latter's dismissal from the civil service and Bose who provided the inspiration and support for Bannerji's rise as early nationalist critic of the excesses of British imperialism.[116] Behind Bose and Bannerji were such articulate politicized Brahmos as Bipin Chandra Pal, Sivanath Sastri, Krishna Kamul Mitra, and Dwarkanath Ganguli.

Keshub was also victim of his preoccupation with the composition of a universal religion which demanded more and more of his time and energy. His American Unitarian friend, Reverend Dall, warned him repeatedly against deserting social reform for the task of constructing a highly intellectualized, highly abstract religious system.[117] But Keshub persisted in his dream of a New Dispensation which would integrate the best elements of all religions.[118] Intellectually, without doubt, the New Dispensation represents one of the major achievements of the Bengal renaissance. The rites, myths, and symbols of all the major faiths underwent a subtle and ingenious transformation to become parts of a new system that it was hoped would replace the limited sectarian system.[119] It was, unfortunately for Keshub, a futile gesture. Many thinking people the world over had by 1884 (the year of Keshub's death) rejected the validity of religious solutions to social problems. Moreover, in the so-called progressive West, virtually every country was becoming an armed yellow dog as Europe before 1914 increasingly resembled a community of hounds on the eve of a fox hunt.

IX. The Challenge of National Identity and the Triumph of Universalism as a Cultural Ideal: The Brahmo Heritage and Rabindranath Tagore

To complete this study of the Orientalist legacy and the problem of Brahmo identity in the Bengal renaissance, one must look carefully at Rabindranath Tagore's reinterpretation of the Adi Brahmo idea of Hindu modernism, which may well constitute his most important ideological contribution to Bengal and to India. Though it is enormously difficult to follow Tagore's intellectual meanderings—indicating a certain cultural rootlessness—I would recommend that we pay heed to the relationship between Hindu modernism and his self-acknowledged adherence to a Hindu Brahmo identity.

Hindu Brahmoism, which I have traced back to 1866 as one consequence of Keshub Sen's schism from the Adi Samaj, was born out of an encounter of modernizing alternatives framed in the context of nationalism and universalism. It was surely no accident that the earliest use of the term *Hindu Brahmo* was in reference to Adi Samajists such as Rajnarian Basu, Debendranath Tagore, and Dwijendranath Tagore. To my knowledge the term was first applied to a Sadharan Samajist in 1890, when Ramananda Chatterji cast off his sacred thread and declared himself a Hindu Brahmo because "Brahmoism was the truest exposition of Hinduism."[120] With the escalation of British imperialism and the consequent rise of militant nationalism, the problem of modernity became even more acute. Here is the setting for Rabindranath's role and contribution as a key member of the Bengali intelligentsia within the Brahmo context.

Though the basic biographical data of Rabindranath's life are well known to the general reader of Indian history, the Brahmo side of his life is relatively unknown in print. Stephen Hay, in a recent monograph on an aspect of Tagore's ideology, claims that the earliest formative influence on Rabindranath was Keshub Chandra Sen.[121] The fact that Rabindranath was born in 1861, during the honeymoon period of relationship between Keshub and Debendranath, is significant to Hay. The fact that Rabindranath was born at the very time Keshub fled his house to live in the Tagore *bari* is also highly significant. Indeed as Rabindranath himself later wrote: "I was fortunate enough to receive his [Keshub's] affectionate caresses at the moment when he was cherishing his dream of a great future spiritual illumination."[122]

No doubt Rabindranath was influenced by Keshub—especially in his ideological development in mature life—since few Brahmos from Debendranath's time onward were not at first favorably attracted to the reformer. But we should also keep in mind that Rabindranath was five years old when the bitter schism radically transformed the affections of the Tagore family and made them deadly foes of Keshub. For all practical purposes, Satyendranath passed out of the Calcutta scene in 1862 when he went to England and upon his return became a covenanted civil servant in west India. The family leadership passed into the hands of Dwijendranath and Jyotirindranath, two of Keshub's deadliest enemies both ideologically and personally.

Indeed, it is Jyotirindranath who became Rabindranath's favorite brother in the years that followed.[123] If Rabindranath experienced anything during the years of Nabagopal Mitra's nationalist enterprises, the *National Paper* with the inflammatory articles by Dwijendranath, the Tagore-supported Hindu Mela, and Rajnarian's presidency of the Adi Samaj, it was assuredly a strong family commitment to Hindu Brahmoism and cultural nationalism. As viewed by Keshub and his followers, the Tagores were drifting back into the Hindu fold. If in his youthful years Rabindranath was still attracted to Keshub's universalism (which is likely, but difficult to prove one way or the other), then we may have isolated the origins of that "traditionalist-westernizer" split in Tagore's personal and ideological makeup which S. C. Sarkar, in an illuminating essay on Tagore and the renaissance, has interpreted as the two most significant currents of thought in the poet's lifetime.[124]

Although Sarkar is in my opinion as close as anyone in identifying this crucial "dialectic" in Tagore's intellectual development, he has unnecessarily imposed his own value judgment on both extreme positions. In terms of the identity problem faced by Brahmos throughout the Bengal renaissance, Sarkar's analysis is from my point of view partial and inadequate. Sarkar evidently approaches Tagore with the idea of the slavophile-westernizer split among the Russian intelligentsia in mind.[125] In the context of the identity problem vis-à-vis the West, this is certainly a valid approach. He splits the sentiments of Bengali intellectuals like Tagore into an Orientalist or traditionalist camp and a westernizer or modernist camp.[126] The difficulty emerges when Sarkar reduces traditionalism to "worship of past glories," "a consciousness of Hindu superiority," and a "tendency to spiritual mysticism and emotionalism."[127] On the other hand westernism equals rationalism and liberalism.[128]

Considering some of the salient aspects of Adi Brahmo Samaj history reviewed in this essay, where in fact does such a definition lead us? Does a defense of one's own tradition always mean traditionalism in the reactionary antimodern connotation employed by Sarkar? The Adi Brahmos in the Tagore family camp were not advocating a defense of status quo traditionalism but were instead aiming to modernize the Hindu tradition through Brahmoism. Nor were any of the Adi Brahmos given to spiritual emotionalism.[129] On the contrary, we find such religious excesses, if you will, among the Keshubites, who were in fact more liberal reformers than the Adi Samajists.[130] The Sadharan Samajists, admittedly the most progressive group of the lot, were no less dominated by religious enthusiasts.[131] Often, those most westernized were also the most passionate theists, whereas Sanskrit College–trained pundits like the famous Vidyasagar—thoroughly exposed to the spirit of the classical tradition—were indifferent to religion. Moreover, belief in the superiority of Hinduism, which was a natural component in the rise of nationalism in India, does not necessarily exclude a belief in constructive change and modernism.

Actually, in terms of cultural identity, nationalism would probably describe the Adi Samaj attitude more accurately than traditionalism. The challenge by the Keshubites, who were professed universalists, only reinforced Adi Samaj loyalty to their own cultural tradition or national heritage. Thus when Sarkar quite rightly points out that between 1882 and 1885 Rabindranath was under Rajnarian Basu's influence,[132] this does not imply that the poet was at the time antimodernist so much as it implies that he identified strongly with Hindu India against the West. Take, for example, the Tagore preoccupation with nationalist projects such as the Hindu Mela or with the national secret society organized in Jorosanko in 1874.[133] Rabindranath, then thirteen years old, was invited to the meetings by Jyotirindranath.[134] Two other conspicuous members were Dwijendranath and Rajnarian. To be sure, the secret society identified itself in no uncertain terms with the Hindu tradition. But in the order of the Swadeshi-like program of the Hindu Mela, the organization promoted, among other things, the industrial development of India, starting with textiles and jute.[135] Was this support of industrialism, in Sarkar's terms, "traditional," "Orientalist," and "reactionary"?

Also, in 1884 when Rabindranath was supposedly in one of his dark and reactionary periods as a prisoner of "Orientalism," he became secretary of the Adi Brahmo Samaj. According to Ramananda Chatterji, who first met Tagore at this time, Tagore was shocked at Bankim Chandra Chatterji's "defense of Hinduism" in the issues of *Prachar Nabajuban*.[136] Ramananda was much taken with Tagore's attitudes at the time. When one considers that Ramananda was in his radical student phase in Calcutta it is difficult to believe that he and his peers would have been attracted by the lectures of a traditionalist reactionary.[137]

In fact, sociologically speaking, the young Rabindranath in the early 1880s was hardly the persevering puritanical type of Brahmo applying himself diligently for some professional career. In comparison with the trio of Satyendranath, Dwijendranath, and Jyotirindranath, Rabindranath was the least educated formally and, in retrospection, the least likely to succeed—judged from the high standards of Brahmo society. Satyendranath was preparing himself for the covenanted service, Dwijendranath was a self-trained technical philosopher, Jyotirindranath was an accomplished musician and erudite musicologist.[138] But as Stephen Hay relates, "Rabindranath in 1882 at 21 years of age had no worldly responsibilities to concern him" as he "lived off income from tenants of the family's large estates."[139] Moreover, having stopped school at thirteen, his education was most irregular.

The 1880s were unsettling years for Rabindranath. He evidently suffered a great loss when his sister-in-law, Kadambani Debi, Jyotirindranath's wife, committed suicide.[140] Five months before that his father had married Rabindranath off to an eleven-year-old girl with little education, the daughter of an employee in the zemindari.[141] This was the period when he moved about in a coarse sheet as a garment and rarely wore shoes.[142] Hay puts great stress on Rabindranath's feeling the rootless outsider during this decade. Then in 1890 he went off to England with his brother Satyendranath for a holiday.

From Sarkar's point of view, Rabindranath was in a pro-Western phase in the period 1886–1898. Using numerous examples from the poet's writings, Sarkar has made a convincing case for Rabindranath's antipathy to Hindu revivalism. This was the era of the newspaper *Bangabasi* under violently anti-Brahmo and generally antiprogressive Jogendra C. Basu.[143] In this period the Hari Sabha branches began to proliferate.[144] This was the age of vicious satires against Brahmos in novels and plays by sharp-witted defenders of the status quo such as Indranath Bannerji.[145] This was the time when Puranic Hinduism and the whole medieval tradition was being defended by such notorious antiwesternizers as S. T. Chadamani and K. P. Sen.[146] The ethos of the era was well captured in 1889 when a Sadharan Brahmo missionary named Bipin Chandra Pal lashed out at what he called "the present social reaction":

> When education, instead of enlarging our minds and making us ready to welcome and fitted to receive the light of other ages and the truth of other countries, simply helps to envelop us in a mist of narrow and selfish patriotism that refuses to acknowledge the existence of any virtue beyond the limits of the narrow hold which we call our country, we may shudder to realize how strong this reaction has already become. In fact, the whole atmosphere seems to be literally surcharged with this virulent poison.[147]

Rabindranath also spoke out against the virulent poison of traditionalism which was mechanical and deadening, but not quite in the westernizing manner suggested by Sarkar. Tagore was, after all, the son of Debendranath and there is no evidence I have seen that indicates a reaction against the Hindu Brahmo style of the Adi Samaj. Most assuredly, Rabindranath was against revivalism, nativism, and xenophobic nationalism. On the one hand, he attacked Bankim Chandra and Nobin Chandra Sen for the dangerous way they wedded some of the worst features of traditionalism with an aggressive nationalism. And he repudiated a static view of the Hindu heritage in the following way:

> A lifeless people, stagnant and immobile
> Its course obstructed by the morass of tradition
> A nation that does not move for its feet are tied
> By scriptural commands and endless incantations.[148]

But on the other hand, Rabindranath seemed to stay clear of that alliance between a westernized Brahmoism and political constitutionalism. His attitude to the Indian Association and the National Congress of Ananda Mohun Bose and Surendra Nath Bannerji is illustrated in an anecdote by Rabindranath's son Ratindranath. One night the poet was invited to a dinner by "anglicized" congressites for the purpose of enlisting his support in the movement. "Father came dressed in a *dhoti* and *chandur* in the midst of the anglicized diners," wrote Ratindranath.[149] He then went on to say that "my father had little faith in their politics" because he "realized the futility of holding meetings and passing pious resolutions."[150]

The fact is the Rabindranath between 1890 and 1900 spent much of his time in rural East Bengal supervising the zemindari.[151] In sharp contrast to the Brahmo professional intelligentsia of Calcutta, who were deeply and directly involved in such issues as modernism, revivalism, and nationalism, Rabindranath was the privileged and poetically gifted son of a

prominent Brahmo zemindar who could drift along the rivers of upcountry Bengal in a houseboat cursing "the organized selfishness of
Calcutta city life."[152] Perhaps no other Bengali poet so captured the
natural beauty and simplicity of East Bengal as did Rabindranath.

Between 1898 and 1906, Sarkar has placed Tagore in another extreme
antiwesternizer phase. There was deep unrest in the poet, while his work
reflected the "shadows of an anguished mind."[153] This was the brief
period of Rabindranath's politicized behavior on behalf of the Swadeshi
movement. In 1904, at his father's birthday celebration, Rabindranath
proudly recalled the Adi Samaj contribution to Indian nationalism. He
is quoted as having said that the greatness of his father lay in refusing
"to dilute our supreme national religion into a vague universalism."[154]
This was also the period in Rabindranath's life when in defiance of Brahmo
social reformism he married off his daughters aged eleven and fourteen
in the traditional Hindu manner.[155]

One should view this phase of Rabindranath's antiuniversalism against
the backdrop of Brahmo defections and the rise of militant nationalism
in Bengal. It was probably a kinship of nationalist feelings that prompted
Rabindranath to invite Brahmobandhab Upadhyay to be headmaster of
the new school at Santineketan in 1901. Rabindranath's own recorded
sentiments during these years resemble those of Brahmobandhab.[156]
Even Rabindranath's notion that "Brahminism and not kingship was our
country's wealth" in ancient times, uttered in 1904, closely followed
Brahmobandhab's own interpretation.[157] Burning with indignation a-
gainst the excesses of European imperialism, which he expressed in poems
on British intervention in the Boer War or in suppressing the Boxer
Rebellion in China, Tagore underwent a Brahmobandhab period, aggressively defying Western racism, militarism, and economic exploitation.[158]

The question may then be asked whether Rabindranath at this point
defected from Brahmoism. Certainly as a militant nationalist, Tagore
was never so suspicious of modernist impulses from the West as during
this period of his life. From a Keshubite or Sadharan perspective, Rabindranath's extreme nationalism would make him appear a defector.
But in the Adi Brahmo tradition, nationalism was more characteristic
than universalism. The question poses a serious dilemma which Tagore
himself quite possibly sought to resolve in his most powerful novel, Gora,
first serialized in Ramananda Chatterji's Probabasi in 1907.[159] In 1907
the poet was clearly beginning to retreat from nationalism back to universalism.

His Gora, the massively built, fair complexioned, and strong-faced hero
who is chairman of the Hindu Patriot's Society[160] and detests anglicized

Brahmos, is according to one contemporary source a caricature of Brahmobandhab Upadhyay. Just as likely is the possibility that Gora was Tagore himself during his Brahmobandhab period between 1898 and 1906. Written at the end of this period, the novel can hardly be interpreted as a propaganda piece on behalf of Hindu nationalism against Brahmo universalism. Instead, it may be seen as a brilliant soul-searching exploration of the dilemma of Hindu modern identity caught between the polarity of nation and world.

On the surface the story is about romantic and other entanglements between Gora's Hindu family and a prominent Brahmo family. On another level it is both a defense and repudiation of Hindu nationalism and a defense and repudiation of sectarian Brahmoism. Only an Adi Brahmo like Tagore, through the character of Gora, could defend Hindu nationalism with such fervor as essential for identity. Take, for example, Gora's reply to the charge of Hindu social abuses and cultural decadence: "It matters not whether we are good or bad, civilized or barbarous, so long as we are but ourselves."[161] Then there is the dialogue between Gora and his closest friend Binoy in which Gora is forced into the position of defending caste, declaring that "since I owe allegiance to society, I must respect caste also."[162] "Are we then bound to obey society in all matters?" Binoy asks. Gora replies that "not to obey society is to destroy it." "What if it is destroyed?" Binoy retorts. Gora's reply: "You might as well ask what harm there is in cutting off the branch in which one is seated."[163]

This same theme is pursued later on in the book when Binoy is sitting with a Brahmo girl discussing "the defects of our society and the abuses of our caste system."[164] He explains to her that Gora feels otherwise because he refuses "to regard the broken branches and withered leaves as the ultimate nature of a tree."[165] Gora regards well-intentioned Brahmo reform as being too often "simply the result of intellectual impatience." Gora maintains that he is not a reactionary because "he does not ask for any praise of the decaying boughs, but asks us to look at the whole tree and then try to understand its purpose."[166]

The alert Brahmo young lady replies that, withered boughs aside, it is the fruits of caste which should be considered and "what kind of fruits has caste produced in our country."[167] Binoy, still representing Gora by proxy, gives a significant answer which again accentuates the need to place the nationalist values of cultural loyalty and self-respect above the Brahmo propensity to expose Hindu social defects:

> What you call the fruit of caste is not merely that, but the result of the totality of conditions of our country. If you try to bite with a loose tooth you suffer pain—for that you don't blame the tooth, but only the looseness of that particular tooth. Because owing to various causes, disease and

weakness have attacked us, we have only been able to distort the idea which India stands for, and not lead it to success. That is why Gora continually exhorts us to become healthy, become strong.[168]

But if Rabindranath sympathetically defended the basic tenets of militant nationalist ideology, he was equally sympathetic to Brahmo modernism and universalism. The book is as much a repudiation of the Brahmobandhab thesis that modernism had to be sacrificed for nationalist goals as it is a defense of the proposition that universalism is not incompatible with the quest for a cultural identity in the modern world. When Gora out of compassion for the poor travels throughout rural India to arouse the masses to their own enormous potential for change, he is greatly disillusioned with his experience:

This was the first time Gora had seen what the condition of his country was like, outside the well-to-do and cultured society of Calcutta. How divided, how narrow, how weak was the vast expanse of rural India—how supremely unconscious as to its own welfare. . . . What a host of self-imposed imaginary obstacles prevented them from taking their place in the grand commerce of the world. . . . Without such an opportunity to see it for himself, Gora would never have been able to observe how inert were their minds, how petty their lives, how feeble their efforts.[169]

That Rabindranath remained faithful to the Adi Brahmo doctrine of modernism proceeding along national lines is quite obvious even when articulated through the defiant nationalist posture of Gora. In one passage after Binoy challenges Gora on the vitality of Brahmo persistence to reform society, the reply is the familiar argument Adi Samajists had been using since the Keshub Sen schism of 1866. Gora says that he too is for change but that "it won't do for those changes to be absolutely crazy ones."[170] In a manner reminiscent of Dwijendranath Tagore, Gora declares that:

A child gradually grows up to be a man but man does not suddenly become a cat or dog. I want the changes in India to be along the path of India's development for if you suddenly begin to follow the path of England's history—then everything from first to last will be a useless failure. I am sacrificing my life to show you that the power and greatness of our country have been preserved in our country itself.[171]

The crushing blow to Gora in the very end of the novel is Rabindranath's vindication of Brahmo universalism against this extremely narrow nation-centered view of change. Throughout the book Brahmos continually argue with Gora that effective change in India is impossible if her cultural frontiers remain shut to the progressive forces in the West.[172] The persuasiveness of the position gradually wins over Gora's friend Binoy, who becomes a Brahmo sympathizer. Then in the final pages Gora, after burying himself deeper and deeper in the pit of his Hindu militancy, learns from the man he viewed as his father that he is not a Hindu after all but the son of an Irishman killed in the Indian Mutiny.[173] Both of Gora's parents had been white Europeans. "In a single moment Gora's whole life seemed to him like some extraordinary dream," writes Tagore. In the following narration, Tagore explodes the myth of a narrow, confining national loyalty and places Gora in the limbo of an uncertain identity:

> The foundations upon which, from childhood, all his life had been raised had suddenly crumbled into dust, and he was unable to understand who he was and where he stood. . . . He felt as though he were like the dew drop on the lotus leaf which comes into existence for a moment only. He had no mother, no father, no country, no nationality, no lineage, no God even. Only one thing was left to him and that was a vast negation.[174]

But the book ends on a triumphant note when Gora begins to accept the wider identity of universal humanism—which Tagore himself was acquiring at this time. Symbolically, it is to Paresh Babu, the most sympathetic to Brahmo in the book, that Gora discloses: "Today I am free . . . today I am really an Indian. In me there is not longer any opposition between Hindu, Muslim, and Christian. Today every caste in India is my caste, the food of all is my food."[175]

Evidently Tagore, after years of brooding despair among the ranks of the nationalists, now returned to the larger tradition of Brahmo universalism. And *Gora* may well have represented his last major reconciliation of opposites leading to a higher synthesis of the nobler features of the Brahmo heritage with the exigencies of contemporary life in Bengal. It is unlikely that he ever deviated much from the vision achieved through the writing of *Gora* but only enriched it with new challenges and experiences moderated by the infirmities of old age.

By 1921, in his beloved ashram at Santineketan, the ever youthful Rabindranath Tagore was busy launching the most ambitious institutional project of his career. Three years earlier, on 22 December 1918, he had assembled the students and faculty of his *vidyalaya* to explain that a new educational experiment known as *Visva-Bharati* would take place at Santineketan.[176] His expressed purpose was clearly in the tradition of earlier attempts to implement the ideal of Brahmo universalism, such as Keshub Sen's efforts through disciples to study major religions by means of primary sources in the original languages. Keshub's home at Lilly Cottage became in fact a virtual meeting place of the cultures of the world. In 1921 it was Tagore's desire to create an "institution which would be a true center for all the existing cultures of the world . . . and where the wealth of past learning which still remained unlost might be brought into living contact with modern influences."[177] The motto, taken from a Vedic text, was "where the whole world forms its one single nest."[178]

In December of that year a meeting was held to announce the formation of Visva-Bharati University. Rabindranath's own dedication speech neatly summarized his last fourteen years of wrestling with the problems of unity and diversity, universalism and nationalism. Why this university? Tagore answered: because "mankind must realize unity."[179] He went on to explain that:

> The first step towards that realization is revealing the different peoples to one another. . . . We must find some meeting ground where there can be no question of conflicting interest. . . . One such place is the university where we can work together in a common pursuit of truth, share together our common heritage, and realize that artists in all parts of the world have created forms of beauty, scientists have discovered secrets of the universe, philosophers the problems of existence, saints made the truth of the spiritual organic in their own lives, not merely for some particular race to which they belonged but for all mankind.[180]

Thus, through the intense problem of finding and maintaining a cultural identity in the modern world, we can establish a causal link between Keshub Sen's New Dispensation Church of the nineteenth century and Rabindranath Tagore's Santineketan experiments of the twentieth. In this sense, the New Dispensation should not be viewed so much as a failure as the first serious attempt within the Brahmo Samaj to make concrete the renaissance ideal of universalism. Bijoy Krishna Goswami, a former Brahmo missionary under Keshub, sought to infuse this spirit into an updated and revitalized form of Vishnavism.[181] Vivekananda, another former Brahmo under Keshub and founder of the Ramakrishna Mission, offered the world neo-Vedantism as the basis for religious and cultural unity. Brahmobandhab Upadhyay, another Keshub disciple, carried the messages of Brahmo universalism into a de-Europeanized form of Roman Catholicism before his final identity crisis and withdrawal into yellow dog national fanaticism.[182] Sasipada Bannerji, one of the most activist of Sadharan Brahmo reformers, started the Debalaya, which aimed to bring representatives of all castes, religions, and creeds together in order to find ways and means of ending hatred and strife.[183]

These experiments, including Tagore's *Visva-Bharati,* were utopian schemes to be sure, especially in light of the more extreme forms of Indian nationalism that followed in the wake of European militarism and imperialism. But so long as these utopian institutions remained true to the original intent of their founders, and to the Orientalist legacy, the Bengal renaissance did not die.

NOTES

1. D. Kopf, *British Orientalism and the Bengal Renaissance* (Berkeley: University of California Press, 1969), pp. 13–21.
2. Ibid., pp. 67–107.
3. Ibid., pp. 22–42.
4. Ibid., pp. 178–213.
5. C. L. Becker, *The Heavenly City of the Eighteenth Century Philosophers* (New Haven: Yale University Press, 1964), p. 103.
6. Kopf, pp. 236–251.
7. H. Kohn, *Prophets and Peoples* (New York: The Macmillan Co., 1961), p. 14.
8. Ibid., p. 13.
9. Macaulay's essay on "Sir James Mackintosh," (1835) quoted in W. E. Houghton, *The Victorian Frame of Mind* (New Haven: Yale University Press, 1957), p. 39.
10. Kohn, p. 15.
11. Macaulay's *Critical Essays*, III, 436–437, quoted in Houghton, p. 123.
12. Kopf, pp. 253–272.
14. Ibid., p. 253–259.
15. Kopf, pp. 108–126, 178–213.
16. Ibid., pp. 263–272.
17. Ibid., p. 266.
18. Ibid., pp. 260–261.
19. The membership of Tagore's Tattvabodhini Sabha soared from nine in 1839 to seven hundred in 1856. See *Annual Report of 76th Brahmo Conference, 1966* (Calcutta: Brahmo Mission Press, 1967), p. 43. According to Professor Muhamed Ali, who has studied closely both the Sabha and the Samaj during this period, the real numerical breakthrough took place in 1845–1846 when the membership increased from 145 to 500, largely as a result of an influx of young college students. See M. M. Ali, *The Bengali Reaction to Christian Missionary Activities* (Chittagong: Mehrub Publications, 1965), p. 47.
20. For an excellent and authentic discussion of Debendranath's contribution in these three areas see P. K. Sen, *Biography of a New Faith* (Calcutta: Thacker, Spink, 1950), pp. 144–176.
21. For a list of the principal converts among the Calcutta intelligentsia between 1832 and 1855, see L. B. De, *Recollections of Alexander Duff* (London: T. Nelson and Sons, 1897), pp. 181–210.
22. A background to the controversy may be found in Kopf, pp. 201–202.
23. L. Carpenter, *Charges Made Against Unitarians and Unitarianism* (Bristol: T. J. Manchee, 1820); R. Roy, *Precepts of Jesus: The Guide to Peace and Happiness* (Calcutta: Baptist Mission Press, 1820).
24. Kopf, p. 202.
25. R. Roy, p. 152.
26. See analysis of Rammohun's position in M. M. Thomas, *The Acknowledged Christ of the Indian Renaissance* (Bangalore: Christian Institute For the Study of Religion and Society, 1970), p. 10.
27. W. Adam, *The Principles and Objects of the Calcutta Unitarian Committee*, vol. CCVI of *India Office Tracts* (Calcutta: Unitarian Press, 1827).
28. Sen, p. 123.
29. *Reprint of a Controversy Between Dr. Tytler and Ramdoss* (Calcutta: Tattvabodhini Press, 1845), p. 2.

30.   Ibid., p. 4.
31.   Ibid., p. 6.
32.   Ibid.
33.   Ibid., p. 7.
34.   Ibid., p. 21.
35.   For a masterful attempt by a convert to establish a historical linkage between comparable religious ideas from Moses and Zoroaster to the Vedic rishis, all culminating in the Christian revelation, see K. M. Bannerjea, *The Arian Witness* (Calcutta: Thacker, Spink, 1875).
36.   For an excellent discussion of the missionary side of the encounter, see Ali, pp. 22–30.
37.   See, for example, R. N. Bose, *Remarks on Reverend K. M. Bannerjea's Lecture on Vedantism* (Calcutta: n.p., 1851).
38.   For an early example by a Bengali convert, see K. M. Bannerjea, *Review of the Munduck Upanishad by Ram Mohan Roy* (Calcutta: Enquirer Press, 1833).
39.   Ibid., pp. 9–10.
40.   Duff quoted in R. Bose, *Vedantic Doctrines Vindicated* (Calcutta: Tattvabodhini Press, 1845), p. 7.
41.   Ibid.
42.   Ibid.
43.   Ibid.
44.   Ibid., p. 8.
45.   Ibid.
46.   This is beautifully articulated in Rajnarian's principle of "unity in essentials, variety in non-essentials and toleration for all," which he develops along with the nationalist position in R. Bose, *A Defence of Brahmoism and the Brahmo Samaj* (Calcutta: Brahmo Samaj Press, 1870), p. 14.
47.   Even during his most "nationalist" period, Rajnarian carried on a lively correspondence with the Unitarian Frances Power Cobbe in which he frankly admitted his debt to Unitarianism. Several of these letters are found in R. N. Basu, *Atma-carita* (Kalikata: Kuntaline Press, 1909), pp. 144–182.
48.   There was in Calcutta between 1855 and 1885 an American Unitarian missionary named C. H. A. Dall who among his many activites arranged for thousands of copies of the complete works of Channing, Emerson, and Parker to be circulated free of cost to Brahmos. For additional information, see "Advantages and Disadvantages of Present Age," *Indian Mirror*, XIV (3 January 1875), p. 4; "American Unitarian Association," ibid. (7 November 1875), p. 1; "Brahmo Samaj," ibid. (25 April 1875), p. 4.
49.   Bose, *Vedantic Doctrines Vindicated*, pp. 8–9.
50.   For background to this momentous decision, see notes by S. C. Charrabarti, editor of D. Thakur, *Atma-jibani*, 4th ed. (Kalikata: Visva-bharatī granthalaya, 1962), p. 377.
51.   For discussion of Brahmo-type nationalism by the man who formulated it during Swadeshi, see R. Chatterji, "Nationality: Past, Present and Future," *Modern Review*, VII (January 1910), pp. 70–75.
52.   For a moving defense by Debendranath of his generation's achievements, see letter from Debendranath Tagore to Keshub Chandra Sen, 8 July 1865, in Sophia Dobson Collet Collection (Sadharan Brahmo Samaj Library, Calcutta).
53.   Ibid., letter from Keshub Chandra Sen to Debendranath Tagore, 4 July 1865.

54. Sivanath Sastri, who was then a follower of Keshub and yet sympathetic to Debendranath, interpreted the controversy largely as a problem of identity. See S. Sastri, *The New Dispensation and the Brahmo Samaj* (Madras: Viyavharatharunjinee Press, 1881), p. 9.

55. Part of this misunderstanding is reflected in a missionary report. See "The Leader of the Brahmo Samaj, Calcutta, and the Author of 'Ecce Homo,' " *Church Missionary Intelligencer*, New Series II (October 1866), pp. 300–308.

56. K. C. Sen, "Jesus Christ: Europe and Asia," in *Keshub Chandra Sen: Lectures and Tracts*, ed. S. D. Collet (London: Straham and Co., 1870), p. 10–11.

57. Ibid., pp. 28, 30–32.

58. Ibid., pp. 5–6.

59. Ibid., p 10–11. 34,

60. Ibid., p. 8.

61. Ibid., p. 23.

62. Ibid., p. 24.

63. Ibid., p. 26.

64. Ibid., p. 27.

65. Ibid., p. 31.

66. Ibid., p. 37.

67. Minutes of a General Meeting of the Brahmo Samaj, 15 November 1866, in Sophia Dobson Collet Collection (Sadharan Brahmo Samaj Library, Calcutta).

68. Ibid.

69. Ibid.

70. R. Bose, "Prospectus to Start a Society for the Promotion of National Feeling Among the Educated Natives of Bengal," April 1866, reprinted in *Modern Review*, LXXV (June 1944), pp. 444–447.

71. Ibid., p. 444.

72. Ibid., p. 445.

73. Ibid., p. 446.

74. D. N. Tagore, "European Model," *National Paper*, III (25 September 1867), pp. 462–463.

75. Ibid.

76. Ibid.

77. Ibid.

78. Ibid., 2 October 1867, p. 474.

79. D. N. Tagore, "Hinduism is not Hostile to Brahmoism," *National Paper*, III (18 September 1867), p. 448.

80. Ibid.

81. D. N. Tagore, "Nationality and Universality," *National Paper*, III (24 February 1869), p. 86.

82. Ibid.

83. D. N. Tagore, "Nationality Indeed," *National Paper*, III (5 May 1869), pp. 208–209.

84. J. Das, "Brahmo Samaj," in *Studies on the Bengal Renaissance*, ed. A. C. Gupta (Jadavpur: National Council of Education, Bengal, 1958), p. 488.

85. *Mandir* inauguration ceremony address, 22 August 1869, reprinted in P. C. Mazumdar, *The Life and Teachings of Keshub Chandra Sen* (Calcutta: Baptist Mission Press, 1887), p. 206.

86. Ibid., p. 208.

87. For an interesting discussion of Keshub's deliberate intent of architectural synthesis, see S. K. Cattopadhyay, *Samanbay marg* (Kalikata: M. C. Sarkar and Sons, Private Ltd., 1961), p. 32.

88. An analysis of some merit on the meaning of the expression may be found in P. N. Bose, *History of Hindu Civilization During British Rule*, vol. 1 (London: Kegan Paul, Trench, Trubner and Co., 1894), p. 150.

89. J. C. Bagal, *Hindu melar itibritta* (Kalikata: Moitri, 1968).

90. Ibid., pp. 13, 16.

91. Ibid., pp. 6, 7, 9, 10.

92. "Mr. Dall and the Brahmo Samaj," *Brahmo Samaj Chronicles* (27 December 1871) in Sophia Dobson Collet Collection (Sadharan Brahmo Samaj Library, Calcutta).

93. Ibid., "Brahmoism and Christianity" (27 January 1871).

94. R. K. Gupta, *Meri Karpentarer Jiban-carit* (Calcutta: Brahmo Samaj Press, 1882), p. 36.

95. D. Tagore, *The Brahmo Samaj: Its Position and Prospects* (Bhowanipore: Satyajnan Sancharini Press, 1855), p. 171.

96. Ibid.

97. "Brahmo Marriages: Their History and Statistics," in *Brahmo Year Book*, ed. comp. S. D. Collet, in Sophia Dobson Collet Collection (Sadharan Brahmo Samaj Library, Calcutta).

98. For details of "truce" see letter from Keshub Chandra Sen to Debendranath Tagore, 13 January 1871, reprinted in *Brahmananda Shri Keshab Chandrer patrabali*, comp. M. Mahalanobish (Kalikata: Bharatvarsiya Brahmo Mandir, 1941), pp. 55–56.

99. *Brahmo Year Book* (see note 97 above).

100. P. C. Mazumdar, "The Relation of the Brahmo Samaj to Hinduism and Christianity," *Theistic Annual for 1872* in Sophia Dobson Collet Collection (Sadharan Brahmo Samaj Library, Calcutta).

101. Ibid.

102. Ibid.

103. "Brahmoism and Christianity," *Brahmo Samaj Chronicles* (see note 92 above).

104. Sir Henry Maine quoted in P. C. Mazumdar, *The Life and Teachings of Keshub Chandra Sen*, p. 251.

105. Ibid., p. 132.

106. See stimulating discussion on Keshub's comparative religion program in J. N. Farquhar, *Modern Religious Movements in India* (New York: Macmillan and Co., 1917), p. 52.

107. Girish Chandra Sen was the Keshubite who translated the Koran into Bengali between 1881 and 1886. See his reference to Islamic interest in G. C. Sen, *Atma-jiban* (Kalikata: Gupta, Mukherji and Co., 1904), pp. 55–56.

108. This is also the Christian missionary Farquhar's assessment. See Farquhar, op. cit.

109. Keshub was not beyond viewing this obsession as a form of madness. See his essays on "The Pagal," *The New Dispensation*, vol. I, 2nd ed. (Calcutta: Brahmo Tract Society, 1915), pp. 77–78, 106–107, 149–151, 186–187, 201–203.

110. For examples of contemporary Brahmo reactions to growing British imperialism, see "Present Struggle for Existence," *Indian Mirror*, XVIII (14 May 1879), p. 2; "Distress of the Middle Class Natives," ibid. (21 May 1879), p. 2; "The Ilbert Act—A Legislative Patchwork," ibid., XXIII (31 January

1884), p. 2; "Practical Closing of the Covenented Civil Service to the Natives," ibid. (21 May 1884), p. 2; "The Term Babu," ibid. (22 May 1884), 2.

111. For examples of contemporary Brahmo reactions to the growing stress and frustration of the younger *bhadralok*, see "Higher Education in India," *Indian Mirror*, XVII (13 February 1878), p. 2; "Grievances of the Native Engineers of Bengal," ibid. (30 January 1884), p. 2; "The Leadership Examination in Bengal," ibid. (27 February 1884), p. 2; "Indian Youths and Technical Education," ibid. (1 March 1884), p. 2; "Indians in the Indian Medical Service," ibid. (13 July 1884), p. 2.

112. One of the earliest conspicuous examples of this was the case of British discrimination against Jessie Bose, the famous Brahmo scientist who was appointed professor of physics at Presidency College in the class iv bracket of the Indian Educational Service at a grade salary only two-thirds that received by a European in a similar position. When Jessie ultimately won equality he became a national hero. See N. C. Nag, "Sir Jagadish Chandra Bose," *Modern Review*, LXII (December 1937), pp. 698–703.

113. Sivanath Sastri, p. 81.

114. The Indian Association, founded on 26 July 1876, was dominated by Sadharan Brahmos of the Ananda Mohun Bose faction made up of Sivanath Sastri, Dwarkanath Ganguli, Krishna Kumar Mitra, Durga Mohun Das, Shib Chandra Deb, and Kali Shankar Sukul. For a good analysis of this faction and their alleged conspiracy against Keshub and the British crown, see D. Datta, *Keshub and the Sadharan Brahmo Samaj* (Calcutta: Nava-Bidhan Press, 1930), pp. 256–257, 261. For a sympathetic point of view by a politicized participant of the Sadharan group who was active in the Indian Association see K. K. Mitra, *Krishna Kumar Mitrer Atma-carita* (Kalikata: Basantī Chakrabartī, 1937), p. 153.

115. For an excellent biography of this unusual Brahmo see H.C. Sarkar, *Life of Ananda Mohan Bose* (Calcutta: A. C. Sarkar, 1910).

116. Ibid., p. 55. Bose employed Bannerji at the City School, a Sadharan Brahmo institution financed by the Boses, after the latter was dismissed from service. For information on Bose's role in forming the Indian Association for Bannerji, see K. K. Mitra, "Amadiger sankat," *Sanjibani*, I (14 April 1883), p. 2.

117. Dall's break with Keshub took place in 1877 after a series of literary exchanges in the press on Keshub's obsession with spirituality, sin, and the quest for a universal religion. To Dall, Keshub had evidently turned his back on social reform. See K. C. Sen, "The Disease and the Remedy," *Indian Mirror*, XVI (6 February 1877), n.p., C.H.A. Dall, "Keep a Warm Head and a Cool Head," ibid. (7 February 1877); Sen, "Prayer and Work—A Reply to Mr. Dall," ibid. (8 February 1877); Dall, "A Real Issue, ' ibid. (4 March 1877); Sen, "On Reverend C. H. A. Dall," ibid. (April 1877).

118. See especially Keshub's fascinating final reply to Dall in K. C. Sen, "Philosophy and Madness in Religion," *Indian Mirror*, XVI (3 May 1877).

119. Some of the New Dispensation rituals, myths, and symbols are explained by Keshub himself in K. C. Sen's *New Dispensation*, pp. 17–20, 39–40, 90–92.

120. N. S. Bose, Ramananda Chatterji (manuscript to be published by Government of India, Publication Division, Ministry of Information and Broadcasting), p. 12.

121. S. N. Hay, *Asian Ideas of East and West: Tagore and His Critics* (Cambridge: Harvard University Press, 1970), p. 23.

122.   Tagore quoted in Hay, op. cit.

123.   Ibid., p. 27.

124.   S. C. Sarkar, *Bengal Renaissance and Other Essays* (New Delhi: People's Publishing House, 1970), pp. 148–183.

125.   Ibid., p. 153.

126.   Ibid., pp. 152–157.

126.   Ibid., p. 153.

128.   Ibid.

129.   In fact it was the early generation of Debendranath Brahmos of the 1840s and 1850s who were the least given to emotional excesses in religious expression but were the most conservative in support of social reform.

130.   On the other hand, the younger generation of the 1860s including their leader Keshub were extreme religious enthusiasts but were also extreme radicals in their zeal for social reform.

131.   Men like Sivanath Sastri, Krishna Kumar Mitra, Sasipada Bannerji, and Bijoy Krishna Goswami—all radical social reformers—were equally devoted to spiritual and theistic concerns within the Samaj.

132.   S. C. Sarkar, p. 132.

133.   B. N. Bandyopadhyay, *Jyotirindra Nath Thakur,* 2nd ed. (Kalikata: Bengiya sahitya parishat, 1956), p. 22.

134.   Ibid.

135.   Ibid., p. 31.

136.   S. Debi, *Ramananda Cattopadhyay o ardha shatabdir bangla* (Kalikata: Prabasi Press, n.d.), p. 126.

137.   Ibid., pp. 12–26.

138.   B. N. Bandyopadhyay, p. 17.

139.   S. N. Hay, p. 26.

140.   Ibid., p. 27.

141.   Ibid.

142.   Ibid., p. 28.

143.   P. N. Bose, *A Hundred Years of the Bengali Press* (Calcutta: Central Press, 1920), p. 99.

144.   Essay on "Sanatan Dharma Rukhshini Sabha" and "Hari Sabha," 24 December 1886, Sophia Dobson Collet Collection (Sadharan Brahmo Samaj Library, Calcutta).

145.   See especially I. Bandyopadhyay, *Kapla-Taru* (Kalikata: Canning Library, 1875).

146.   B. C. Pal, *Memories of My Life and Times,* vol. I (Calcutta: Modern Book Agency, 1932), p. 437.

147.   B. C. Pal, *The Present Social Reaction: What Does It Mean?* (Calcutta: Brahmo Samaj Press, 1889), p. 3.

148.   Tagore quoted in Sarkar, p. 166.

149.   R. N. Tagore, *On the Edges of Time* (Calcutta: Orient Longmans, 1958), p. 9.

150.   Ibid., p. 9.

151.   S. N. Hay, p. 31.

152.   Ibid., p. 32.

153.   S. C. Sarkar, p. 168.

154.   Tagore quoted in Sarkar, p. 171.

155.   S. N. Hay, p. 32.

156. R. Tagore, *Towards Universal Man* (Calcutta: Asia Publishing House, 1967), pp. 49–66.
157. Ibid., p. 64.
158. S. N. Hay, p. 33.
159. P. R. Sen, *Western Influence on the Bengali Novel* (Calcutta: Calcutta University Press, 1932), p. 46.
160. R. Tagore, *Gora* (London: Macmillan and Co., 1924), p. 6.
161. Ibid., p. 24.
162. Ibid., p. 42.
163. Ibid.
164. Ibid., p. 87.
165. Ibid.
166. Ibid.
167. Ibid.
168. Ibid.
169. Ibid., p. 132.
170. Ibid., pp. 329–330.
171. Ibid., p. 330.
172. Ibid., pp. 44–56.
173. Ibid., p. 402.
174. Ibid.
175. Ibid., pp. 405–406.
176. P. C. Mahalanabis, "The Growth of Visva-Bharati," *Visva-Bharati Quarterly*, VI (April 1928), pp. 79–94.
177. Ibid., p. 92.
178. Ibid.
179. *Visva-Bharati and Its Institutions* (Santiniketan, 1961), p. 19.
180. Tagore quoted in ibid.
181. B. C. Pal, *Saint Bijoykrishna Goswami* (Calcutta: Bepin Chandra Pal Institute, 1964), p. 69.
182. For a good biography of Brahmobandhab, see P. C. Singha, *Upadhyay Brahmo-Bandhab* (Uttapara, West Bengal: Amarendra Nath Cattopadhyay, n.d.).
183. Sir A. R. Bonerji, *An Indian Pathfinder: Memoirs of Sevabrata Sasipada Banerji* (Oxford: Kemp Hall Press, n.d.). pp. 92–95.

The Reinterpretation of Dharma in Nineteenth-Century Bengal: Righteous Conduct for Man in the Modern World

RACHEL VAN M. BAUMER
University of Hawaii

This essay, in slightly modified form, was originally written for and read to the symposium on Aspects of Religion in South Asia, conducted in the spring of 1971 at the School of Oriental and African Studies, University of London. It will also appear in a forthcoming publication of the symposium papers and is included here by permission of the editor of that volume. Inclusion of the essay in this volume, however, seems particularly appropriate for two reasons. It explores the nature of synthesis in nineteenth-century Bengali thought by examining in detail the change in one fundamental idea brought about by intellectual arguments of that period. Perhaps even more importantly, it examines the philosophical and psychological mechanism which laid the basis for acceptance in the Hindu community of ideas of patriotism, independence, the nation, and democracy. Seen in this light, the reinterpretation of dharma is an intellectual development having basic usefulness and importance to the Indian nationalist movement.

There are several important motifs in Hindu thought, the history of which may be traced in continuity from very ancient times. Among these, the concept of dharma[1] has exerted a dominant influence on both the society and the individual. Conversely, in its treatment by scholars and sages from age to age, it has reflected the modifications of the social order and attendant changes in social usages with the flow of history. Examination of the various views of dharma in chronological sequence would provide a fascinating study of the expansion of social, religious, and political ideas by Hindu scholars. It is my purpose, however, to confine this study to the last major reinterpretation of dharma, which evolved in Bengal during the nineteenth century. As the quality and style of life changed under the impact of historical events, Hindu society everywhere in South Asia was compelled to reexamine its understanding of the order of things, but nowhere were the motivation and response stronger than in Bengal, the center of British and Indian interaction. In the vigorous intellectual ferment of that remarkable century, the ancient concept of dharma was not discarded but, rather, accommodated to changing society. The manner and extent of its accommodation can be more thoroughly appreciated by reviewing a few simple, yet basic, aspects of the development of ideas of dharma prior to the modern period.

The ideas of dharma and its close associate, karma, are manifestations of a primary concern in Hindu thought from ancient times for maintenance of order. The emphasis in the Vedic period was placed upon upholding the cosmic order. Priests viewed the sacrifice as the vehicle by which this goal could be reached. In their zeal to sustain the cosmic balance, they developed an exceedingly elaborate ritual of sacrifice and gave primary significance to exact performance of the ritual. In an extension of this elementary idea,[2] the conduct of human life was seen as contributing to preservation of the all-important order and, in fact, many relationships and interactions in human life were believed to be parallels to divine relationships and behavior. Just as complex rules developed around the ritual of the sacrifice in an early period, a detailed set of rules regulating human life was gradually formulated. This development was accompanied by a subtle shift of emphasis from exclusive concern with cosmic order. Order in human society itself became a valuable objective.

The code of ethical behavior which was the outgrowth of this process was given systematic treatment by a number of early scholars, most prominent among them the legendary sage Manu. His work, believed to have been composed early in the Christian era,[3] classified the various dharmas into two main categories under which were listed an inventory of duties obligatory in each. The one category, *varṇāśramadharma*, concerned duties imposed upon an individual by the circumstances of his birth, i.e., caste, and by his stage in life, i.e., *āśrama*. A parallel can be seen between the earlier idea of sustaining the cosmic order by the proper performance of all the acts which supported it and the later system of *varṇāśramadharma* in which the world order, that is, the social order, was to be maintained through proper actions of the individuals who made up its component parts. Concern for social order had gained strength through the belief that the individual benefits directly from a society in which all services and actions are functioning in harmony. Thus, if the individual faithfully performed the duties obligatory upon him through his caste affiliation, he provided a necessary service to the society from which he benefited. If he carefully fulfilled the duties attached to his particular *āśrama,* he contributed to the moral and spiritual well-being both of society and of himself. Manu's second category, *sādhāraṇadharma*, consisted of duties imposed on every individual as a human being regardless of his position in society or his stage of progress in life. These duties were steadfastness, forgiveness, application, nonappropriation, cleanliness, repression of the sensibilities and sensuous appetites, wisdom, learning veracity, and restraint from anger.[4] The righteous man was the individual who, with no thought of self, made rigorous efforts to perform all his duties in accordance with the sacred law.

The individual's chief concern, nevertheless, was with himself, for he was responsible for his action alone and not that of any other. His motivation did not lie in a sense of public responsibility but rather in an understanding of the importance of keeping the sacred law for the purpose of his own welfare. In one respect, as noted above, the proper performance of one's dharma secured the welfare of the social order and hence his own derived welfare. In the other respect, the strict performance of one's dharma secured his own spiritual well-being in the future experience of release from rebirth, *mokṣa*. In whatever way it is viewed, the individual's concern was self-directed, though in no sense was it permitted to be selfish. "Hindu morality primarily aimed at the autonomy of the individual, i.e., at making him self-sufficient and self-dependent and free from all external bonds, physical and social."[5]

This notion of dharma, allied as it was with the doctrine of karma, maintained an important place in subsequent Hindu speculative and religious thought. Moreover, its effect on the history of the Hindu people, while difficult to measure, cannot be cast aside. Ideas of dharma submerged individual personality in a fixed role on the one hand and, on the other, strengthened individualism along the lines of individual responsibility, individual action and, in a particular sense, detachment. Furthermore, they implied a worldview and historical perspective in which group roles were fixed and the interaction among them was a reflection of divine action. On this point Bankimcandra was to write in modern times deploring the view of ancient Hindus who saw human history as the history of the gods.[6]

These primary characteristics and effects of the concept of dharma remained essentially unchanged during the course of the medieval centuries. Even reinterpretations which seemed to set forth sharply contrasting views revealed upon examination the same core of understanding.

Whether in speculative thought such as the teaching of *viśiṣṭādvaita,* or in religious movements, as, for example, the cult of the god Dharma,[7] or in purely social reaction such as that of Hindu society under Muslim rule, the concept of dharma remained little altered in scope at the end of the medieval period in comparison to that of the code of Manu. Dharma remained an intensely personal code of conduct, limiting the individual's perspective to his immediate relationships and to his own progress in life. Obligations to society were those due family, caste, and immediate community. Political ideas consisted chiefly of the duties and obligations of the individual to the king (or, in the case of the king, his duties and obligations to his subjects). Spiritual fulfillment was pursued on the basis of one's own style of life based on the classical four āśrama. Furthermore, the entire code was constructed on a principle of relativity. What signified obligation for one man did not necessarily constitute another man's duty.

The devoutly religious man of late-eighteenth-century Bengal was surrounded by an unsurmountable barrier of duties, obligations, practices, and taboos which effectively cut him off from deep involvement in his fellow man. His entire way of life was directed inward as he strove to maintain his dharma. Nevertheless, not all men of late-eighteenth-century Bengal were devoutly religious. A substantial number of high-caste, educated, and influential Bengalis of that period had developed a worldly-mindedness which gave little place to concentration on observing rigid rules of righteous conduct. While having a certain emotional attachment to the traditional teachings of the fathers, many prominent Brahman families of Bengal had adopted a secular style of life molded by the necessities of position and survival under the Muslim power. At the time of assumption of authority by the British, there existed an elite society in Bengal whose tastes and manners were cosmopolitan, who were often more learned in Persian than in Sanskrit, and who were caught up in administrative and commercial affairs. Members of this group were quick to reach out for a place in the new system, not only in the areas of administration and commerce but in the spheres of culture and social exchange as well.

The elite Hindu society clearly perceived the urgency of accommodation and synthesis in the various arenas of life. They could look for success under the new authority only by becoming familiar with the methods and manners of the new rulers. Despite British efforts to bring a certain continuity to administrative organization and to suppress disruptive influences on the Hindu way of life, a sense of drastic change must have been apparent to those Hindu elite who were in direct contact with the British. The lifestyle of the British stood in direct contrast to Hindu culture. Perceiving the motivating influences of action—psychological, philosophical, moral—would have been formidable. In addition to meeting the practical demands of establishing a *modus operandi,* Hindu society had to meet the challenge of superior British technology. Although it took several decades for the significance of that challenge to penetrate Bengali intellectual circles, a superficial appreciation of the British technological superiority was evident from the beginning. The first ventures of

British missionaries into the field of education at the end of the eighteenth century added to the impetus toward learning, understanding and, where possible, making accommodation to British culture, worldview, and philosophy. It became an important means for disseminating British procedures in practical affairs. Thus the pressures to investigate and to assimilate the ideas of the new rulers were many.

The obstacles to smooth accommodation were many, also. The psychological crises brought about by a relationship of superiority versus inferiority were continuous throughout the history of British rule in India. In Bengal they covered a wide range of reactions from anglophilia to anti-British terrorism. The emotional problem was inherent in the situation and could never quite be overcome. A further obstacle to the synthetic process was intellectual: widely disparate points of worldview and attitudes toward life were held by the two cultures. Western views and Western thinkers were often misinterpreted because Hindu understanding and perception rested on Hindu assumptions and conditioning. In yet another area, the challenge to religious belief thrown out to Hindus at an early period by the Christian missionaries evoked from the beginning the strongest response from Hindu society. The resulting schism between orthodox and universalist groups was in one sense an obstacle to the process of synthesis, yet in other ways it was extremely helpful in that it provided the forum in which philosophical views argued out. It is, in fact, this aspect of nineteenth-century development that I would call one of the most influential factors in helping Bengalis to define their social and political views, the results of which have shaped the course of their recent history.

Several aspects of Hinduism in Bengal at the beginning of the nineteenth century should be noted here. There was, of course, that characteristic of Hinduism evident in many ages, a basic flexibility, a tendency to absorb new religious practices and symbols. Furthermore, Bengal had had a long history of religious heterodoxy. Several major reform movements in eastern India had threatened orthodox Brahmanism in centuries past. There was, on the other hand, an increasing lack of interest in piety on the part of certain privileged groups in Bengal. Their wealth and influence made it possible for them to exert considerable pressure for relief from the more irksome rules of dharma and to urge a liberal reformation of religious belief. Among the notable examples of their public efforts are the petitions of several rajas to Brahman courts for permission to arrange the marriages of widowed daughters. A final and particularly important condition of the period was the fact that a small number of Brahman families had become thoroughly secularized, thus making available respected channels for penetrating reinterpretations of basic Hindu beliefs. From just such a family came Rammohan Ray, first of the great Bengali intellectual leaders of the nineteenth century.

In the year 1800, Rammohan, then twenty-six years of age, was occupied in looking after property belonging both to himself and to his father, a well-to-do Brahman landlord.[8] His father was a Vaisnava and his mother Sakta, but the Rays seem to have been much like other high-caste families who had been engaged for several generations in serving the Muslim administration.[9] Their tastes and lifestyle were entirely secular, and their chief interest lay in the pursuit of business affairs. It was Rammohan's early venture as a moneylender that brought him into close contact with members of the British community. For ten years he was associated with two of them, both civilians, either in an official capacity or by private arrangement. Early in this period, he wrote his first tract, *Tuhfat-ul-Muwahiddin,* in which he expounded his belief in monotheism. The tract suggests a fair knowledge of Muslim theology on Rammohan's part and testifies to his knowledge of Persian and Arabic before he learned Sanskrit. He studied the latter language, along with the Hindu *śāstra,* during his stay in Rangpur from 1809 to 1814. There is some evidence that the pandit with whom he studied, and who was a lifelong friend, initiated Rammohan into Tantrism. It was after he moved to Calcutta in 1815 that Rammohan had closer contact with Christian doctrine through his associations with Christian clergymen both in Calcutta and in Serampore. Writing of Rammohan's life in Calcutta, De comments that he entertained friends and distinguished visitors in his two Calcutta houses, a practice which brought him "in closer contact with a larger world, in which prevailed in those days three divergent types of culture, Hindu, Muslim and Christian."[10]

Rammohan's interest in religious inquiry was thoroughly stimulated through these contacts, although he maintained his former business and social interests too. From his investigation of the three religions emerged a strong universalist conviction which manifested itself mainly in his writings on the nature of God. His religious tracts, really begun in a major way at the age of forty, were devoted primarily to advocating worship of a Supreme Being without form or symbolic representation. While Rammohan is remembered chiefly for his preaching of the worship of one God and for his attacks on idolatry, his writings in that connection also contained the first significant change in the understanding of righteous conduct to be voiced in the nineteenth-century Hindu community.

In a strong statement in his *Second Defense of the Monotheistical System of the Veds,* Rammohan denounced the traditional Hindu doctrine of karma, pointing out the distinction between the Sanskrit term and the English word *works.* Yet at the same time he cited, in support of his position, the great Hindu authorities Manu and Sankaracarya, who placed the highest value on knowledge of God through contemplation and worship:

> To English readers, however, it may be proper to remark, that the Sunskrit word which signifies *works*, is not to be understood in the same sense as that which it implies in Christian theology, when works are opposed to faith. Christians understand by works, actions of *moral merit*, whereas Hindoos use the term in their theology only to denote religious rites and ceremonies prescribed by Hindoo lawgivers, which are often irreconciliable with the commonly received maxims of moral duty: as, for instance, the crime of suicide prescribed to widows by Ungeera, and to pilgrims at holy places by the *Nursingh* and *Koorma* Poorans. I do not, therefore, admit that works, taken in the latter sense (that is, the different religious acts prescribed by the Sastra to the different classes of Hindoos respectively) are necessary to attain divine faith, or that they are indispensable accompaniments of holy knowledge; for the Vedant in chapter 3rd, section 4th, text 37th, positively declares that the true knowledge of God may be acquired without observing the rules and rites prescribed by Sastra to each class of Hindoos; and also, examples are frequently found in the Ved, of persons, who, though they neglected the performance of religious rites and ceremonies attained divine knowledge and absorption by control over their passions and senses, and by contemplation of the Ruler of the universe, Munoo, the first and chief of all Hindoo lawgivers, confirms the same doctrines in describing the duties of laymen, . . . the illustrious Sankaracarya declared the attainment of faith in God, and the adoration of the Supreme Being, to be entirely independent of Brahmanical ceremonies. . . .[11]

The pursuit of the knowledge of God, through proper worship[12] and exercise of self-restraint,[13] was in Rammohan's view the highest aim of the righteous man. Closely associated with this aim was the manifestation of righteous conduct in relation to one's fellow man. This was not the older notion of occupational duties to be carried out conscientiously for the efficient working of society. Rather, Rammohan's concept of service to one's fellow man was associated with moral ideas of consideration, compassion, and the Golden Rule.[14] One aspect of his views on worship formed a parallel in principle to the old idea of obligation to exact performance of caste duties, or even exact performance of the sacrifice, to maintain order and balance of the whole. Rammohan taught that each believer was responsible for performing his act of worship completely and with care. If he did not do so, the worship of none of the group could be complete.[15]

In explaining the distinction between the popular understanding of karma and the Western notion of merit, Rammohan led to an important distinction to be made within the context of Hinduism—the distinction between customs and fashions (traditions and usages) and scriptural authority. It was a distinction that was to be widely used throughout the century by men of various persuasions,[16] and it was related both in origin and usage to another crucial principle of Rammohan's, namely, the necessity of rational approach to textual criticism in the interpretation of the Scriptures. In his introduction to the *Kena Upanishad*, he wrote of his work:

> It will also, I hope, tend to discriminate those parts of the Veds which are to be interpreted in an allegorical sense, and consequently to correct those exceptional practices, which not only deprive Hindoos in general of the common comforts of society, but also lead them frequently to self destruction, or to the sacrifice of the lives of their friends and relations.[17]

The principles of criticism which Rammohan employed seem to have been based on rudimentary perceptions of rational judgment, lacking the scholarly refinements of a later day; but his courage in leading the way to a critical interpretation of the most sacred of Hindu texts was remarkable and its results far-reaching. Contrary to the practice of some later Bengali intellectuals, he made the sacred texts the sole authority for his arguments, but his method of interpretation made it possible for him to prove his point of view.

The teachings of Rammohan's literature led away from a notion of righteousness based on performance of karma. Righteousness consisted in cultivating knowledge of the Supreme Being through adoration and contemplation. Along with this righteousness was a sense of moral social behavior which directed the individual's thoughts and attitudes outward to an awareness and consideration of other men's feelings and conditions. These ideas reveal a dramatic change of interpretation of righteous conduct. While individual responsibility remained strong and personal, the individual's freedom of action and sense of social involvement were quite different. Men were obligated to act toward other men in a way they themselves wished to be treated. They were to respond to other men's needs with compassion and sympathy. Dharma placed few other demands or restraints upon them than these attitudes toward others and the performance of the true worship of God. Although Rammohan's message of moral conduct was liberal and opposed to the sanction of tradition, he was still careful, despite both his luxurious style of life and his writings on religious doctrine, to keep intact his caste standing, a consideration of greatest importance in his day.[18]

Rammohan's ideas on worship were put into practice in the meetings of the Brahmo Sabha, which he founded, and later in those of its successor, the small but highly influential Brahmo Samaj. The main lines of emphasis put forward by the Brahmo Samajists during subsequent decades were essentially those of Rammohan, but they were much more fully developed and, in some instances, considerably changed. The pursuit of the knowledge of the Supreme Being through worship and contemplation retained primary emphasis. In this connection, a great deal was said also about the cultivation of all the human faculties as part of the discipline of true worship. The attainment of the full potential of humanity was the result of a fruitful search for the knowledge of God. The man who had this quality of complete humanity had developed all the human faculties to their full potential, and he had complete control over them.

Involvement in the well-being of others was an equally strong principle of the Brahmo Samaj, and the ideal was transformed into practice through a variety of social services. The Brahmos were extremely active in the field of social reform, particularly as it related to the status and treatment of women, education, and medical service. The motivation, in part, was similar to Rammohan's ethical ideal of the Golden Rule, but it had curious overtones of the older notion of a properly functioning society. In the first edition of *Tattvavodhini Patrika,* the official organ of the Brahmo Samaj, an editorial signed by "A" (undoubtedly Aksay Kumar Datta) pointed out the dependence of human beings on each other for survival, as compared to other animals. He argued that God had given man this nature, and the person who ignored that fact did so at his own peril. The essay challenged traditional views and customs on several levels. It completely rejected the traditional practice of asceticism implied in the third and fourth stages of *āśramadharma* and equally endorsed the first and second stages. Man, it said, belonged in human society in an active way, not only because men depend on each other's help in the material and temporal affairs of life but also because men depend on each other for the transmission of knowledge and wisdom. This particular line of argument operates somewhat on the "vested interest" aspects of *varṇadharma,* that is the proper performance of man's duty to uphold a society which, in return, offers him the necessities for maintaining his own life.

The Brahmo Samaj generally took a rather sympathetic view of the division of society into castes.[19] But the Sadharan Brahmo Samaj, a splinter group from the Brahmo Samaj, took a strong position against caste, advocating and performing intercaste marriages.

While the Brahmo Samaj carried forward ideas of Rammohan's with regard to righteous conduct, it also revived aspects of older concepts which played a much more minor role in Rammohan's writings. The idea of maintaining order and balance of the whole by the proper performance of worship, the idea of interdependence of human beings as an underlying motive for service, and the emphasis put upon discipline of the human faculties and control of the passions—all were in harmony with age-old Hindu beliefs.

There were several other streams of religious and social thought in Bengal contemporaneous with the Brahmo Samaj movement. In the first half of the century, the most radical group was Young Bengal, a faction of young men who formed themselves into the Society for the Acquisition of General Knowledge. Their early activities created a furore in Calcutta's upper-class Hindu society, the effects of which reverberated through the controversies of the remainder of the century. They held nothing of the old customs and taboos sacred. Their whole effort was directed toward denying completely their Hindu heritage. Although a few members of the faction converted to Christianity, most of them came to maturity with a satisfying, if somewhat curious, blend of a restored general belief in Hinduism with European rationalism. It was their youthful fascination with the latter that had resulted in their rebellious pranks against Hindu customs and institutions. Fondness for the philosophies of the West was to remain constant with others as well, who, coming after them, were also recipients of Western education.

The intellectual and social reforms of the Brahmo Samaj and the radical actions of Young Bengal were not without counterreaction in conservative circles. The preaching of Rammohan Ray had aroused several prominent defenders of traditional Hinduism to response. In the days of the Society for the Acquisition of General Knowledge, the name of the poet and editor, Isvarcandra Gupta, became closely associated with the cause of the traditionalists who argued mainly in defense of the use of images and symbols in worship and social regulations in common usage, deriving from the doctrines of *varṇāśramadharma* and *sādhāraṇadharma*. They represented both the Sakta and Vaisnava sects of traditional Bengali Hinduism.[20]

In the latter part of the century, Vaisnavism itself was reinterpreted[21] by a number of Bengali intellectuals, foremost of whom had been, in his youth, a protégé of Isvarcandra Gupta. The label of conservatism inherited from Isvarcandra has attached itself to the name of Bankimcandra Chatterji to this day. Yet a careful reading of his literature reveals an astonishing mixture of Saktism and Vaisnavism, traditional and Brahmo Samaj doctrines, Sankhya philosophy and European positivism. From a point early in his career,[22] his literature was devoted increasingly to the theme of Hindu nationalism, a theme which was supported by a defense of Hindu institutions. During the 1870s and 1880s, Bankimcandra was, perhaps, the most influential novelist and journalist of Bengal. When, finally, his religious monographs appeared, it is doubtful whether they created the same sensation aroused by his earlier literature; yet they were to exert a strong influence on the development of twentieth-century thought through such channels as Aurobindo.

It was particularly Bankimcandra's monograph, *Dharmmatattva,* which provided the doctrine of nationalism used so widely in twentieth-century Bengal. But this monograph is also among the most significant of the nineteenth-century statements of dharma. Bankim's reinterpretation of the ancient concept brought together the various strands of nineteenth-century thought into a whole that reflected the synthesis of ideas which had been achieved by the last quarter of the century. Bankimcandra cannot be credited with great originality of thought. Most of his ideas can be traced to other sources. But he was able to write down those ideas with greater power and appeal, and in a somewhat more systematic fashion, than any of his Bengali contemporaries. Furthermore, his formulation of a systematic theology and moral code was more extensive than most works written in that century with the possible exception of the Rammohan Ray literature.

Bankimcandra's religious background was Vaisnava. In his monographs,[23] the sole basis in Hinduism for his arguments was Vaisnava faith and doctrine. He supported that branch of Vaisnavism which views the world as primary reality and the relationship between the soul and the Supreme Being as dualistic. Without a fundamental perception of this kind, there would have been a certain difficulty in developing his doctrinal statement in *Dharmmatattva.* His delineation of the character of Krishna provided him with an example of his meaning in the definition of dharma, a method similar to some aspects of Christian teaching concerning Christ. On the theological level, Bankim's position was quite different from Rammohan's. It opposed the idea of a quality-less God and supported belief in an *avatār,* namely Krishna. It was founded upon the Gita and related texts, but owed little, or nothing, to the Vedanta.

To the interpretation of the ancient Vaisnava texts, however, Bankimcandra brought the same principle of textual criticism which had guided Rammohan's interpretation of the Scriptures. Bankimcandra had received a more extensive training than Rammohan in Western philosophical thought through the medium of Western education, and he borrowed widely, not only from its method but from its content as well. In this respect, he differed from Rammohan in that he took materials for developing his doctrine from a broad variety of sources. Quite contrary to Rammohan and the Brahmo Samajists, he was prepared to argue the value of certain traditional social views on the basis of custom and usage.[24] But even though he generally supported caste as an efficient means of organizing society and the traditional role of women in society, he was completely intolerant, as were these others, of the endless ritual demands and taboos established through the centuries by priestly Brahmans[25] in the name of dharma.

Dharma, in Bankimcandra's definition, was a matter of the heart. Oppressive social rules and taboos, he wrote, were a devilish invention, but "devotion to God, love for mankind, and quietness of heart, this, indeed, is dharma."[26] True dharma, he taught, was founded on purity of heart (*cittaśuddhi*). This was the foundation of the Hindu religion, and whoever had this purity of heart needed no other religion.[27] The manifestation of *cittaśuddhi,* in Bankim's view, was control of the senses, the sensual appetites. The theme of self-discipline, or firm control over the physical being, is very old in Indian thought. Like the idea of dharma itself, the ideal of self-control appears over and over in various guises in the many religious and philosophical systems indigenous to South Asia. In the nineteenth century, it was advocated by Rammohan, the Brahmo Samaj, traditional Hinduism, and ultimately by later religious thinkers such as Bankimcandra, Ramakrishna Paramhansa, and Vivekananda. In this connection, Bankimcandra taught the necessity of cultivating all the human faculties, mental as well as physical, to attain *manusyatva*,[28] one of the primary goals of dharma. On this point, he not only gleaned inspiration from the teachings of the Brahmo Samaj, but also anticipated the philosophical basis of Rabindranath's *Mānuṣer Dharma*.[29]

From these general views of dharma, as well as from his investigation of the philosophies of Spencer, Comte, and Mill,[30] Bankimcandra, in the later years of his life, formulated a doctrinal view of dharma which was set forth mainly in his monograph *Dharmmatattva* and, in part, in the monograph *Kṛṣṇacaritra*. His teachings incorporated long-standing views of Hindu tradition and new ideas introduced from Western thought. In this synthesis, dharma was still, in fact, the principle by which the fully developed man conducted his life in the modern world:

> The expression and maturing, the consistency and fulfillment, of all our physical and mental faculties in every part is *dharma*. This *dharma* is dependent on cultivation, and cultivation is dependent on actions [*karma*]. Therefore *karma* is the chief means to *dharma*. This *dharma* may be called duty[31] [*svadharmmapālan*].[32]

Dharma was not to be understood as having two categories, each with its separate code of obligatory duties. Although Bankimcandra supported the organization of society into castes, he did not endorse the distinction between *varṇadharma* (one's duties to others) and *āśramadharma* (one's duty to oneself). Rather, Bankim he believed that man, in the cultivation of all his mental and physical faculties, having achieved completeness,

satisfied the demands of dharma in all its aspects and in one operation.[33]
In effect, he denied special rules of conduct applying to certain men according to the circumstances of their birth and taught a code of conduct
to be followed by all men in all conditions, a code analogous to *sādhāraṇadharma*. The great example of the complete man was Krishna, who
satisfied all the ideals of manhood—physical, mental, intellectual, and
ethical. Following his example, modern man could attain these high
ideals by keeping righteousness itself as his primary motivation:

> The cultivation and fulfillment of all the faculties, indeed, is dharma. That
> you will do neither for yourself nor for others. You will do it because it *is*
> dharma.[34] Those faculties are related to oneself and to others; in their cul-
> tivation, one's own welfare and the welfare of others [are] accomplished
> together. Consequently, if you understand dharma in this way, removing
> the distinction between one's own welfare and another's welfare is an ob-
> jective of the theory of culture.[35]

Although one should perform the actions of dharma not with regard to
self or to others but because they were dharma, he believed in a motivating
agent which led the righteous man to maintain his high standard of
conduct and self-development. That motivating agent he called *prīti,* love
which is completely selfless and all-transcending. He identified this love
with bhakti, which he defined as that state of mind existing when one has
become a follower of God, having cultivated all the human faculties. The
manifestation of *prīti* and bhakti in respect to man's outward conduct
corresponds to an ethical principle Bankim claimed to derive from two
sources: the words of the ancient Hindu *śāstra*, "*ātmavat sarvvabhūteṣu
yaḥ paśyati sa paṇḍitaḥ*"; and the words of Christ, "Therefore all things
whatsoever ye would that men should do to you, do ye even so to them."[36]

The objects of *prīti* were ranked by Bankim in their order of importance,
and the actions associated with each level were commented upon. In each
case the primary concern of action was for saving the particular object of
prīti. He defined the four great stages of love, at once similar to Darwin's
theory of evolution, Herbert Spencer's three stages of social development,
and the Hindu four *āśrama* of life. The development of *prīti* began with
love for oneself. The remaining stages were love of family, love of country
and, last and highest of all, love of God. Although love of God was the
highest stage of *prīti,* the highest level of its manifestation in earthly
relationships was love of country, a theme based largely on Herbert
Spencer's view of the importance of the life of the social organism over the
life of its units.[37] The presentation of his message, however, bore a great
likeness to Vaisnava doctrine.

> The result of this *bhakti* is love for the world because God is in every being.

There is no contradiction between love for the world and love for one-self, love for one's own people, love for one's own country. To begin with, whatever conflict we feel arises because we do not exercise care to develop all of these faculties with lack of desire. That means that there is a lack of proper cultivation. Moreover, I have understood that saving one's own people is a much greater duty than saving oneself, and saving one's own country is much greater than saving one's own people. When *bhakti* toward God and love for all people are the same thing, it can be said that, apart from *bhakti* toward God, love of country is the greatest duty of all.[38]

In Bankim's definition, one's duty in the matter of saving his country included giving his life for it when called upon to do so.

Bankimcandra's nineteenth-century doctrine of dharma rested upon the ancient notion of a code of righteous duty for which each individual was completely responsible. Moreover, it restated the importance of the idea of karma, although the term was given a quite different meaning. It seems significant to later use of Bankim's doctrine that, in writing of karma, he reemphasized a philosophical view which Hindus understood well and which had been denied by such nineteenth-century religious thinkers as Rammohan and leaders of the Brahmo Samaj. The definition and description of righteous duty were changed considerably, making all of man's obligations acts of love toward God, expressed in acts of love toward his fellow men and country.

In his doctrine, however, was woven the Brahmo Samaj idea of culti-vation of all the faculties. Rammohan's concept of achieving one's full potential of righteousness through adoration (that is, worship) of God, though Vedantist, was not very different in principle from Bankim's Vaisnava view of bhakti as the essential element in the operation of dharma. These two systems of thought, moreover, emphasized a new aspect of righteous conduct. While still directed inward in the sense of teaching strong personal responsibility and negation of desire, they put a sharply different emphasis on human relationships. Actions and attitudes toward others were based on an ethical principle which included empathy, the feeling of care toward others that one experiences for oneself. This new dimension laid the foundation for the great social service programs conducted by a number of Hindu groups, chief among them the Brahmo Samaj and the Ramakrishna Mission.

The new concept of relationships moved the circle of concern and responsibility beyond one's own people, that is, family or community, to a much larger unit. The maximum unit indicated by Bankimcandra was the whole world. But in practical application, one could not save the whole world. One was responsible for saving the largest unit to which he be-longed on the basis of cultural affinity. Thus emerged the concept of the nation. The object of political action was defined, and, indeed, the completely foreign concept of political action was brought within the fold of traditional Hindu dogma. At a later period, Aurobindo was to write in emotional terms of Bankimcandra's having given the mantra and converting a whole nation in a day; but the fact cannot be denied that with Bankim's doctrine of dharma, an acceptable philosophical, religious, and psychological basis had been laid for the twentieth-century nationalist movement.[39]

Not the least important of these aspects was the influence exerted by the nineteenth-century religious writers in asserting that textual criticism on a rational basis was the only acceptable procedure for the intelligent man in approaching the interpretation of the scriptures. This principle was founded upon and, in turn, supported the idea of individual judgment. The growth of that idea among the educated people of India could only serve to strengthen not merely the emergence of views of self-determination but also the very acceptance of democracy as a form of government.

At the close of the nineteenth century, the synthesis was complete. Dharma remained intact, but redefined. With it was associated still the concept of karma, though drastically reinterpreted. Primary concern was still directed inward in the sense of responsibility for one's actions and morality in an attitude of selflessness. But dharma was no longer compartmental. It was a moral principle which operated in all aspects of a man's life, directing the whole and integrating all the noble faculties of humanity. It was motivated by love of God, a love manifested in one's view of all other men in whom God resided. It demanded that one give himself completely to the service of all men who held the truth as he did and were bound together by this view of life. The preservation of that society held first priority over all other demands of life. In its breadth of scope, it could give place to Rabindranath's concept of Universal Man or it could also support Hindu nationalism, depending on where the emphasis was placed. The events of history proved to be decisive. The emergence of the state fulfilled the greatest dharma of all apart from love of God— saving one's own country.

NOTES

1. The word *dharma* was used by various religious and philosophical systems of ancient India to denote a number of concepts and ideas having considerable difference of meaning. The word *dharma* is used in this essay to denote a code of ethics, social law, customs, duty—those principles, having divine origin and divine imperative, which were intended to guide each individual on his journey from birth to death.

2. The idea of emphasis on social order being an extension of the emphasis on

order in the sacrifice is, admittedly, just one of many views on the subject.

3. A. L. Basham, *The Wonder That Was India* (New York: Grove Press, Inc., 1959), p. 80.

4. S. K. Maitra, *The Ethics of the Hindus* (Calcutta: The University of Calcutta, 1925), pp. 7, 8.

5. Ibid., p. 8.

6. Bankimcandra Chatterji, *"Bāṅgālār Itihās," Baṅkim Racanābalī,* vol. II (Calcutta: Sahitya Samsad, 1959), p. 330. This volume is referred to hereafter as *BR.*

7. For a description of this cult, see Shashibhusan Dasgupta's *Obscure Religious Cults* (Calcutta: University of Calcutta, 1946), pp. 297–396.

8. Sushil Kumar De, *Bengali Literature in the Nineteenth Century,* 2nd ed. (Calcutta: Firma K. L. Mukhopadhyay, 1962), p. 503. Facts of Rammohan's life and career contained in this essay are taken mainly from De's work.

9. Ibid., p. 503: "His ancestors, in the latter half of the 18th century, served the Muhammedan rulers of Murshidabad and acquired property in some capacity or other."

10. Ibid., pp. 514, 515.

11. Rammohan Ray, "A Second Defence of the Monotheistical System of the Veds," *English Works of Raja Rammohun Roy,* vol. I (Calcutta: Brahmo Samaj Century Committee, 1928), p. 117. (This volume is referred to hereafter as BSCC.) The tract was published originally in Calcutta in 1817.

12. To be understood as prayer and contemplation of the Supreme Being.

13. Ibid., p. 14.

14. Ibid., pp. 48, 79.

15. Rammohan Ray, *"vājasaneyasaṁhitopaniṣader bhāṣā bibaraṇer bhūmikār curṇak," Tattvabodhini Patrikā, "sakaler ucit ye āpan āpan anuṣṭhān yatna pūrbbak karen, sampūrṇa anuṣṭhān nā karile upāsanā yadi siddha nā haẏ, tabe kāhāro upāsanā siddha haite pāre nā."*

16. Among the more prominent of this number were Isvarcandra Vidyasagar and Bankimcandra Chatterji.

17. BSCC, p. 35.

18. S. K. De, op. cit., p. 528. Another of Rammohan's contemporaries, Ram Ram Basu, expressed his inability to convert to Christianity in spite of his attraction to its teaching because of the importance to him of maintaining his caste standing. His *Rājā Pratāpādityacaritra* gives further evidence of the great importance he placed on caste affiliation.

19. For example, see Sridhar Nyayaratna's sermon to the Brahmo Samaj printed in *Tattvabodhini Patrikā,* vol. 1, no. 8, p. 61.

20. These two sects are not mutually exclusive.

21. The reinterpretations of Vaisnavism in Bengal over the past five centuries are manifold.

22. His second novel, *Kapālkuṇḍalā,* published in 1866, gave the first real hint of the emerging theme.

23. One intriguing aspect of Bankimcandra's literature is the Vaisnava doctrine of his monographs and the Sakta appeal of his novels. While the latter have certain Vaisnava elements, the overwhelming religious and emotional appeal is made through the *devī.*

24. His position on Hindu widow remarriage was based on this argument.

25. Bankimcandra, like Rammohan, was a Brahman.

26.   B. C. Chatterji, *"dharma ebaṁ sāhitya," BR*, vol. II, p. 258. See also *"samya,"*
       BR, vol. II, pp. 838, 384.
27.   B. C., Chatterji, *"cittaśuddhi," BR*, vol. II, p. 259.
28.   The completely developed state of all the qualities of humanity.
29.   Rabindranath, a Brahmo, undoubtedly was influenced to some extent by
       Bankim's writings.
30.   These were foremost among the many Western philosophers he quoted.
31.   *Duty* is Bankim's word. He wrote the English word in parentheses after the
       Bengali word *svadharmmapālan.*
32.   B. C. Chatterji, *"kṛṣṇacaritra," BR*, vol. II, p. 433.
33.   B. C. Chatterji, *"kām," BR*, vol. II, p. 271.
34.   The italicizing of the word *is* translates the Bengali emphatic particle.
35.   B. C. Chatterji, *"samya," BR*, vol. II, p. 384.
36.   Ibid.
37.   For another discussion of this aspect of Bankim's literature, see T. W. Clark's
       "The Role of Bankimcandra in the Development of Nationalism," in *His-
       torians of India, Pakistan and Ceylon*, ed. C. E. Phillips (London: Oxford
       University Press, 1961), pp. 432–435.
38.   B. C. Chatterji, *"dharmmatattva," BR*, vol. II, p. 661.
39.   An interesting analogy suggests itself between Bankim's doctrine of national-
       ism based on dharma and the relationship of dharma and *mokṣa* in ancient
       Hindu thought. The role of dharma in providing a basis for the idea of *mokṣa*
       (i.e., as defined in the Upanishadic context, freedom) is, in part at least, that
       of demonstrating the necessity of freedom by creating awareness of being in
       bondage. National freedom could, in part, be seen as necessary on the basis
       of public and private bondage; but this perception could be greatly streng-
       thened by the view of dharma as a binding obligation toward one's country
       from which he would gain release only as the country achieved freedom.

Bengal and Britain: Culture Contact and the Reinterpretation of Hinduism in the Nineteenth Century

JOHN N. GRAY
University of Hawaii

I

During the nineteenth century, two cultures, each with a long history and rich traditions, intensely interacted in Bengal. The arena for this interaction was the city of Calcutta. The participants in the interaction were the colonial officers, professionals (educators, scholars, doctors, and lawyers), businessmen, and missionaries from England and the urban, Western-educated, Hindu upper-caste Bengali elite. These Bengalis were not a homogeneous group; rather they may be seen to be divided into two groups based upon their attitudes toward Hinduism and social reform. The orthodox Bengali elite supported Puranic and Tantric Hinduism with its emphasis on Siva and Sakta and opposed British social reforms such as the abolition of *sati*. The more progressive segment of the Bengali elite felt that Puranic/Tantric Hinduism was one cause of Indian backwardness and that Vedic Hinduism was more compatible with a modern society. They advocated social reform and government intervention in effecting these reforms. Both groups within the Bengali elite were composed of Brahmans, Kayasthas, and Baidyas who had received a Western education and who secured professional, commercial, and government employment in Calcutta. As a result of their interaction with the British, both groups of the Bengali elite, by the end of the nineteenth century, felt they were ready to approach the problems of modernization and eventual independence.

It is possible to classify the interaction between the British and the Bengali elite with other culture-contact situations on three counts: first, as is common to the colonial situation, the representatives of British

99

society were clearly dominant in the interaction; second, as the subordinate partner in the interaction, the Bengali elite assimilated British ideas and values into their culture; and third, the Bengali elite maintained an identity with and a continuity with their own culture.

These three attributes are commonly used in historical descriptions of nineteenth-century Bengal. Rachel Van M. Baumer, for example, portrays the Bengali elite as a group which "perceived the urgency of accommodation and synthesis in various arenas of life."[1] She suggests that the motivation for the Bengali elite to effect a synthesis of British and Bengali cultures was the practical need of the Bengalis to learn the ways of the British and to develop a *modus operandi* in their interactions with them.[2] On the other hand, Baumer indicates that the superior-inferior relationship between the British and the Bengali elite and the Bengali's wide variation in attitudes toward British culture were two of the obstacles that prevented a synthesis of British and Bengali cultures.[3] By delving into the motivations for and against a synthesis of British and Bengali culture, Baumer identifies an important area of investigation. These motivational forces, however, have a more complex relation with the synthesis effected by the Bengali elite. If we analyze the motivations, attitudes, and interactions of the Bengali elite as a process that results in a synthesis, then we find that these factors are not simply positive or negative forces. Depending on additional circumstances, namely the British attitude toward Bengalis and the shifting economic and political conditions, the superior-inferior relationship between the British and the Bengali elite may be seen as a deterrent to synthesis at one time and a stimulus to synthesis at another; and practicality as a motivation for adopting British customs and values may vary in its importance in stimulating a synthesis.

David Kopf's analysis of the British Orientalists of the early decades of the nineteenth century pursues similar themes: an encounter with a dominant culture and an identity quest on the part of the Bengalis who had assimilated attitudes and values of the British culture.[4] His analysis demonstrates the importance of the status differential between the British and the Bengali elite, the British attitude toward the Bengali culture, and the stress felt by the Bengali elite who assimilated British customs and values.[5]

It is the literary creativity of Bengalis in the nineteenth century that is often used to demonstrate the synthesis of British and Bengali cultures. Baumer, Kopf, and other Bengal specialists have explained the synthesis in the following motivational framework: first, the superior-inferior relationship between the British and the Bengali elite; second, the attitudes of the British toward the Bengalis and vice versa; third, the alienation experienced by the Bengalis who imitated the British; fourth, the maintenance of a "Bengaliness" even though much British culture was assimilated; fifth, the practicality of adopting aspects of the British lifestyle; and sixth, the economic and political policies of the British colonial administration. An important factor that seems to be missing from these analyses is the Bengali elite's perception of the interaction. Some significant questions arise as a result of considering their perception of the situation. Even though historians claim that the British were clearly dominant in the interaction, how did the Bengali elite view their own status? If they, too, considered themselves in a subordinate position, how did they react to it? How is their perception of subordination related to the synthesis they effected? Similar questions can be asked concerning their perceptions of the British attitude toward Bengali culture and the economic and political conditions during the nineteenth century. Furthermore, we need to delineate the changing relationship between the motivations as their strengths vary and as other social conditions vary during the evolving process of synthesis. We also need to explain the specific relationship between the motivations and the synthesis. For example, why did the superior-inferior relation move the Bengali elite to incorporate British ideas and values into their culture?

It is my aim to answer these questions while expanding previous explanations of nineteenth-century Bengal by employing a combination of two orientations: a consideration of the Bengali elite's perception of their own culture and of British attitudes; and an analysis of the continually evolving synthesis to show the shifting relationships between the significant motivating factors for and against the synthesis. As a chronological framework for the analysis, I divide the nineteenth century into three periods—1800–1830, 1830–1870, 1870–1905—based on the shifting British attitudes toward Bengali culture and the Bengali elite's perception of these shifts and their perceptions of themselves. As the discussion proceeds, the basis for choosing these criteria will become evident.

Before moving into the analysis of the events of nineteenth-century Bengal, I should make some comments about the object of study—the Bengali elite. I have chosen to focus on this group for two reasons. First, historical studies of nineteenth-century Bengal concentrate almost exclusively on the Bengali elite in Calcutta. This emphasis indicates the group's historical importance. Second, it is they who did most of the writing which is the basic source of data for my analysis. To generalize beyond this group of Bengalis, who as a result of the interaction with the British became less and less like other segments of Bengali society, would not be warranted. Yet at various times during the century and for various reasons, the Bengali elite sought to influence these other segments of Bengali society.

Martin Orans has observed a similar synthesizing process among a variety of groups. After studying the Santal tribe of India,[6] the Jatars of Agra city, the Burakamin of Japan, and the American Negroes,[7] he developed the theory of the rank concession syndrome (RCS) to explain the synthesis effected by these groups. His theory is relevant to the Bengali elite of the nineteenth century because, like the groups he studied, they were in a subordinate position and accommodated ideas and values from the dominant culture.

The RCS theory describes the processes that result when a subordinate society concedes rank to a dominant society.[8] As a result of conceding rank a society will emulate rank attributes of the dominant society in an attempt to raise its status. Associated with rank concession is power concession, which indicates that the subordinate society also concedes that the dominant society is technologically more powerful. A society will borrow technology from the dominant society not because of inferiority feelings but to attain some practical goal (crops, health, victory in war). Although a society concedes power when it concedes rank, power can be conceded independently of rank.

There is a motivation which is in opposition to the motivation to borrow that results from rank and power concessions. This opposing motivation is what Durkheim terms *solidarity*.[9] Solidarity refers to those shared cultural characteristics that bind a society together. These characteristics also serve as a boundary between two societies and inhibit the mutual assimilation of traits. The binding effect of the shared cultural characteristics is termed *internal solidarity*; their boundary effect is termed *external solidarity*.[10] According to Durkheim, individuals of a society want to be like other individuals in that society and will be motivated to preserve the society's solidarity. Thus emulation is in conflict with solidarity, given that a society concedes rank. Orans calls this an *emulation-solidarity conflict*.

Emulation is not distributed evenly among the individuals within a rank-conceding society. Those with greater economic and political power are more apt to emulate because of their more frequent interactions with members of the dominant society. Such "differential emulation"[11] is destructive of internal solidarity. Nevertheless, an individual cannot be successful in raising his status without economic and political power. Therefore, an emulation-solidarity conflict occurs among those who have the economic and political resources to pursue higher status by borrowing and being accorded higher rank by members of the dominant society.

Hence there is a relation between the strength of the emulation-solidarity conflict and the economic and political conditions under which mobility attempts are made. If individuals pursue an "economic rank path,"[12] there is less conflict because the solidarity requirements of this path are less important than in a political rank path. Solidarity is less emphasized in the economic rank path because, in a market economy, economic success requires individual initiative. Ties with the family or other groups can hamper the economic success of an individual because he may be socially required to distribute his wealth. A political rank path supports the solidarity of a society because, in democratic governments, political success requires the backing of a majority of a society's members. Thus in the political rank path, while emulation and the motivation to borrow remain, solidarity requirements are stronger and this produces a more severe emulation-solidarity conflict than does an economic rank path.

Orans identifies five means of synthesis by which individuals may attempt to resolve their emulation-solidarity conflict:

1. Indigenous claims—through the history-mythology of the culture, individuals demonstrate that what is borrowed is really a forgotten indigenous custom.

2. Syncretism—"naturalizing" borrowed customs by combining them with indigenous customs.

3. Innovative combination—a fusion of indigenous and borrowed customs that results in a change in both.

4. Pattern emulation and trait maintenance—incorporating the deep values of the dominant culture while vigorously emphasizing distinctive indigenous traits.

5. Redefinition of relevant group identification—escaping the conflict by establishing an identity with a group outside the boundaries of the subordinate culture (for example, the proletariat, a different religion).

The most severe emulation-solidarity conflict develops when individuals, after pursuing rank economically, switch to a political rank path. Mobility attempts via the economic rank path emphasize borrowing, and successful individuals will have internalized many of the borrowed customs and values. When they shift to a political rank path, where solidarity is paramount, they find they are alienated from their own society and may have difficulty reacquiring indigenous customs. Under these conditions a "cultural movement"[13] results. Cultural movements are evidenced by a proliferation of literary creativity. The motivation underlying this creativity is the severe emulation-solidarity conflict. The literature produced is directed at resolving the conflict by employing some, if not all, of the techniques noted above.

Of the many anthropological theories of social changes, Orans' RCS theory seems to be the most powerful. By using it we are able to describe the complexity of the varying relations among the motivations for a synthesis and the process whereby the Bengali elite in dealing with these motivations developed a synthesis.

II

The city of Calcutta was founded by Job Charnock in 1690 as a commercial settlement. Thus even in 1800 Calcutta was a relatively new city. It had no traditional inhabitants whose behavior might serve as a standard for the Bengalis migrating to the city for economic reasons. Yet Calcutta was the major arena for interaction between the Bengalis and the British. For both, Calcutta was a new environment in which they could work out their modes of interaction without any of the influences that would have been present had Calcutta been a city with a longer history. Both groups had the opportunity to adapt or ignore their own traditional customs if they proved to be detrimental to their commercial interests. It seems to me that such an environment was conducive to the Bengali elite's adoption of British customs and values because of the geographical, if not social, distance from the inhibiting influences of traditional customs and attitudes. Thus, at the behavioral level of analysis, I infer an urban/rural dichotomy with reference to Calcutta and the rest of Bengal. Whether or not this dichotomy exists at the level of values and abstract social rules is a question beyond the scope of this essay.[14]

1800–1830

After the British established their control over Bengal in 1757, many Hindu upper-caste Bengalis (Brahmans, Kayasthas, and Baidyas) entered into relations with British commercial, financial, and administrative organizations in Calcutta, from which they realized great economic benefits.[15] Thus began a long period of economic interaction between the British and the Bengali elite which continued well into the nineteenth century.[16] It is difficult to sort out from the available data how much the Bengalis borrowed from the British culture and what motivation lay behind such borrowing. We may be able to get some indications of the Bengali elite's attitude toward British culture and the kind of borrowing that took place during this period by looking at the family backgrounds of several influential personages of the Bengali elite in the latter half of the nineteenth century.

The earliest of this group, Devendranath Tagore, who led the most westernized reform group in the 1840s and 1850s, was brought up in a family which had amassed wealth in commercial relations with the British in Calcutta.[17] His father, Dwarkanath, had started an agency house in Calcutta and also managed industrial concerns.[18] Ananda Mohan Bose, a prominent figure in the Sadharan Brahmo Samaj, was born to a Kayastha family in 1847. His grandfather had become wealthy through a salt business, and his father had been a government officer. Ananda Mohan received an English education.[19] The family of Sasipad Benerje, who was born in 1840, was in government service in a suburb of Calcutta.[20] He, too, was given an English education. Bipin Chandra Pal's father was also in government service. Giving up his government post, his father moved the family to Sylhet, where Bipin Chandra could receive an English education.[21] Sivanath Sastri (born 1840) at the age of nine went to Calcutta to live with his uncle, who edited a Bengali journal. He was educated at Sanskrit College but chose the English medium course.[22] Bankim Chandra Chatterjee, whose literature flourished in the late nineteenth century, was born in 1838. His father was in the civil service. Bankim attended an English medium school and Presidency College. Vivekananda was born to a Kayastha family in Calcutta. His great-grandfather had become wealthy as the managing clerk and associate of an English attorney. His descendants retained that wealth and position by going into the professions.[23] In fact, most members of the Sadharan Brahmo Samaj (which is considered by many historians to be the most westernized reform group in the latter part of the nineteenth century) came from families associated with the British, either in the professions, commerce, or civil service.[24] Almost all these Brahmos had an English education, many with college degrees.[25]

What I have been trying to demonstrate with this summary is that many fathers and grandfathers of the Bengali elite had successfully interacted with the British during the early decades of the nineteenth century. With respect to the RCS theory, the family histories suggest that these Bengalis borrowed British behavior patterns because successful economic interaction demanded it. Because the British dominated the government, commercial, and professional life of Calcutta, the Bengalis had to conform to the British lifestyle if they wished to establish lucrative relations with them. The least I can say about the motivation of these Bengalis is that they borrowed British customs for their economic interactions because it was beneficial to their success. If this was the case, then we may hypothesize that the members of the Bengali elite who were involved with the British borrowed customs because they had conceded power. Whether or not these same Bengalis had conceded rank is difficult to establish with the data available to me.

We may get further indications of at least power-incorporative borrowing on the part of the Calcutta Bengali elite by looking at the rise of Western education in the early nineteenth century. The reason for the establishment of Hindu College in 1817 exemplifies the attitudes of many of the Bengali elite toward Western education. According to Kopf, "such families as the Mullicks, Debs, Tagores, and Ghoshals owed much of their recently acquired wealth to European relationships. They valued highly competence in the English language and training in European fields of study."[26] Further, Hindu College was the Calcutta elite's expression "of a practical need to provide the sons of that group with an advantageous European education."[27] If Kopf's conclusions are correct, one may infer that the elite, who themselves had been quite successful in their interactions with the British, felt that Western education was an important prerequisite for further successful relations. It is significant that they chose Western education and not the traditional one because this choice indicates a concession that English education would give their sons a practical advantage.

It is also significant, as Kopf points out, that the Bengali elite did not feel their culture threatened by Western education:

> It was the Orientalist understanding and respect for Hindu civilization that probably impelled the founders to favor the idea of a Hindu College in the first place. The Orientalist belief that western education should serve not as an end in itself but as the stimulus for changing the indigenous culture from within explains why Bengalis accepted the experiment without a recorded murmur of dissent. It was therefore not really secular knowledge in western dress that was to be imparted at Hindu College, but useful knowledge from the West transmitted without ethnocentric bias.[28]

If Kopf's analysis is valid, then it appears that the elite did not feel Bengali solidarity was being disrupted by the formation of Hindu College. Thus, in terms of the RCS theory, power concession and power-incorporative borrowing are not perceived to conflict with a society's solidarity maintenance. If this is the case, then concession of inferiority, not mere borrowing, is the crucial factor in the process of effecting a synthesis.

Another point should be made concerning the formation of Hindu College: there was some resistance from the orthodox Hindus. David Hare and Rammohun Roy appear to have been the originators of the idea to open a school like Hindu College. After approaching Sir Edward Hyde East, the Chief Justice of the Supreme Court, who agreed with the idea, they received approval from other members of the Bengali elite.[29] However, the orthodox Hindus of Calcutta "refused to have any connection with the school if Rammohun was included in the College Committee."[30] They presumably felt this way because they viewed Rammohun's seemingly westernized theology and his appeals for social reforms (such as the abolition of *sati*) as a threat to their culture. They did not want their sons to incorporate these ideas while obtaining an education, though it appears that they did want their sons to have a Western education. This episode may indicate the beginnings of a conflict between a desire for Western education and a desire to maintain Hindu solidarity on the part of the orthodox Hindus. However, the motivation behind the elite's support of Western education is still unclear. With the evidence of the resistance to Rammohun's involvement with Hindu College we open the possibility of rank concession along with power concession on the part of the orthodox elite in Calcutta. In any event the wide support for Western education instead of traditional education suggests that the elite felt that Western education was superior for at least practical purposes (power concession).

Although there seems to be no concrete evidence for rank concession with respect to the Bengali attitude toward Western education, there are some indications of feelings of inferiority among the progressive Bengali elite, as exemplified by Rammohun Roy. Rammohun's early education consisted in learning Persian under a Maulavi and Arabic in Patna.[31] His later education included a study of Sanskrit language and literature in Benaras.[32] He acquired knowledge of English and Western culture while working as a civil servant under John Digby.[33] By 1815 Rammohun had been exposed to the culture and religion of India, the Muslims, and the West. His theology was an attempt to synthesize all these traditions into a universal monotheism which closely resembled the Unitarianism of the West.

That Rammohun conceded rank to the West, especially Christianity, is evidenced in a letter he wrote to Digby in 1817: "I have found the doctrine of Christ more conducive to moral principles, and better adapted for the use of rational beings, than any other which [has] come to my knowledge."[34] Further, Rammohun states: "Genuine Christianity is more conducive to the moral, social and political progress of a people than any other known creed."[35] In general, Rammohun's theology and social reforms were a response to the morally degraded condition into which he felt Hinduism had fallen. He believed that women suffered from moral degradation and inhuman social customs and therefore championed the abolition of *sati* and the general emancipation of women.[36] Realizing the "degraded" state of Hindu society and blaming the Puranas and the later Sastras, Rammohun seems to concede that Christian principles provided a means of morally regenerating Hinduism. Rammohun experienced an emulation-solidarity conflict in that he always considered himself a Hindu and tried to incorporate—by means of indigenous claims, syncretism, and innovative combination—Western social reforms and Christian Unitarian principles into Upanishadic philosophy and theology. The founding of the Brahmo Sabha in 1828 can be seen as the expression of the emulation-solidarity conflict felt by Rammohun because he attempted to demonstrate with Brahmo religion that Western ideas, values, and behavior patterns were indigenous to Hindu tradition.

Rammohun's attitude toward Western education was mentioned in connection with the formation of Hindu College. It appears that Rammohun felt Western education was an important ingredient in India's progress toward moral regeneration, social reform, and modernization. He opposed the formation of Sanskrit College, an institution proposed by H. H. Wilson which would stress "the traditional Sanskritic studies of rhetoric, sacred literature, law, and grammar"[37] along with Western subjects. in 1823, when the government decided to organize Sanskrit College, Rammohun wrote a letter of protest to Lord Amherst:

> If it had been intended to keep the British nation in ignorance of real knowledge, the Baconian Philosophy would not have been allowed to displace the system of Schoolmen, which was the best calculated to perpetuate ignorance. In the same manner the Sanskrit system of education would be best calculated to keep this country in darkness, if such had been the policy of the British legislature. But as the improvement of the native population is the object of the government, it will consequently promote a more liberal and enlightened system of instruction embracing Mathematics, Natural Philosophy, Chemistry, Anatomy, with other useful sciences, which may be accomplished with the sums proposed by employing a few gentlemen of talents and learning, educated in Europe.[38]

Relying solely on these remarks, we have difficulty deciding whether Rammohun conceded rank and power or just conceded power with regard to Western education. Clearly, he though that Western education was better suited to India's progress. But did he also think that Western society in general was better than Hindu society? He probably felt that Western society was better than contemporary Hindu society. Assessing his attitudes toward Christianity and Western education, I feel that he did concede rank to Western culture and that he also experienced an emulation-solidarity conflict, the expression of which was his attempts at synthesizing Western moral principles and social reforms into the Upanishads, the formation of the Brahmo Sabha, and the sharp criticisms his view received from the orthodox Hindu community.

According to Kopf, 1800–1830 was the age of the Orientalist.[39] In order to train British civil servants for the posts in India, the British Orientalist scholars had to systematize Indian language and translate Hindu texts into English. As a result of their work, the Orientalists and the Bengali pundits who worked with them found that India had a long history and "discovered" the Indian golden age in Vedic times. The Bengali pundits became conscious of their ancient civilization and developed a pride in it.

The concept of an Indaan golden age of Vedic times subscribed to by the British Orientalist scholars and their pundits suggests that both these groups thought that contemporary Hindu society was in a degraded state. In addition, this same concept indicated to the Orientalists and the Bengali pundits that India possessed an indigenous model for revitalizing its culture without the wholesale adoption of Western culture. The Orientalists also introduced the idea of renaissance to the Hindus which, combined with the idea of an Indian golden age, could have encouraged the intelligentsia to seek cultural revitalization through the renaissance of their golden age.[40]

When viewed in terms of the RCS theory, the Orientalists and the Bengali pundits of the College of Fort William present a perplexing picture. There does not seem to be any evidence indicating that the Bengali intelligentsia of the college felt that their culture was inferior, except perhaps for contemporary Hinduism.[41] Equipped with historical consciousness and a pride in their golden age, it appears that these Bengalis felt their culture needed a regeneration from its present state and that their civilization contained the ingredients of the progress they envisioned. Modernization could take place but it could be consistent with Indian tradition. The major legacy of the Orientalists was a sympathetic attitude toward Indian culture and a historical consciousness of a golden age to which Bengalis of the latter nineteenth century turned in their attempts to reduce the emulation-solidarity conflict.

In sum, the 1800–1830 period of Bengali history displayed no clear-cut evidence for rank concession, though I suspect it was present in Rammohun Roy's theology and social reforms. However, I think there is concrete evidence for power concession and borrowing in the elite support of education and the success in their economic interactions with the British, although it is hard to tell whether their power-incorporative borrowing was associated with rank concession and emulation. I suspect that much of the difficulty in distinguishing between "pure" power-incorporative borrowing and rank-concession borrowing with the associated power-incorporative borrowing is due to Orans' insufficient explication of these concepts. His only statement on this problem is that "emulation and power-incorporative borrowing are often intermingled in particular acts."[42] However, I hope to show that these phenomena crystallized during the next period (1830–1870) as a result of the defense of Hinduism against attacks by such Englishmen as Macaulay and Duff.

1830–1870

When Bentinck became governor general in 1828, the growing tide of anti-Hindu criticism that had been expressed by some Englishmen for more than a decade attained the status of official policy. This change in British attitude—from the Orientalists' respect for Hindu Vedic civilization to the vehement anti-Hinduism of the anglicists and evangelists—produced a defensive response by the Bengali elite which crystallized the incipient emulation-solidarity conflict of the previous decades. Since the latter years of the eighteenth century, many Englishmen had held a rather low opinion of Indians and their Hinduism and had felt that Christianity and Western education were needed to civilize the subcontinent. However, the Orientalist position was well entrenched in the administrative structure because of the efforts of men like Wellesley, Wilson, Colebrook, and other scholars connected with the College of Fort William. One might assume that the anti-Hindu opinions of the early nineteenth century did not have a great impact on the Calcutta Bengali elite because such opinions were tempered by the Orientalists and because missionary activity was held to minimum until 1813.

Exemplifying this anti-Hindu criticism of the early nineteenth century were the attitudes of Charles Grant. Upon his return from India in 1794, Grant started advocating missionary activity in India "to transform and deliver a whole people from superstition to light through the educational process."[43] For Grant, "Indian civilization was barbaric because its religion was degrading. It was both dangerous and a violation of the Christian spirit even to tolerate such a culture."[44] The continuing controversy about allowing missionary activity in India brought to light further indications of anti-Hindu feelings in England. Lord Teignmouth, in supporting the evangelical position in 1813, maintained that "only the strong ethical content of Christianity could eradicate the deeply rooted deceit, obscenity, and tendency toward corruption" that he found so common in Hindus.[45] Both Grant and Wilberforce in their strong support for missionaries in India "portrayed Hinduism as rotten to the core and incapable of any sort of restoration, reform, or renaissance."[46] And Wilberforce argued before Parliament that "the Hindu divinities were absolute monsters of lust, injustice, wickedness, and cruelty. In short, their religious system is one grand abomination."[47] Against this criticism, the Orientalists could not prevent Britain from allowing the establishment of Christian missions in India.

James Mill's *History of British India* was another source of anti-Hindu criticism. The following passage demonstrates the attitude of at least one British scholar toward India:

> Even in manners, and in the leading parts of the moral character, the lines of resemblance [between Indians and Chinese] are strong. Both nations are to nearly an equal degree tainted with the vices of insincerity; dissembling, treacherous, mendacious, to an excess which surpasses even the unusual measure of uncultivated society. Both are disposed to excessive exaggeration with regard to everything related to themselves. Both are cowardly and unfeeling. Both are to the highest degree conceited of themselves, and full of affected contempt for others. Both are in a physical sense disgustingly unclean in their persons and houses.[48]

Such opinions of Indians and Hinduism forcefully and officially confronted the Bengali elite in Calcutta under the administration of Bentinck
and in the statements and actions of Macaulay, Duff, and the Young
Bengal group. Bentinck dismantled the College of Fort William, nearly
drove to extinction the Calcutta Madrassa and Sanskrit College, rendered
impotent the Calcutta School and School Book Societies, forced the
anglicization of the curriculum of Serampore College and strongly supported Western education for Indians.[49]

The Bengali elite of Calcutta also encountered the derogatory statement of Macaulay and Duff. In the Minute of 1835 Macaulay wrote:

> It is I believe no exaggeration to say that all the historical information
> which has been collected to form all the books written in the Sanskrit lan-
> guage is less valuable than that what may be found in the most paltry
> abridgements used at preparatory schools in England. In every branch of
> physical or social philosophy, the relative position of the nations is the
> same.[50]

Macaulay felt that contemporary English culture and knowledge were
the zenith of civilization and that westernization was the only true form of
modernization.[51] That Macaulay sought modernization through Western
secular education is clear when he said, "We must do our best to form a
class who may be interpreters between us and the millions whom we
govern; a class of persons Indian in blood and color, but English in tastes,
in opinion, in morals, and in intellect."[52]

Alexander Duff, a Scottish missionary who arrived in India in 1831,
was the religious counterpart of Macaulay's secular westernization. Duff
also believed that Western education was an important ingredient of
modernization for India, so long as it was "in close and inseparable
alliance with the illuminating, quickening, beautifying influence of the
Christian Faith."[53] The need for the combination of Western education
and Christianity in modernizing India was predicated on Duff's harsh
opinion of Hinduism. In *India and Indian Missions,* Duff wrote:

> Of all the systems of false religion ever fabricated by the perverse ingenuity
> of fallen man, Hinduism is certainly the most stupendous—whether we
> consider the boundless extent of its range, or the boundless multiplicity of
> its component parts. Of all the systems of false religion it is that which
> seems to embody the largest amount and variety of semblances and
> counterfeits of divinely revealed facts and doctrines.[54]

The impact of these British opinions was multiplied when Bengalis
themselves leveled similar criticisms at Hinduism. The appointment of
Henry Louis Vivian Derozio to the faculty of Hindu College in 1828
signaled the beginning of a wave of loud and vehement Bengali criticism
of Hindu religion and civilization. The students of Derozio at Hindu

College, who came to be known as Young Bengal, felt that revitalization of India was not to be found in her past but in opening "Indians' minds to the cultural offerings of the west so that India might once more share the benefits of human progress."[55] That Young Bengal had a low opinion of Hinduism is clear from Madhab Chandra Mallek's statement in the college magazine: "If there is anything that we hate from the bottom of our heart, it is Hinduism."[56] The debates held by the students of Hindu College generally revolved around the so-called vileness, corruptness, and unworthiness of Hindu religion and its unfitness for rational beings.[57]

Along with their denunciation of Hindu religion, Young Bengal advocated westernization as a better way to modernize India. Derozio had instilled in his students a spirit of free thought and revolt against Hindu society and customs. These students were inspired by the writings of Voltaire, Locke, Hume, and Paine and by European history. Krishna Mohan Bannerjee, a Christian convert, in the first address given before the Society for the Acquisition of General Knowledge echoed the feelings of Young Bengal:

> If the study of history be of such immense consequence to mankind in general, it is by far more so to persons of our present situation. We are by no means satisfied with the state of things around us. We wish we were not surrounded with such wretched and degraded fellow-men. . . . Dissatisfied with our present intellectual and moral condition and desiring to improve ourselves and countrymen, we have come to the determination of organizing this very society. . . . There are nations that at one time groaned under the wretched degradation but who stand conspicuous now for everything that is good and great. . . . Can we observe with attention the rise of European Communities from the lowest depths of barbarism without getting some insight into the secret of human emancipation from corruption and misery?[58]

In 1833 Young Bengal started a journal, *Bijnan Sar Sangraha,* the purpose of which was "to communicate, chiefly among the natives of Bengal, such selections from works of European literature and science as may tend to enlarge the sphere of their moral sentiments and infuse a spirit of activity and enterprise in all those pursuits which conduce to the happiness or glory of man."[59] Young Bengal felt that Hinduism was the cause of the so-called social and moral corruption and backwardness of Hindu society and that by imitating Western culture and with Western science and philosophy India could be a great country.

Young Bengal's imitation of the West went beyond education. Descriptions of their lifestyle provide further evidence of their attitudes toward Hinduism and Western culture. Bose reports that these radical students shouted at orthodox Hindus that they ate beef, and that they greeted the image of Kali with "Good morning, madam."[60] Benoy Ghosh reports that the main characteristics of members of Young Bengal were "their love of the West and intoxication with the English."[61] Heimsath quotes K. A. N. Sastri's description of these students: they "adopted an agressive attitude to everything Hindu and openly defied the canons of their inherited religion, while some of them offended public opinion by their youthful exuberance such as drinking to excess, flinging beef bones into houses of the orthodox, and parading the streets shouting 'we have eaten Mussulman bread.' "[62] S. Mukerjee states that "there was a rush for everything English, and English ideals dominated our lives and thoughts."[63] In a Calcutta periodical in 1851 the students of Hindu College were described as having a "smattering of English," dressing fashionably, carrying around Shakespeare and Milton, eating beef, and drinking wine.[64]

With reference to the RCS theory, the members of Young Bengal had conceded rank to English culture in the early 1830s. However, as the decade progressed a large portion of the Bengali orthodox community harshly criticized their ideas and behavior. The orthodox elite's attempts to check the westernization of the members of Young Bengal revealed their growing concern with the solidarity of Bengali society. The Dharma Sabha, formed in 1831, protested against the radical trends of Young Bengal. Parents withdrew their sons from Hindu College and forced the firing of Derozio. The Young Bengal members were threatened with excommunication from Hindu society. The orthodox community forced the suspension of the progressive periodical *Parthenon,* published by the students of Derozio, after its first issue in 1830.[65] The attacks by the orthodox elite became more vehement after the Christian conversion of about fifty of the students, among them Mahesh Chandra Ghosh and Krishna Mohan Bannerjee.[66]

Two points must be made about the reaction of the orthodox elite to Young Bengal. First, the feelings of alienation felt by Young Bengal were the result of these attacks. In terms of the RCS theory, the alienation of these students was an important factor in the emulation-solidarity conflict they experienced toward the end of the 1830s. Most members of Young Bengal joined Devendranath Tagore in revitalizing the Brahmo Samaj in 1842. The Brahmo Samaj of 1842 was an extension of the ideas of Rammohun Roy which, as demonstrated above, were attempts to solve the emulation-solidarity conflict. In other words, most members of Young Bengal returned to the position of espousing social reform and modernization while attempting to maintain their Hindu solidarity by using the techniques of synthesis and indigenous claims of Brahmoism. I will have more to say about the Brahmo Samaj shortly.

Second, the reaction to Young Bengal of the members of the Dharma

Sabha demonstrated an emulation-solidarity conflict on the part of even the most orthodox Hindus of the Calcutta Bengali elite. According to Kopf, the members of the Dharma Sabha were not against modernization but against the total westernization of India.[67] That the members of the Bengali orthodox community were in favor of Western education eventually is demonstrated in their support of Hindu College. The organization of the Dharma Sabha followed Western lines with a president, board of directors, secretary, and treasurer. They conducted their meetings according to the strict rules of parliamentary procedure.[68] They tended to agree with the British criticism of Hinduism—that the customs and practices of eighteenth-century Hinduism were inferior and that reform was needed. Their ideas for social reform, such as their plan for aiding the rural poor and their proposal for aiding Calcutta's poor by building a charitable institution and hospital, were derived from their contact with and emulation of Western society.[69] Yet they resented the forceful intrusion of Western culture and the harsh criticisms of the British. As a result, they sought to maintain their solidarity by defending the Hinduism reconstructed by the Orientalists.[70]

The Brahmo Samaj of Devendranath Tagore presents the clearest example of the emulation-solidarity conflict felt by the more progressive Bengali elite between 1830 and 1870. In general, they agreed with the derogatory opinions of Puranic Hinduism held by the British. The members of the Brahmo Samaj believed there was much that was better in Western culture. However, they were also defensive of Hinduism as reinterpreted by Rammohun Roy. Therefore they attempted to maintain their Hindu solidarity through the Brahmo religion.

When Devendranath Tagore assumed the leadership of the Brahmo Samaj in 1843, that organization had passed through a period of stagnation since the death of Rammohun in 1833. It is probable that Devendranath had conceded rank to British culture. Because his father, Dwarkanath, had been successful in his business relations with the British in the 1800–1830 period, it is assumed that he internalized many English customs that his family had adopted because of presumed power-incorporative borrowing of his father. Devendranath attended Hindu College in 1831 and continued his studies there for four years. Although I lack evidence, it seems probable that he held attitudes similar to those of the Young Bengal students of the college. We get indirect evidence of his sympathy with the ideas of Young Bengal and his rank concession to Western culture by the fact that he joined the Society for the Acquisition of General Knowledge in 1838. We also get indirect evidence of his emulation-solidarity conflict, for in that same year he was converted to the Brahmo faith. In his autobiography, Devendranath mentions a spiritual loneliness which was lessened when, after coming across a part of the Upanishads dealing with monotheism, he took up the Brahmo faith.[71]

The formation of the Brahmo Sabha by Rammohun Roy in 1828 was an expression of his emulation-solidarity conflict. There seems little reason not to accept that when Devendranath assumed the leadership of the organization in 1843 it was still an expression of the members' emulation-solidarity conflict. Most members of the Brahmo Samaj were Western-educated Bengali elite who had conceded rank in the sense that they admitted that the Puranic/Tantric Hinduism, which the British criticized, was inferior. But the blind imitation of Western culture by Young Bengal was viewed as a threat to Hindu solidarity.

In an attempt to stem the tide of westernization and to provide a means of identifying with Hindu civilization while incorporating many of the social reforms and institutions of the West, Devendranath formed the Tattvabodhini Sabha in 1839, which became a subsidiary of the Brahmo Samaj when he joined it. The journal of the Brahmo Samaj, *Tattvabodhini Patrika,* emphasized Bengali solidarity symbols by stating the need for developing the Bengali language, studing science and theology, and battling against the superstition and idolatry of medieval Hinduism if moral and material uplift were to be realized.[72] They confronted the criticism of the missionaries by publishing rejoinders in defense of Vedic Hinduism: "We will not deny that we consider the Vedas and the Vedas alone as the authorized rule of Hindu theology. They are the sole foundation of all our beliefs and the truths of all other Shastras will be judged of according to their agreement with them."[73] It seems that the members of the Brahmo Samaj indirectly admitted the inferiority of medieval Hinduism by using Vedic Hinduism as their foundation of Brahmo religion.

Brahmoism provided an alternative to westernization and Christianity. "They offered the Western-educated a reformed Indian religion—Vedantism—which they argued was free of superstition and priestly tyranny. At the same time, Brahmos claimed to offer an ethical system based on Hindu scriptures but reflecting the identical sentiments of the Sermon on the Mount."[74] If Kopf is right, the Brahmos were clearly attempting to deal with an emulation-solidarity conflict.

The Brahmoism of Devendranath was not wholly successful in resolving the emulation-solidarity conflict. The Brahmo Samaj did manage to check missionary proselytizing and put an end to the wholesale imitation of the West by providing the Bengali elite of Calcutta with a form of Hinduism that denied the so-called superstition, idolatry, and moral and social corruption of medieval Hinduism.[75] However, the same religion, Brahmoism, which synthesized the Western-inspired reform of the position of women, education, and *sati* with the Hinduism of the Vedas and Upanishads also alienated the Brahmos from the orthodox Bengali elite. In the 1850s Devendranath stated that "we Brahmos are situated amidst a community which views us with no friendly feelings" because we attack "their Puranic and Tantric systems."[76] Another factor which added to their alienation from the more orthodox segment of the Bengali elite was their continued sympathy toward American and British Unitarianism.[77] The orthodox Bengali elite probably believed that this sympathy was a further Western influence that would destroy traditional Hindu religion. Raj Narain Bose, in a reaction to this alienation, attempted to demonstrate the superiority of Hinduism over Christianity. The Hinduism he chose to support was that of classical Vedanta while attacking that of the Puranas and Tantras.[78] These efforts failed the convince the orthodox community of the Brahmos' Hindu identity because the Brahmos attacked the very religion in which they believed. Thus the Brahmos in the 1850s were still experiencing an emulation-solidarity conflict.

When Keshab Chandra Sen joined the Brahmo Samaj in 1858, the organization switched from an emphasis on religious reinterpretation of Hinduism and incorporation of Western ideas to an emphasis on social reform.[79] Keshab quickly became the leader of many younger Brahmos by advocating campaigns against *kulin* polygamy, child marriage, and caste while promoting widow-remarriage, intercaste marriage, and women's emancipation through education.[80] These reforms were too radical for Devendranath because he felt they would alienate the Brahmo even further from Hindu society. With more data I might have been able to demonstrate that Devendranath agreed with many of the reforms proposed by Keshab Chandra and that because of the emulation-solidarity conflict he chose to identify more closely with Hinduism than did Keshab Chandra.

In any event, Keshab Chandra's speech "Jesus Christ: Europe and Asia," delivered in 1866, was interpreted by Devendranath and his faction as an apologia for Christianity and led to a split in the Brahmo Samaj in that same year. Keshab's group formed the Brahmo Samaj of India; Devendranath and his followers formed the Adi Brahmo Samaj.

Devendranath attacked the Brahmo Samaj of India and started programs aimed at the modernization of India. At this point the solidarity focus of the emulation-solidarity conflict was extended by the Adi Brahmo Samaj. They realized that their Brahmoism must be spread among a wider segment of Hindu society so that a majority of Bengalis could have pride in their culture. Thus the Hindu Mela was started by Dwijendranath Tagore. The program included a display of Hindu industrial goods, physical training to restore the manliness of Bengali youth, the establishment of a school of Hindu music, the founding of a school of Hindu medicine, and the encouragement of Indian antiquities. These programs were a response to the "degradation" of Bengali society.[81] Dwijendranath, recognizing the danger of westernization but also recognizing the "inferiority" of Bengali society, attacked the Brahmo Samaj of India in 1869:

> With all our present inferiority and infirmities we are little better respected by the world than the Christian negro of North America who speaks English, dresses himself with the jacket and pantaloon, and whose habits of life in fact are mostly borrowed from the European settlers there. And why so? Simply because his civilization is nothing more than an image of European manners and habits, and he is no more like the true European than the monkey in the red-coat riding on the she-goat is like a human being. By means of mere imitation we can be just so much like the Europeans as slaves are like their masters.[82]

While the Tagores and the Adi Brahmo Samaj were dealing with their emulation-solidarity conflict by creating the Hindu Mela to increase the internal solidarity of Hinduism and uplift the masses and instill pride in Hindu civilization, the Brahmo Samaj of India was becoming more and more westernized and more and more alienated from Hindu society. The Brahmo Samaj of India under Keshab continued to push for social reforms as a response to their agreement with the criticisms of the West. Their alienation attained a de jure status with the Marriage Act of 1872. This act stated that intercaste marriages would be legally recognized if the partners declared that they were neither Hindu, Christian, Muhammadan, Parsi, Buddhist, Sikh, nor Jain.[83]

Why the Adi Brahmo Samaj experienced a more severe emulation-solidarity conflict and started programs aimed at fostering the internal solidarity of Hindu society and massing support for their program of nationalism and why the Brahmo Samaj of India did not seem to experience the same degree of conflict may be explained by reference to rank path. The Adi Brahmo Samaj chose a political rank path as evidenced by the nationalistic tenor of their programs. According to the RCS theory, the choice of a political rank path results in an increased emulation-solidarity conflict which can be resolved by syncretizing indigenous and emulated customs and by emphasizing the indigenous customs in order to gain the support of the masses. The Hindu Mela was just such a program with the added ingredient of instilling pride in Hindu culture. Because Keshab's program was universalist in tone, he spoke of solidarity with mankind more than solidarity with Hindus. Thus there was not the severe emulation-solidarity conflict and less motivation to emphasize indigenous customs and symbols in their program and philosophy. Keshab's group did experience an emulation-solidarity conflict as evidenced by their derogatory opinion of Hinduism. However, in speaking of a solidarity with all mankind they relieved the self-hatred that accompanies rank concession without "the exigencies of social unity aimed at improving status."[84] In sum, the difference between the Adi Brahmo Samaj and the Brahmo Samaj of India was the choice of rank path and the focus of solidarity. The former group by choosing the political rank path of nationalism experienced an increase in the emulation-solidarity conflict. Consequently they had to gain mass support through the Hindu Mela. The latter group, though experiencing an emulation-solidarity conflict, did not switch to a political rank path but rather attempted to resolve their conflict by speaking of a solidarity with all mankind. Such rhetoric may decrease overt solidarity attempts, and thus they were free to pursue their Western reforms without the inhibiting influences of a nationalistic solidarity with their own society.

1870–1905

The organizations, theology, and events of the 1830–1870 period were a reaction by the Bengali elite to the change in attitude of the British. Instead of the Orientalist sympathy for Hindu Vedic religion and civilization, the anglicist scorn for all that was Indian prevailed. The British attitude indicated to the Bengalis that the only way India could purge herself of the so-called backwardness, corruption, and idolatry of medieval Hindu civilization was the wholesale adoption of British culture. Although the Bengali elite seemed to agree that Puranic/Tantric Hinduism was inferior, they reacted in defense of Vedic Hinduism through such organizations as the Brahmo Samaj and Dharma Sabha. Brahmoism incorporated Western-inspired social and religious reforms into Vedic and Upanishadic Hinduism as a defense against British criticism of the entire civilization and history. By doing so, the Brahmos indicated that they were experiencing an emulation-solidarity conflict. At the beginning of the 1870–1905 period, there was another shift in British attitude and policy toward Bengalis. According to Kopf, this shift was shown in three ways:

> In the first place, there was a sharp rise of the educated unemployed who could not find suitable jobs. Secondly, gifted Bengalis were discriminated against openly by Britishers who resented "niggers" in high positions. Thirdly, the nonofficial British community blocked every effort to give Indian magistrates the power to judge cases involving whites as well as nonwhites.[85]

In other words, now that many Bengalis had emulated and borrowed British customs—a course which had been advocated by the British in the 1830s—the British reversed their position and displayed hostility toward the kind of westernized Bengali they had sought to produce.

The changing economic conditions of the nineteenth century were an important factor in the Bengalis' view of British attitudes. Between 1800 and 1850 the Bengali upper castes in Calcutta were highly successful in their commercial dealings with the British.[86] Around 1850, Bengalis were withdrawing from commercial affairs because of a series of commercial crises and increased British exclusiveness.[87] At the time the commercial ventures were failing, there were increasing opportunities of white-collar employment for the Bengalis who had an English education.[88] These employment opportunities, together with the opening of government appointments for Bengalis, increased the stimuli for Bengalis to acquire an English education. The members of the Bengali elite were successful in obtaining most of the white-collar positions as well as the government appointments.[89] After 1870, the Bengali elite were almost entirely left out of commercial development. In addition, because of rising population, land fragmentation, and lack of agricultural improvements, their revenue from landholdings was decreasing.[90] This loss of agricultural revenue in the 1870s forced more of the Bengali elite to seek public service and professional employment.

Since English education was necessary for professional and public service employment, there was a sharp increase in school and college enrollment in the 1870s. The increasing numbers of English-educated Bengali elite meant stiffer competition for civil service and government jobs.[91] However, the number of job opportunities did not keep pace with the number of qualified Bengalis.[92] Thus many educated Bengalis found themselves unemployed in the latter part of the nineteenth century and they blamed the British for their situation. In 1876 the British government sought to lower the maximum age limit from twenty-one to nineteen for the open competitive examination for civil service posts.[93] This action was a prime example of what the Bengalis viewed as British attempts to keep Indians out of government service.

Those Bengalis who did secure employment in the professions or in civil service found themselves discriminated against by the British in attaining higher positions. For example, Bankim Chandra Chatterjee "felt that there was little chance of his extra labors receiving recognition since he was not an Englishman."[94] It appears that Bengalis did not receive the promotions that less-qualified Englishmen received because the British believed that the educated Bengalis were cunning, deceitful, and lacked manly courage. A handbook for British administrators in India stated that: "The physical organization of the Bengali is feeble even to effeminacy. . . . His mind bears a singular analogy to his body. It is weak even to helplessness for purposes of manly resistance but its suppleness and tact move children of sterner climates to admiration not unmingled with contempt."[95] Furthermore, educated Bengalis who did find employment were subject to demands of servility from their British superiors. In addition, as John R. McLane points out elsewhere in this volume, Bengali professionals, particularly lawyers, had a difficult time "gaining access to the highest position in the bar" because of the poor training they received and the belief on the part of many Indians that an Indian lawyer was less likely to be successful in winning court cases.[96]

Another expression of the shift in British attitude was the failure of the Ilbert Bill to become law. Since the "Black Acts" of 1849, Indians had been trying to bring "British-born subjects under the jurisdiction of the local courts, thus abolishing the existing privilege of trial by the Calcutta supreme court alone."[97] The Ilbert Bill of 1882 sought to legalize the rare practice of trying Englishmen by Indian magistrates. But the European community, organized by Branson, successfully killed the bill by pressuring Lord Ripon.

The unemployment of the educated Bengalis, together with economic and legal discrimination, clearly displayed the British attitudes toward Bengalis in the 1870s. The change in attitude forced the Bengalis to reconsider the rank path they had chosen to raise their status. Until the 1870s, the Bengalis had been pursuing higher status via their economic interactions with the British and religious reform. As mentioned, the economic rank path produces a less severe emulation-solidarity conflict because it is a more individual avenue of mobility. The fact that the Bengali elite was pursuing an economic rank path may explain the greater emphasis on emulation of Western culture in previous periods. This is not to say that the elite was not concerned with solidarity; rather that, in relation to the period with which we are now dealing, they seemed to be emphasizing the borrowing of Western customs more than attempting to affirm their likeness with their own culture. Dwijendranath's comments about the Brahmo alienation from the rest of Bengali society were a recognition of the fact that both the orthodox community and the Brahmos were concerned with Bengali solidarity.

The situation we encounter in the 1870s is different from those that Orans considers.[98] The increased emulation-solidarity conflict for the Santal, Jatars, Burakamin, and Negroes resulted from the opening of the political rank path. In the Bengali case of the nineteenth century, we see the *closure* of the economic rank path. The result is that the Bengali elite was forced to pursue a political defense of the position they had gained through the economic rank path. In other words, the closure of the economic path, together with British discrimination against the Bengali elite, forced the Bengalis to attempt to organize politically to maintain, if not improve, their positions and numbers in the professions and in civil service jobs. Thus there was a shift from an economic to a political rank path not because of new political opportunities but because of diminishing economic ones.

The switch from the economic to the political rank path brought about more severe emulation-solidarity conflict. In fact, it might be hypothesized that the Bengal elite did not experience a severe emulation-solidarity conflict until the 1870s, when they were forced to pursue rank politically and thus wider their base of support. The Adi Brahmo Samaj was exceptional because it expanded the focus of its solidarity attempts in 1866 as a reaction to the alienation they experienced and the programs advocated by Keshab Chandra. The Hindu Mela was an expression of their expanded focus.

If the Bengali elite did shift from an economic to a political rank path with the resultant increased emulation-solidarity conflict, then we should expect a "cultural movement" in which the elite attempts to increase their solidarity with Hindu civilization in order to gain wider support for their programs of modernization. Further we should expect literary creativity to proliferate, practicing the techniques of syncretism, innovative combination, and indigenous claims in order to naturalize the borrowed ideas and values from the West and to increase Bengali solidarity. The neo-Vaisnava and neo-Vedanta movements of the last quarter of the nineteenth century were stimulated by the increased emulation-solidarity conflict resulting from the shift to the political rank path.

To exemplify the cultural movement of the last quarter of the nineteenth century, I turn now to the literary works of Bankim Chandra Chatterjee with respect to the increased emulation-solidarity conflict of this period. Bankim Chandra was born in 1838 of a *kulīn* Brahman family. He probably had close contact with Western culture because his father had been in the civil service and because he had an English education. His upbringing therefore included many English values which became internalized during his youth.

Bankim Chandra experienced an emulation-solidarity conflict. That he felt Bengali society was inferior is evident: "Moreover, the people of our country, particularly the humble people, are exceedingly lazy."[99] According to Bankim, Hindu society was backward because of the mastery of the Brahmans and the lack of moral strength to resist on the part of the common people: "At first the mastery of the Brahmans increased through the passiveness of the other castes. Because of the loss of intellectual strength on the part of the other castes, their minds became especially susceptible to superstition. Superstition is produced by fear."[100] And Bankim showed equal disdain for the westernized Bengali babu:

Whose words are one in his mind, ten in speech, a hundred in writing, and a thousand in a quarrel, he is a babu. Whose strength is one thing in his hand, ten times greater in his mouth, a hundred times greater on the written page, and out of sight at the time for work, he is a babu. Whose intelligence in his childhood is in books, in youth in a bottle, in adulthood in his wife's *ancal,* he is a babu. Whose god of good fortune is the British, whose guru is the teacher of the Brahmo religion, whose Veda is the native newspaper, and whose place of pilgrimage is the National Theatre, he is a babu. Who is a Christian to the missionaries, a Brahmo to Kesabcandra, a Hindu to his father, and an atheist to Brahman beggars, he is a babu. Who takes water at home, liquor in his friend's house, a tongue lashing in the prostitute's quarters, and a collaring at his Master Sahib's house, he is a babu. Who despises the use of oil at bath time, his own finger at meal time, and his mother tongue at conversation time, he is a babu. Whose concern is only with clothing, whose diligence is pursuing a good job, whose only respect is for his wife or mistress, and whose anger is only for good books, without doubt, he is a babu.[101]

Not only did Bankim view Hindus as inferior but he also conceded that the British were superior: "That the English are generally superior to the people of this country, no one will deny except the man blinded by conceit. The English are superior to us in strength, culture, knowledge, and glory."[102] Bankim admired the bravery and dedication to duty of the British; and he felt that Indian backwardness was due to the lack of self-confidence and moral strength of his generation.[103]

Although Bankim conceded rank to British culture and especially admired the strength and courage of Englishmen, he did not feel that westernization should be the form of modernization for India, as evidenced in his description of the babu. Further, he did not advocate the program of social reform as did the Brahmos; rather he felt that a moral regeneration and a nationalistic spirit were the answer to the problem of Indian backwardness. "He believed that social and political reform would follow naturally upon religious regeneration."[104] His reinterpretation of Vaisnavism was an attempt to naturalize those values of the West which he admired by demonstrating that the values were actually part of Vaisnava tradition. As such, his neo-Vaisnavism, together with Vivekananda's neo-Vedanta, was part of the "cultural movement" stimulated by the increased emulation-solidarity conflict resulting from the switch to a political rank path.

Because Bankim Chandra regarded religion as the basis of moral regeneration, he viewed it as a system of ethics, not merely a belief in gods:

I am not one of those who think that a belief in God, or in a number of gods, or in a future existence, or anything else which does not admit of proof, constitutes religion. But when such belief, or any belief whatever, furnishes a basis for conduct of the individual towards himself as well as towards others . . . it is religion. . . . Religion viewed thus is in theory a philosophy of life; in practice it is a rule of life.[105]

In order for India to solve the problems of her backwardness, Bankim Chandra advocated a two-pronged program: the creation of a righteous kingdom with moral and ethical regeneration, and the fostering of a national spirit by developing self-confidence and strength. Since religion was the key to both these programs, he reinterpreted Vaisnavism in order to naturalize the ethics and national feeling necessary for creating his righteous kingdom. Bankim Chandra demonstrated that there did exist a righteous kingdom in Hindu tradition. He portrayed the Aryan culture of Vedic times as one of enlightenment and morality. Yet this righteous kingdom had degenerated because the masses of Hindus were too lazy to resist the corruption introduced by the Brahmans through fear and superstition.

The proper ethics of moral regeneration were to be found in the Krisna portrayed in the *Mahabharata*. Krisna displayed the social and ethical activism, the devotion to humanity, and the moral strength to resist evil. In *Krsnacharitra* ("Biography of Krisna") Bankim presented the goal of moral regeneration as the kingdom of righteousness and claimed that it would be attained if Hindus upheld their dharma. Dharma, however, was not the multiplicity of particularist ethics of Puranic Hinduism but a universalist ethic of devotion exemplified by Krisna in the *Mahabharata*. All Hindus should emulate Krisna's code of ethic—*karmayoga,* the path of works as service to man rather than the performance of rituals.[106] Bankim portrayed Krisna in *Krsnacharitra* and in *Anandamath* as the ideal man. Together with his ascetics, Krisna devoted himself to the creation of a nation in which "the truth of the eternal religion will triumph. Bankim Chandra pictured the creation of the Indian nation as a triumph of religious truth."[107] Thus the moral regeneration of Indians would foster a national feeling among Hindus because of their pride in their kingdom of righteousness.

Bankim also portrayed Krisna as powerful warrior, a good tactician and administrator, just, good, forgiving, brave.[108] In order to carry out his dharma of creating a righteous kingdom and working for the good of humanity, Bankim believed that a man should cultivate all his faculties. He was against the ascetics' physical withdrawal from the world and their consequent physical degeneration. Physical and mental strength were necessary for spiritual regeneration.[109] For Bankim a major message of the *Mahabharata* was that a man should be physically and mentally prepared to resist evil with violence, if necessary, in order to creat the kingdom of righteousness.[110] As mentioned, Bankim felt that India had degenerated because the people were too lazy to resist the corruption of the Brahmans. Thus he advocated physical training along with spiritual uplift as the way to prepare Hindus for their dharma of creating a righteous kingdom.

Another important factor in Bankim Chandra's reinterpretation of Vaisnavism using Krisna was asceticism. In the novel *Anandamath,* he portrayed a band of *sannyasin* who fought "to create a golden age of material and moral progress when the eternal religion would flourish."[111] As mentioned above, Bankim was against a *sannyasa*'s withdrawal from the world. Instead he advocated a this-wordly asceticism by which man would attempt to perfect not only himself but also his society. In *Krsnacharitra,* "Krisna is ideal because he worked for the good of his people and for the creation of the good society."[112] Bankim believed that a *sannyasa* should sever his family ties so that he could be wholly dedicated to his dharma of working for the good of his motherland. In sum, Bankim advocated a this-worldly asceticism in which man should become a *sannyasa* by severing his family ties, by developing his physical, mental, and spiritual strength and courage, by devoting himself to work in this world for the good of his fellow man, by spreading the eternal religion, by resisting evil with force if necessary in the pursuit of righteousness, and by building the confidence and national feeling of the people of India. In both *Krsnacharitra* and *Anandamath,* Krisna and his *sannyasin* were portrayed as possessing all these virtues, and they sought the moral regeneration of their people in creating a kingdom of righteousness.

Bankim Chandra did not exclusively use Vaisnava symbolism in his reinterpretation of Hinduism. In fact, the major symbol for his nation when the eternal religion reigned was Sakta. The goddess Kali was used as the symbol of the Hindu nation. Kali represented both the degradation of Hindu society and the source of strength and power to whom *sannyasin* should dedicate their works.[113] For Bankim, Kali was the symbol of the nation which would stimulate a national feeling among Hindus. She would stimulate the moral and physical courage to resist evil; she would stimulate an active dedication to the creation of a righteous nation.[114] The new nation, symbolized by Durga, would be based on the ethic of love of humanity. Bankim believed that the moral regeneration of India depended on love of others. Love of God was the highest stage of human love, but because civilization was imperfect, love for one's countrymen would suffice until a higher ethical stage was reached by man. The three stages leading to the development of love of God were love of self, love of family, and love of nation.[115] Bankim translated these stages of love into an ethic of works:

> Saving one's own people [family] is a much greater duty than saving oneself, and saving one's own country is much greater than saving one's own people. When *bhakti* toward God and love for all people are the same thing, it can be said that, apart from *bhakti* towards God, love of country is the greatest duty of all.[116]

Thus Bankim Chandra used the symbol of Kali and an ethic of love to stimulate a national feeling among the Hindus.

In his reinterpretation of Vaisnavism and Sakta symbolism, Bankim Chandra naturalized, through indigenous claims, several of the Western values he admired. Two of these values were bravery and dedication to duty, and it is clear that he emphasized these in his interpretation of the dharma of Krisna and the *sannyasin*. Choudhury's description of the Western ideas which influenced Bankim's reinterpretation of Vaisnavism indicates the extent of his borrowing from the West:

> Like the Sadharan Brahmos, Bankim Chandra had also been greatly influenced by his readings in western philosophy. He was a great admirer of Auguste Comte and his concept of a religion of humanity. Bankim's emphasis on humanitarianism and his doctrine of cultivation of all human faculties seem to have reflected the influence of John Stuart Mill. *But Bankim Chandra insisted that these basic ideas and ideals existed in Hindu thought in a better form.* The Comtean religion of humanity is imperfect because it did not include a belief in God. In the life of Krisna Bankim Chandra found a similar religion of culture which included belief in God and was based on the incarnation of God. He also found in the life of Krisna the principle that the criterion of true religion is what is good for humanity, which he says is similar to the utilitarian philosophy of Bentham and Mill. According to Bankim Chandra the spiritual principles necessary for a moral regeneration can be found in Hinduism and did not need to be imported from outside. The true principles of Hinduism must be rediscovered and reapplied for religious reformation and regeneration. Bankim Chandra stated that religious reform must evolve from within Hindu religious tradition. Western religious and philosophical thought could only act as a stimulus to reexamination of the real meaning of the Hindu tradition.[117]

A further indication of Bankim's borrowing and incorporation is evident when he said:

> Religion in its fullness cannot be found in the qualityless god of the Vedanta, because he who is without qualities cannot be an example to us. . . . The basis of religion is a god with qualities *such as is mentioned in our Puranas and in the Christian Bible,* because He and only He can be our model. The worship of an impersonal God is sterile; only the worship of a personal God has meaning to man.[118]

Bankim Chandra Chatterjee was part of the cultural movement of the last quarter of the nineteenth century—a movement that was stimulated by the increasing emulation-solidarity conflict resulting from the switch from an economic to a political rank path. Through his literary creativity he sought to resolve his own emulation-solidarity conflict by advocating the solidarity of his people. His literary creativity is demonstrative of Orans' RCS theory in that he attempted to naturalize British ideas and values into Hindu tradition, principally through the technique of indigenous claims. Furthermore, he chose the god of the Puranas as the god of his new Hinduism. This is significant in that the Puranas were singled out for criticism by the British missionaries earlier in the century and therefore carried low status value. Emphasizing low status attributes is, according to Orans, ideally suited to stimulating external solidarity because these attributes are the most distinctive.[119]

Space does not permit a similar analysis of the neo-Vedanta of Vivekananda. But if my understanding of his theology is correct, he too naturalized several ideas and values from the West. The disciples of Bijoy Krisna Goswami, many of whom converted from Brahmoism, also displayed the emulation-solidarity conflict in their attempts at synthesizing Western values and indigenous tradition. The fact that several of his disciples converted from Brahmoism is significant in that, as the nineteenth century drew to a close, the members of the Sadharan Brahmo Samaj found themselves more and more alienated from the rest of the Calcutta Bengali elite. Although these Brahmos advocated social reforms similar to those of the neo-Vaisnavas, neo-Vedantists, and the Adi Brahmo Samaj, they did not attempt to naturalize the programs as thoroughly as did the other groups. It appears that the Sadharan Brahmos were not so concerned about solidarity because they felt that their group was the core of Bengalis who would interact with the British for the betterment of Hindu society. I think that they underestimated the solidarity requirements of a political rank path. It was not until the partition of Bengal in 1905 that the Brahmos saw the futility of agitating a small group to gain British concessions in political, economic, and social matters. Their activity failed because they were alienated from the rest of the elite and therefore lacked the wide support necessary in the political rank path. They did not try to counter their alienation by thorough attempts at naturalizing the Western ideals and values they emulated The post-1905 political activity was based upon the more indigenous reinterpretations of Hinduism of Bankim Chandra and Vivekananda. For it was these philosophies which combined the social activism, universalist ethics, free thinking, and social reform ideas borrowed from the West with the solidarity attributes of Hinduism.

III

By considering the entire nineteenth century, this analysis of the Bengal elite in Calcutta has been more suggestive than comprehensive. In terms of Orans' RCS theory, the behavior and attitudes of the Calcutta Bengali elite can be seen as a long process of conflicting motivations and ideas culminating in the sweeping reinterpretations of Hinduism which synthesized the cultures of Britain and India in the last quarter of that century. It was these neo-Hindu theologies which were philosophical foundations of the more radical, and sometimes violent, political events of the first quarter of the twentieth century.

The phenomenon of the Bengali elite borrowing ideas, values, and customs from the British while continuing to proclaim themselves Hindus was more than a need for synthesizing two cultural traditions. It was also a result of two conflicting motivations: first, the motivation to imitate the British after having conceded rank to them; and second, the motivation to maintain group solidarity in the face of the increasing alienation, due to borrowing, of the rich and powerful Bengali elite of Calcutta. These motivations and the behavioral consequences were closely related to changing British attitudes and colonial policies in India. Decreasing economic opportunities after 1850 forced the elite to seek political means of maintaining their position in British economic and political institutions and of securing a significant voice in the modernization of their region and country. The switch to a political rank path increased the severity of the emulation-solidarity conflict, motivating a cultural movement in which Bengalis sought to demonstrate that the values they borrowed from the West were actually indigenous to Hindu civilization.

The process of synthesis that evolved in Calcutta during the nineteenth century had a unique character due to the time, place, and participants. On the other hand, this analysis has identified characteristics of the synthesis which enable us to view it in the wider context of culture contact where one society is dominant. In this the history of nineteenth-century Bengal may tell us something about the colonial situation in general, given that the subordinate society concedes rank. Such optimism is enhanced by the similarities of the process of synthesis between nineteenth-century Bengal and the societies studied by Orans.

The case of the Bengali elite of Calcutta in the nineteenth century suggests at least one new aspect of Oran's RCS theory. In the cases that Orans considered, the switch from an economic to a political rank path occurred when political democracy offered a significant alternative for mobility. As we have seen, when the Bengali elite switched to the political rank path, it was not because political democracy had become a real opportunity but because the economic path was closed off to them. Thus the British compelled the Bengalis to use the political path before it was viable.

To be sure, this analysis has not made nineteenth-century Bengal fully comprehensible. However, by adopting the approach I have taken, scholars may gain significant insights into culture change in general and nineteenth-century Bengal in particular by analyzing the events, organizations, and personages of shorter periods within that century.

NOTES

1. Rachel Van M. Baumer, p. 85 of this volume.
2. Ibid.
3. Ibid. pp. 85, 86.
4. David Kopf, *British Orientalism and the Bengal Renaissance: The Dynamics of Indian Modernization, 1773–1835* (Berkeley: University of California Press, 1969).
5. Kopf uses the "identity quest" theme of analysis in his description of Bengal from 1835 to 1900 in his essay in the present volume.
6. Martin Orans, *The Santal: A Tribe in Search of a Great Tradition* (Detroit: Wayne State University Press, 1965).
7. Martin Orans, "Caste and Race Conflict in Cross-Cultural Perspective," in *Race, Change, and Urban Society,* eds. P. Orleans and W. R. Ellis, Urban Affairs Annual, vol. V (Beverly Hills, Calif.: Sage Publications, 1971).
8. Orans uses the term *encysted* to denote what I have termed the subordinate society. Though he never explicitly defines *encysted,* it appears to mean a group that is either a structural segment of the dominant-superior society or is geographically surrounded by the dominant-superior society. Since I feel that it is the subordinate position of the inferior society that is crucial, I will refer to it as such and not use the term *encysted.* The summary of Orans' RCS theory which follows is taken from his works cited in notes 6 and 7 above).
9. Emil Durkheim, *The Division of Labor in Society,* transl. George Simpson (New York: Macmillan Co., 1933), p. 130.
10. Orans, *The Santal,* p. 3.
11. Ibid., p. 42.
12. Ibid., p. 129.
13. Ibid., p. 93.
14. For a more detailed discussion of the question of the rural/urban dichotomy in Bengal, see Ralph W. Nicholas, "Rural and Urban Cultures in Bengal" (unpublished paper presented to a seminar on Bengal, University of Hawaii, 1972).
15. N. K. Sinha, *The Economic History of Bengal from Plassey to the Permanent Settlement,* vol. 11 (Calkutta: K. L. Mukhopadhyay, 1967), p. 225.
16. For a more thorough description of the economic relations between the British and the Bengalis during the first half of the nineteenth century, see Blair Kling's essay in this volume.

17. Kopf, *British Orientalism,* p. 60.
18. Kling, op. cit.
19. Barbara Southard Choudhury, "Neo-Hinduism and Militant Politics in Bengal, 1875–1910" (unpublished Ph. D. diss., University of Hawaii, Honolulu, 1971), p. 127.
20. Ibid., p. 130.
21. Ibid., p. 133.
22. Ibid., p. 138.
23. Ibid., p. 246.
24. For lists of the members of the Sadharan Brahmo Samaj, their backgrounds, and education, see Choudhury, op. cit., pp. 117–211.
25. Ibid., pp. 117–119.
26. Kopf, *British Orientalism,* p. 180.
27. Ibid., p. 180.
28. Ibid., p. 181.
29. N. S. Bose, *The Indian Awakening and Bengal* (Calcutta: K. L. Mukhopadhyay, 1960), p. 61.
30. Ibid., p. 61.
31. Ibid., p. 10.
32. Ibid., p. 11.
33. Ibid., p. 12.
34. Cited by Bose, op cit., p. 16.
35. Cited by Bose, op. cit., p. 25.
36. Ibid., p. 20.
37. Kopf, *British Orientalism,* p. 183.
38. Cited by Bose, op. cit., p. 64.
39. Kopf, *British Orientalism.*
40. Ibid., p. 175.
41. Ibid., p. 39.
42. Orans, *The Santal,* p. 125.
43. E. Stokes, *The English Utilitarians and India* (Oxford: Clarendon Press, 1959), p. 30.
44. A. Embree, *Charles Grant and the British Rule in India* (New York: Columbia University Press, 1962), p. 148.
45. Memoir of the Life and Correspondence of John, Lord Teignmouth, pp. 142–143. Cited by Kopf in *British Orientalism,* pp. 141–142.
46. Ibid., p. 142.
47. Great Britain, *Hansard's Parliamentary Debates,* XXVI, 22 June 1813, p. 164. Cited by Kopf in *British Orientalism,* p. 142.
48. James Mill, *History of British India.* Notes and Continuation by H. H. Wilson. 9 vols., 4th ed. (London: James Madden and Co., 1840), II:135. Cited by Kopf in *British Orientalism,* p. 240.
49. Ibid., pp. 241–242.
50. Minute of 2 February 1835. Cited by Kopf in *British Orientalism,* p. 250.
51. Ibid., p. 243.
52. Cited by Bose, op cit., p. 66.
53. Cited by Bose, op. cit., p. 75.
54. Alexander Duff, *India and Indian Missions* (Edinburgh: John Johnstone, 1839). Cited by Bose, op. cit., p. 87.
55. Kopf, *British Orientalism,* p. 256.
56. Cited by Bose, op. cit., p. 39.

57.   Ibid., p. 40.
58.   Krishna Mohan Bannerji, "On the Nature and Importance of Historical Studies," in *Awakening in Bengal,* ed. G. Chattopadhyay (Calcutta: Progressive Book Publishers, 1965), pp. 22–23.
59.   Book review in *Calcutta Magazine,* 1933, p. 176. Cited by Chattopadhyay, op. cit., p. xxv.
60.   Bose, op. cit., p. 42.
61.   Cited by Chattopadhyay, op. cit., p. xlviii.
62.   Charles H. Heimsath, *Indian Nationalism and Hindu Social Reform* (Princeton: Princeton University Press, 1964), p. 13.
63.   S. Mukerjee, "Studies in Bengalee Literature 1," *Hindustan Review* (May 1907), p. 480. Cited by Heimsath, op. cit., p. 13.
64.   Kopf, *British Orientalism,* p. 258.
65.   Chattopadhyay, op. cit., p. xxi.
66.   Fallon, "Christianity in Bengal," in *Studies in the Bengal Renaissance,* ed. A. C. Gupta (Jadavpur: The National Council of Education, Bengal, 1958), p. 456.
67.   Kopf, *British Orientalism,* pp. 271–272.
68.   Ibid., p. 271.
69.   Ibid., p. 272.
70.   Ibid.
71.   Bose, op. cit., p. 84.
72.   Ibid., p. 86.
73.   *Tattvabodhini Patrika,* cited by Bose, op. cit., pp. 87–88.
74.   Kopf, p. 47 in this volume.
75.   Bose, op. cit., p. 95.
76.   Cited by Kopf on p. 61 of this volume.
77.   Ibid., p. 52.
78.   Ibid.
79.   Bose, op. cit., p. 150.
80.   Kopf, p. 53 of this volume.
81.   Ibid., p. 57.
82.   Cited by Kopf on p. 59 of this volume.
83.   Ibid., p. 63.
84.   Orans, "Caste and Race Conflict," p. 140.
85.   Kopf, p. 64 of this volume.
86.   Choudhury, op. cit., p. 26.
87.   Kling, pp. 37, 38 of this volume.
88.   Choudhury, op. cit., p. 28.
89.   Ibid., p. 28.
90.   Ibid., p. 29.
91.   Ibid., p. 41.
92.   Ibid., pp. 41–42.
93.   Bose, op. cit., p. 178.
94.   Choudhury, op. cit., p. 178.
95.   John Strachey, *India: Its Administration and Progress* (London, 1888), pp. 411–412. Cited by L. I. Rudolph and S. H. Rudolph in *The Modernity of Tradition* (Chicago: University of Chicago Press, 1967), pp. 164–165.
96.   John R. McLane, pp. 153, 154 in this volume.
97.   Bose, op. cit., p. 160.

98. Orans, "Caste and Race Conflict."

99. Bankim Chandra Chatterjee (BCC), "Bangakeser Krsak," *Bangadarsan* (Phalgun, 1279 B.S.), *BR*, vol. II, p. 303. Translated by Rachel Van M. Baumer in *Bankim Chandra Chatterjee: Bengali Artist and Intellectual*, revision of unpublished Ph. D. diss., "Bankimchandra Chatterjee and the Bengal Renaissance" (University of Pennsylvania, Philadelphia, 1964), p. 223.

100. BCC, "Bangadeser Krsak," *BR*, vol. II, p. 302. Translated by Baumer, op. cit., p. 227.

101. BCC, *Bangadarsan* (Phalgun, 1279 B.S.), vol. II, p. 12. Translated by Baumer, op. cit., p. 225.

102. BCC, "Jatibair," *Sadharani* (Krattik, 1280 B.S.), *BR,* vol. II, p. 885. Translated by Baumer, op. cit., p. 229.

103. Choudhury, op. cit., p. 178.

104. Ibid., pp. 180–181.

105. BCC, "Letters in Hinduism," as reprinted in *Bankim Racanabali*, vol. III, p. 237. Cited by Choudhury, op. cit., pp. 182–183.

106. Ibid., pp. 188–189.

107. Ibid., p. 195.

108. Ibid., p. 188.

109. Ibid., p. 188.

110. Ibid., p. 191.

111. Ibid., p. 187.

112. Ibid., p. 188.

113. Ibid., p. 193.

114. Ibid., p. 193.

115. Ibid., pp. 197–198.

116. BCC, *Dharmatattva*. Translated by Rachel Van M. Baumer, op. cit., pp. 20–21. Interpretation in brackets is my own.

117. Choudhury, op. cit., pp. 189–190. Italics are my own.

118. BCC, *BR,* vol. 111, p. 593. Translated by T. W. Clark in "The Role of Bankim Chandra in the Development of Nationalism," in *History of India, Pakistan and Ceylon,* ed. C. H. Phillips (London: Oxford University Press, 1962), p. 423. Italics are my own.

119. Orans, "Caste and Race Conflict," p. 95.

The Social and Institutional Bases of Politics in Bengal, 1906-1947

J. H. BROOMFIELD
University of Michigan

The recent revolution in Bangladesh must have revealed to nonspecialists what has always been evident to the specialist in Bengal studies: that our knowledge of the twentieth-century political history of this major world region is woefully inadequate. No detailed narrative of the Indian nationalist movement in the old undivided British province is available, and the development of Muslim politics has been even more thoroughly neglected. One turns hopefully from English to Bengali language sources, but there, apart from some interesting memoirs and less reliable biographies, the situation is no better.

It is this state of neglect which has encouraged me to consider the following questions: What political institutions existed in undivided Bengal? How did those institutions change through the forty years up to independence? And what do the changes tell us about the shifting social bases of politics?

One great merit of institutional analysis is that it permits us to say something reasonably exact about the extent of political participation and the nature of leadership. The analysis of membership and executive committee lists, if combined with painstaking biographical compilations, is certainly less slippery ground for generalization than the claims of politicians about their following and influence, all too frequently relied upon by historians. Similarly, an examination of the stated purposes of institutions and their practical achievements is a salutary test of political rhetoric.

CHRONOLOGY

To provide a chronological framework for the discussion, and also to

132

provoke thought about the major political movements of the half century, I shall first divide Bengali politics into chronological phases. I assume there would be general agreement in reckoning 1971 and 1947 as milestones in the region's history. Most historians would also add 1905 but, as the title of this essay indicates, I reject that date in favor of 1906. Opposition to the partition of Bengal had begun as soon as the proposal was announced in 1903, but the agitation followed the pattern of "polite" protest characteristic of the late nineteenth-century Congress. It was 1906 that brought radical departures: the mobilization of the Congress volunteer brigades; a militant campaign of economic boycott and Swadeshi; and the first spectacular strikes by the terrorist *samiti*. The year also saw serious communal rioting and the formation of the All-India Muslim League at Dacca. Here were many of the elements that characterize twentieth-century Bengali politics.

I select 1918 as the beginning of the next period, again passing by (this time with less assurance) a commonly accepted milestone—provincial reunification in 1912. The moderates lost control of the Bengal Congress in 1918, and with the rising star, C. R. Das, in the vanguard, the new leadership began the construction of a genuine party machine to give Congress the capability of engaging in mass politics. This strategy involved the extension of recruitment and organization to the district towns, in itself a major reorientation. The revitalized party attracted even the terrorists, and for a time there was a lull in revolutionary violence. Muslim politicians also were rudely confronted with the problems of mass political participation in 1918 when the frustrations of their coreligionists in Calcutta resulted in fierce rioting. This outburst precipitated the formation of new communal organizations, most notably the Khilafat committees, and influenced their organizational efforts among industrial labor.

Eight years later Calcutta suffered even more serious communal rioting, which marked another turning point in the province's political history. Congress had splintered after Das' tragically early death in 1925, and the Hindu-Muslim Pact which he had laboriously negotiated was repudiated by his successors. The slide toward Hindu communalism, accompanied by a reactivation of the terrorist *samiti*, was matched on the Muslim side with an open advocacy of separatism. A vigorous attempt was made to organize the Muslim voters behind communalist candidates in an effort to gain control of all elective institutions. This effort was sustained into the 1930s, and was largely successful.

The appointment of A. K. Fazlul Huq, Krishak Praja party leader, as chief minister of Bengal in 1937 opened the next phase. Four million additional peasants had been enfranchised in 1935, and many and varied were the politicians who stood forth claiming to speak in the name of the tenantry. Among them were the new converts to Marxism, recently graduated from British prisons. Huq held the premiership for six years, and his succession of ministries produced an impressive body of rural economic and social reform legislation.

Huq fell in 1943, M. A. Jinnah claiming that his defeat was a triumph for the ideals of the Muslim League, by then committed to the achievement of Pakistan. From 1943 to 1947, the final phase, the league held office in Bengal, and the prospect of the incorporation of all or part of the province within Pakistan was the overriding political issue.

THE NINETEENTH-CENTURY LEGACY

For each of these five periods, let us examine the institutional framework of politics. In doing so we shall be well advised to place the broadest possible construction on the term *political institution*. Many institutions which are nominally economic, social, or religious are used for political ends, and we shall limit our understanding of the political process if we do not take them into account. Here, however, I exclude the political role of government administrative institutions and, at the opposite pole, the political role of the family. Almost all that lies between may be termed voluntary association.

At the opening of the twentieth century Bengal already had an extensive network of political institutions—to the annoyance of the British imperial administrators who regarded this situation as an unhealthy characteristic of the province. The British themselves had been responsible for introducing some of the institutions, but to their displeasure they had been progressively taken over by Bengalis to serve indigenous purposes. The Bengal Legislative Council, almost forty years old by the turn of the century, remained a small consultative body under tight British control. This was less true of the Calcutta Municipal Corporation and the district and local boards of the other municipalities. Election or appointment to these bodies was prestigious, and they had sufficient local power to make membership attractive to landholders and lawyers, the two occupational groups then most active in Bengali politics.

For this reason, the landholders and bar associations to be found in most district towns and in the capital had a lively political involvement. Coordination of their activities, though only intermittently attempted, was supplied from Calcutta in the former case by the aristocratic and influential British Indian Association and in the latter by the High Court Bar Library Club.

In Calcutta there were also chambers of commerce to represent the interests of bankers and merchants, plantation, colliery, mill, and factory owners. These chambers were organized on communal lines, with separate

British, Marwari, Muslim, and Bengali Hindu organizations. In the mofussil, however, almost all prominent bankers and merchants (Marwari, Muslim, and Bengali Hindu) also held land; so we find the landholders associations representing their interests locally.

Lawyers and landholders were prominent on the executive committees of the district and people's associations, but here were also to be found college professors, schoolteachers, journalists, and government officials. A few of these organizations were active in the district headquarters towns, but most were based in Calcutta, where the prominent professional and commercial men had gone to further their careers and where the most effective lobbying for district interests could be done. Functioning as their central organization, in a manner parallel to that of the British Indian Association and the Bar Library Club, was the Indian Association of Bow Bazar.

What we do not find at the beginning of this century is a Congress organization. Many members of the associations described called themselves congressmen; most members of the Indian Association were so identified. But the institutional activities of Congress were limited to the annual national convention and the annual provincial conference, organized jointly by the Indian Association executive and the district association of the host district. The Bengal Provincial Congress Committee, though in existence on paper, was in effect a subcommittee of the Indian Association.

One of the most prevalent distortions in historical writing on modern India is the equation of nationalism with politics, and it bears repeating that in the early twentieth century there was much politics to which nationalism was irrelevant or only marginally important. One obvious area of this kind in Bengal was educational politics. At every level, from the senate of Calcutta University to the school boards of subdivisional towns, the most prominent local men were engaged in voluntary educational administration, which had assumed extraordinary importance for Bengalis as one of the few avenues of constructive public endeavor open to them in their circumscribed colonial society.

This was one field in which the Muslims were very active. Apart from the affairs of their own *madrassah* and *maktab*, they were taking an increasing interest by 1900 in general educational politics, with associations at the provincial and national levels (the Central National Mahommedan Association being the most renowned) lobbying for remedial help for the community on the ground of educational backwardness. The District Islamia Anjumans, parallel bodies to the Hindu-run district and people's Associations, also gave educational affairs priority.

To complete this picture we should take note of the college students' associations, themselves arenas for lively political contests and a fertile recruiting ground for nationalists. Less directly involved with politics, but important as centers for educated gathering and discussion, were the private libraries, reading rooms, and cultural societies (Sahitya Parishad, Saraswat Sabha, and Sanskriti Samaj) found in many towns. As one may guess from their Bengali titles, these were primarily Hindu societies, concerned with the Hindu cultural heritage of particular localities. It is indicative of how much less lively was the cultural life of Bengal's Muslims that they had few such societies outside Calcutta, and many of those were patronized by the Urdu, rather than the Bengali-speaking, community.

At this point a word of caution is necessary: institutional development had not proceeded evenly throughout the province. Calcutta, of course, was in a category by itself, but between the districts there was also a marked variation in the level of institutionalization. In Midnapore and Hooghly, for instance, we find greater activity than in neighboring Bankura, Burdwan, and Birbhum. Dacca and Chittagong had many more political institutions than did the districts which lay between. We can guess at some of the reasons for these disparities, but the very fact that we are still speculating about such fundamental features of Bengal's political system is a mark of how limited is our knowledge.

PHASE ONE: 1906–1918

Lord Curzon's partition gave an extraordinary boost to politics in Bengal, one indicator being an immediate jump in newspaper circulation. In the latter half of the nineteenth century Calcutta had been justly famous for its lively journalism, but we must be careful in retrospect not to exaggerate the size of the profession or its influence. It was only from 1906 onward that readership expanded sufficiently to support a sizeable number of professional journalists, and the newspaper and periodical offices became the focal points of important political groupings. Dacca, capital of the short-lived Province of Eastern Bengal and Assam, was now able to sustain a daily paper; other mofussil towns intermittently produced weeklies. These were most often a sideline of small commercial presses, and their publishers could afford to dabble in nationalist politics only when they had financial backing from local congressmen to compensate for the inevitable loss of their staple government advertising. This was one of the small, but effective, ways in which the British discriminated against the Hindu nationalists. Expressions of support for Muslim political positions did not bring similar punitive action.

The British had good reason to be disturbed by institutional developments in Bengal in 1906 and the years immediately following. Inspired by Garibaldi's Red Shirts, the younger, militant congressmen organized volunteer brigades to lead the boycott of stores selling imported cloth and to hawk Swadeshi goods produced by the experimental economic self-help societies founded since the turn of the century. This ideal of economic self-reliance was paralleled by the ideal of national education, which inspired the establishment of schools and colleges independent of the British-dominated Calcutta University and state systems. The curricula of the new institutions combined an emphasis on the glorious cultural heritage of Hindustan with a stress on technical and physical education. As in the establishment of sports clubs and gymnasiums at this time, no great effort was made to conceal the intended connection between physical training and the preparation for a disciplined struggle against the imperialists.

More clandestine were the revolutionary *samiti,* which attracted recruits from the college generation with a heady doctrine of political self-sacrifice as service to Ma Kali, the avenger. Elaborate rites of initiation bound the members with vows of loyalty, secrecy, and celibacy, and, for the most trusted, there was training with revolvers and bombs in preparation for attacks upon British officials. Calcutta and the peri-urban areas to the north along the Hooghly, Dacca and Barisal, were the initial centers of organization. But as the British reinforced their Committee for Imperial Defence and hit back with arbitrary arrest and deportation, the terrorists were forced to scatter across the province, spreading the legend of revolutionary violence which has become so important a part of Bengal's political tradition.

Less spectacular but also working to establish the link between religious tradition and nationalism were the *jatra* (folk theater) and *loksangit* (folk song) parties, which now went out from the urban centers to spread the message of resistance and national regeneration to a wider audience. Gurudev Rabindranath Tagore supplied songs and dramas for their repertoire.

The period also saw new religious institutions spreading into the mofussil from Calcutta. Throughout much of the nineteenth century, the metropolis, and one or two of the larger towns, had witnessed a lively conflict between reform groups like the Brahmo Samaj and their traditionalist opponents, but in rural Bengal religious organization had retained its traditional familial form. Vivekananda's Ramakrishna Mission, whose *math,* ashrams, schools, hostels, libraries, and dispensaries were soon to be found all over Bengal and beyond, supplied a new model—and, incidentally, a new arena for politics.

The social service ideal which inspired the mission's work also inspired a host of smaller societies, many of them secular. To meet the recurrent disasters of famine, flood, cyclone, and epidemic to which Bengal is tragically prone, these organizations raised funds, assembled relief supplies, and ministered to the needs of the suffering. Many a political reputation was made through hard work and effective organization during emergency relief operations.

The initiatives in nationalist politics produced a flurry of counteraction among the Bengali Muslims, and this activity was sustained by the succession of crises which beset the community through the subsequent decade. The foundation of the All-India and Bengal Presidency Muslim Leagues following the December 1906 conference in Dacca was an event of major importance, but surprisingly this was the only significant Muslim institutional innovation in this period.

PHASE TWO: 1918–1926

Engaged in the winter of 1917–1918 in a struggle to wrest control of the Bengal Provincial Congress Committee (BPCC) from the Indian Association, C. R. Das and his fellow extremists organized an All-Bengal Political Conference in Calcutta to which they brought more than a hundred rural delegates. Acting with their approval, they seized control of the BPCC and immediately reconstituted it to provide direct representation for district associations.

This was the beginning of the construction of a Congress machine in Bengal, the organizational effort reaching its high point during the noncooperation movement in 1921. By that time the BPCC had its own office in Calcutta, from which Das' staff of full-time workers directed the affairs of the four divisions into which the metropolitan area had been divided and kept in regular communication with the Congress committees now active in each district. A Congress News Service dispensed party propaganda and the Congress volunteers, more numerous and more formally organized than in the partition period, were at work throughout the province collecting for the Swaraj Fund, the party purse.

Women made their first appearance in any numbers in political agitation, and the new *mahila samiti* began educational and social welfare work in the towns. The national schools and colleges, most of which had expired in the years since the partition agitation, were revived to encourage a boycott of government educational institutions, and in some places Congress arbitration boards were offered to mediate disputes withdrawn from the law courts. Although this effort at parallel government could not be sustained for more than a few months, it did set a pattern which was repeated with increasing success in each of the other civil disobedience campaigns up to—and beyond—independence.

To carry Congress' influence outside the towns, the Gandhians built up rural ashrams where the lessons of village reconstruction and cottage industry were patiently taught through the example of personal labor. In all these activities Muslims as well as Hindus were involved, for this period from 1918 to 1925 was the high point in Muslim involvement in Indian nationalist politics in Bengal.

In addition the Muslim politicians had their Khilafat committees, the product of the discontent—international and local—accompanying the end of World War I. These committees, with a central headquarters in Calcutta and branches in every district town, paralleled the Congress organization, with which they were encouraged (unsuccessfully) to merge. The Khilafatists also showed vigor in taking over the District Islamia Anjumans, and with the support of many mullahs they had a reliable communications network among their coreligionists.

It was they who took the initiative, quickly followed by the Congress, in trade union organization. Agitation among transport workers, miners, mill laborers, and, later, tea garden coolies produced a rash of strikes in the immediate postwar years, but the organization was weak, with scarcely any strike funds available to it, and the workers involved suffered severely. It took another twenty years of organization before the trade union movement in Bengal became a powerful force.

These efforts were obviously directed toward agitational recruitment. There were other organizational initiatives inspired by the enfranchisement in 1921 of almost a million new voters among the urban lower middle class and the prosperous cultivators. We find prominent and aspiring politicians busy with the formation of associations of teachers, mukhtar, nongazetteered government officers, and joatdar. The electoral stakes were now worth playing for. The provincial Legislative Council had been given control over some government departments; power in the Calcutta Municipal Corporation was transferred by mid-decade from official nominees to the elected members; and an expanded system of local boards was taking over functions of the district and subdivisional officers. Even at the height of their success in 1921, the noncooperators were uncomfortably aware of the risks involved in leaving these institutions to their opponents, and in 1923 they returned to the hustings.

Another major institutional development of the years between 1915 and 1925 must be noted: the caste associations. Some caste sabha in Bengal dated from much earlier, but it was in this period that many more of the middle and lower castes were organizing. The new associations appear to have had little connection with the traditional caste panchayet, a few of which still survived in Bengal to settle marriage and other intracaste disputes. The normal pattern of the new associations was for a handful of educated and professionally employed members residing in a district town or, more frequently, Calcutta to form a committee. Through printed circulars and at meetings called in the district town most conveniently located for the majority of the caste members, they explained the objectives of the proposed association.

Typically these aims included the improvement of the caste's ritual practices to conform with the higher status (Kshatriya, Vaisya, or clean Sudra, whichever it might be) to which the caste was "unquestionably" entitled. Stress was laid upon ensuring that this "correct" status, and a caste name appropriate to it, be recorded at the decennial census. In some cases the abolition of endogamous subgroups within the caste was urged; in others, particularly where there was marked occupational differentiation between the divisions, a complete split was advocated. In view of the new powers vested in local boards and the legislature, attention was drawn to the opportunities open to the caste if its members gave solid support to those of their fellows who were candidates for elective office. Caste members were urged to subscribe to the association to support the educational campaign needed to effect these reforms and to enable the association to aid indigent caste members. When the appeals were successful, the associations usually began the publication of caste journals, but few were sustained for any length of time.

PHASE THREE: 1926–1937

Criticism of the privileges and power of high-caste men in the literature of some of the caste associations was one of a number of disturbing developments which led to the formation of the Bengal Hindu Sabha in 1923. The prime movers were Brahmins, and their stated purpose was to resist the growing disunity among Hindus, which, they asserted, endangered Hindu social order and political power. From 1926 onward the Bengal Hindu Sabha had many battles to fight.

Congress' repudiation of C. R. Das' Hindu-Muslim Pact, and the subsequent brutal communal rioting in mid-1926, convinced many Bengali Muslims that they should follow those leaders who were urging an end to all alliances with the Hindu nationalists. With the approval of the provincial government, and with the assistance of British officials in some districts, there was a successful consolidation of the local Muslim associations to ensure more efficient electoral management. This consolidation resulted in the return of many separatist candidates to the Bengal Legislative Council in the December 1926 elections; it also created a large increase in Muslim representation on the local boards when those elections were held in the following year. In the early 1930s more and more seats were captured, and inroads were made on the Hindu-controlled college and school boards.

In rural areas there was now evidence of growing collaboration between the Muslim and low-caste Hindu peasantry, to the detriment of the interests of the higher landed classes. The Krishak Samitis, which had struggled ineffectually to organize the peasantry since their foundation after World War I, now began to attract a much wider following as the world depression throttled Bengal's economy. They were given central leadership and spokesmen in the legislature when Fazlul Huq formed the Krishak Praja party in July 1929. At the same time Depressed Classes (Scheduled Caste, as they later came to be called) Associations were formed to unite low-caste *sabha* in a lobby against the high-caste Hindus in the constitutional debates which opened with the appointment of the Simon Commission. Pursuing the same objective of political visibility, the tribals—a large but generally disregarded minority in Bengal—were also attempting to build intratribal links between their traditional village councils. They had only limited success, the Santals being perhaps the most enterprising.

These were violent years, with extremist organizations of many kinds active in Bengal. The fascist and communist parties of contemporary Europe provided models for some of the younger Bengali agitators. The home-grown terrorist *samiti* had extended their networks throughout much of rural as well as urban Bengal, and their coercive tactics were now used against their Muslim and Hindu political opponents as well as against the British. During the civil disobedience campaigns between 1930 and 1934, they gained sufficient strength and weapons to engage the British police and military in guerrilla warfare. In Midnapore district their repeated assassinations of British officials temporarily broke British control, and the Congress was able to run a parallel government for a time.

Aggressive Muslim revivalist groups, like the Ahmadiyyas from north India, did battle (and the word is not used metaphorically) with equally aggressive Hindu organizations like the Arya Samaj, also an import from the Panjab. Societies to oppose cow slaughter and music before mosques fervently sought evidence of offenses by their communal opponents. To complete a dismal picture there were Calcutta's *goonda dol*, which enterprising politicians of both religions (H. S. Suhrawardy and Sarat Bose among them) found useful as hired auxiliaries in interparty fighting.

The period also gave thousands of Bengali nationalists institutional experience of another kind: incarceration in British jails or detention camps. No humor is intended in describing these as political institutions. By crowding together prisoners of widely differing ages, experience, ideological persuasion, and region of origin, the British inadvertently created an environment in which parties, platforms, manifestos, and conspiracies flourished. The nationalists emerged from these political "staff colleges" with a great deal besides their accolade of Prison Graduate.

PHASES FOUR AND FIVE: 1937–1947

The decade from 1937 to 1947 was so full of political excitement and tragedy for Bengal that although it seems lame to describe its institutional history as simply more of the same, such a characterization is not far wide of the mark. There were some new developments. The cooperative movement, which had limped along since early in the century, was given new vigor in the late 1930s by the zeal of the Krishak Samitis and the commitment of a provincial government armed with an electoral mandate to reduce rural indebtedness and provide new sources of agricultural credit. This was the first administration to take office under the 1935 Government of India Act, which established responsible government in the provinces. Its legislative backing included the Krishak Praja and Scheduled Caste parties, the latter an important new element in Bengali politics.

Radical legislation could also count upon the support of the host of Marxist cells, which had hatched in the peculiarly favorable conditions of the British prison camps. Many of the younger terrorists had been converted to communism during their internment, and their release in the late 1930s added to the complexity of Bengali politics. Muslim politics in Bengal had always been notorious for its factionalism, and after Das' death the provincial Congress had seemed determined to follow suit. With the expulsion of the dominant Bose group at Gandhi's instigation in 1939, and with the formation of the Forward Bloc, all chance of a unified nationalist movement in Bengal was destroyed. Throughout the political infrastructure—municipalities, student associations, trade unions, District Congress Committees, Krishak Samitis—rival parties now struggled for control. Adding to the clamor in Calcutta, and reflecting a growing mood of regional exclusivism throughout India, were new representative associations formed by non-Bengalis. These groups had the dual function of providing social welfare for their fellows and lobbying for the protection of their corporate interests, particularly their employment.

In the last phase—the years immediately before independence—we see some strikingly divergent developments. One was the neighborhood *puja* committees, which progressively were transmuting the great Hindu festivals, most notably Durga and Saraswati Puja, from family to community functions. Given their detailed knowledge of their localities built up through a number of years of fund raising, and the rivalries which were generated with the sponsors of adjacent *pandal*, these committees became useful adjuncts to the formal political parties.

Many of the Marxists, meanwhile, had set to work among Bengal's proletariat—the industrial and plantation laborers, and the landless tribals—and among the peasantry to foment social revolution, for they saw the opportunities offered by the disruptions which would inevitably accompany the departure of the British. In some places in support of their campaign for agricultural rent and tax resistance, they revived the *loksangit* and *jatra* techniques employed many years before during the first partition.

At the international level, Subhas Bose's daring escape and alliance with the Axis powers to form the Indian National Army set the seal on the romance of violence in Bengal. Less romantic and more immediately violent were the vigilante groups and militia, organized by communal extremists of both the major religions. These private armies skirmished throughout the early 1940s and finally closed in pitched battle in 1946. The bloodshed ensured the partition of Bengal.

THE SOCIAL BASES OF POLITICS

If our understanding of the institutional history of twentieth-century Bengal is imperfect, how much worse is the state of our knowledge on the social bases of politics. No more than a beginning has been made with the detailed research necessary to trace the shifting regional, status, class, and age composition of the political leadership or its following.

The institutional changes which have been sketched here provide clues to those shifts, but they are no more than clues. Besides, we must be cautious of reading too much into them. Observing the preeminence of the landholder associations at the beginning of the century, and their precipitate decline in importance from the mid-1920s, we may rightly conclude that the old zamindari class was losing power. We shall be misled, however, if we also conclude from this example that all institutional decline reveals a shift in power to a new social stratum. For instance, after 1918 the Indian Association sank into insignificance, but the leadership of the Bengal Congress, which superseded it, came from the same *bhadralok* status group that had dominated nationalist politics in Bengal since the late nineteenth century.

Elsewhere I have described the *bhadralok*: "a socially privileged and consciously superior group, economically dependent upon landed rents and professional and clerical employment; keeping its distance from the masses by its acceptance of high-caste proscriptions and its command of education; sharing a pride in its language, its literate culture, and its history; and maintaining its communal integration through a fairly complex institutional structure that it had proved remarkably ready to adapt and augment to extend its social power and political opportunities."[1] It has been a frequent cause for comment that the *bhadralok* have continued to dominate political institutions, providing leadership even after independence in West Bengal and even in parties as radical as the Communist Party Marxist and the Naxalites. This appearance of continuity is perhaps illusory. The *bhadralok* category is probably too inexact for detailed analysis, concealing rather than revealing subtle changes in the social bases of power over the half century.

It is of no help, for instance, in measuring the effects of the generational conflicts which periodically beset Bengali nationalist politics—for example, during the first partition agitation and again in the late 1920s when dissatisfaction with the infighting and ideological bankruptcy of the Congress bosses led the younger intellectuals to form the Socialist party. Similarly, we must not overlook class tensions within *bhadralok* society which appear on some crucial occasions, for example during the noncooperation debate of 1920, to have forced major changes in political tactics.

This institutional analysis has revealed a reorientation from 1918 of nationalist organization toward the district towns, and we find a parallel in the late 1920s in Muslim reorganization. What this reflects is the growth of new wealth in the Bengal countryside. To explain this growth we must look at Bengal's topography, which has always hindered easy communication, and at its shifting river courses, treacherous climate, and debilitating endemic diseases, which together have caused repeated fluctuations in population density and agricultural productivity. These fluctuations meant that even into the early years of the present century there remained underused areas of Bengal and its hinterland—for example, the Sunderbans, the *char* along the Brahmaputra, the Terrai, and the sal jungles of the Chota Nagpur fringe—which were available for economic enterprise as transportation, agricultural, and health technologies were improved. There has as yet been no study of who profited from the opening of these new lands, nor is there an accurate measure of the capital reinvested in agricultural land from East Bengal's jute trade, North Bengal's tea industry, and West Bengal's mines. We do, however, observe the emergence by 1920 of a parvenu class (Muslim as well as Hindu) residing in the district towns and controlling sections of the surrounding countryside through powerful patronage networks.

It was this class which was best situated to take advantage of the devolution of power to the district and local boards, as also of the enlargement of the provincial legislature and the extension of the franchise. It was they who most frequently gained the organizational backing of the caste associations and the consolidated Islamia Anjumans. They were the moving force in the *joatdar* associations, and their investments sustained, among other ventures, the district cooperative banks.

The existence and activities of a parvenu class should alert us to the danger of assuming that once outside the cities and past the *rājbāri* of the great zamindars, all that was to be seen in Bengal was an undifferentiated peasant mass. There were, of course, a number of "fat cats" among the generally poor rural populace. The thinnest of all—the dispossessed tribals and other landless laborers—had no institutional representation before independence. The nonoccupancy *raiyat* and the poorer share-croppers appear to have had to wait until the 1940s for the Marxists to give them a lead with the Tebhaga and similar movements. It was the occupancy *raiyat* who were the prime movers in the Krishak Samitis, and the mainstay along with some of the higher tenure holders (*joatdar, talukdar,* and *patnidar*) of the agricultural cooperatives. Thus what appear at first sight to be institutions of the rural poor prove on closer inspection to be new sources of strength for the moderately well-to-do.

The political mobilization of the industrial proletariat in Bengal, as we might predict from the European experience, preceded that of rural landless labor by three decades. The years immediately following World War I were seminal. War demands had artificially stimulated industrial and mining development in Bengal, but early in 1920 there was a severe trade recession. To make matters worse a succession of natural disasters in 1918 and 1919, including the great influenza epidemic, had led to a sharp rise in the price of foodstuffs and cotton goods. Wages did not respond to the price inflation. The work conditions for industrial labor and the terms of employment were generally deplorable.

We have already observed that the Khilafatists and congressmen saw in this situation a fine opportunity for agitational recruitment, and their initial successes added strength to the noncooperation movement. In the long run, however, the politicians were faced with a thorny problem: they were Bengalis while almost all the industrial laborers were from Bihar and the United Provinces. The sustained disinclination of these men to accept Bengali leadership, as also their refusal to identify themselves with the region in which they lived out their working lives, has been the source of serious instability for twentieth-century Bengal, East and West. The periodic resort to violence by the "Biharis" should serve as a reminder that not all politics is institutionalized. Historically the mob has been a potent political force.

NOTES

1.   *Elite Conflict in a Plural Society: Twentieth-Century Bengal* (Berkeley: University of California Press, 1968), pp. 12–13.

   Note: Regarding this as an interpretive essay, I have taken the liberty of excluding references. Should the reader be interested in the research sources on which

I base my assertions, I would refer him to the above book and to my published articles:

"A Plea for the Study of the Indian Provincial Legislatures," *Parliamentary Affairs*, vol. XIV, no. 1 (Winter 1960–1961), pp. 26–38.

"The Partition of Bengal: A Problem in British Administration, 1830–1912," *Indian History Congress, Proceedings of the 23rd Session, Aligarh 1960*, vol. II, pp. 13–24.

"The Vote and the Transfer of Power: A Study of the Bengal General Election, 1912–1913," *Journal of Asian Studies*, vol. XXI, no. 2 (February 1962), pp. 163–181.

"The Regional Elites: A Theory of Modern Indian History," *Indian Economic and Social History Review*, vol. III, no. 3 (September 1966), pp. 279–291.

"The Forgotten Majority: The Bengal Muslims and September 1918," and "The Non-cooperation Decision of 1920: A Crisis in Bengal Politics," in *Soundings in Modern South Asian History*, ed. D. A. Low (London: Weidenfeld and Nicolson, 1968), pp. 196–260.

"Four Lives: History as Biography," *South Asia*, vol. I, no. 1 (June 1971), pp. 74–92.

Bengal's Pre-1905 Congress Leadership and Hindu Society

JOHN R. McLANE
Northwestern University

THE PROBLEM

In its first twenty-five years, the Indian National Congress failed to fulfill two of its primary goals. First, the Congress did not succeed in persuading most nationalists outside the English-speaking professions that it welcomed their participation or represented their vital concerns. Second, it was unable to convince Muslim leaders that it was in their interest to join the Congress. Not only did Muslim leaders generally remain aloof from the Congress prior to founding the All-India Muslim League in 1906 in opposition to the Congress; they also persuaded the small number of Muslims who had attended the Congress sessions to withdraw. Only a handful of Muslims were delegates to the 1907, 1908, and 1909 Congresses.[1] The first elections under the Morley-Minto reforms of 1909 confirmed that the anti-Congress position of the Muslim League was widely supported by Muslim voters. Members of the league won "all the Muslim seats on the provincial Legislative Councils of Eastern Bengal and Assam, Bengal, the United Provinces, Bombay, and Madras." They also gained a number of general seats.[2]

An examination of the organizational and programmatic goals of the Congress does not yield an adequate explanation of the Congress' failure to attract Muslim support. Congress leaders actively sought Muslim participation in the early years. The avoidance of specifically Hindu themes and symbolism and the reliance on the English language in the early Congress meetings were intended to make Muslims feel welcome, although the resulting cultural drabness and neutrality undoubtedly diminished the Congress' appeal for many Hindus. A Muslim (Badruddin

Tyabji) was offered the Congress presidency in 1886, 1887, and 1883,[3] Muslim delegates were given free transportation and lodging at early Congresses, and Muslims were promised that no new resolutions to which Muslim delegates as a body objected would be passed. With the important exceptions of Congress proposals for representative institutions and competitive examinations for the civil services, the core of the Congress program was generally not opposed by educated Muslims. Yet Muslims generally avoided the Congress.

The key to understanding this abstention is to be found in Muslim perceptions of what the Congress movement stood for. A number of recent studies have attempted to define Muslim perceptions.[4] However, insufficient attention has been given to developments within Hindu society which may have affected the ways Muslims viewed the Congress. Nor has there been much study of the religious identity of Congress leaders or of their efforts, or lack of efforts, to reassure Muslims of their security in the new competitive society. It has not been explained, for example, why the secular-minded Hindu Congress leaders relied upon the initiative of their English colleagues in appealing for Muslim support. Why did A. O. Hume in the earliest years of the Congress and William Wedderburn in 1910[5] assume responsibility for making overtures to Muslim leaders on behalf of the Congress? How can the stated goal of communal cooperation be reconciled with the failure of cosmopolitan Congress leaders to react creatively to incipient Muslim separatism? How does one explain the immobility, helplessness, and resignation of Congress leaders when faced with communalization of politics after the 1905 partition of Bengal?

A partial answer to these questions may be found in a reconstruction of the professional and private lives of leading Congress members. It will be seen that their roles tended to be discrete, unrelated, and perhaps incompatible. As members of a nation-building movement, they were expected to subordinate their individualistic ambitions, pride, and Hinduness to the collective interest of a multicommunal organization. As members of the legal, journalistic, and teaching professions, they were engaged in highly competitive enterprises whose language and milieu were English and whose personnel were rarely Muslim. As members of *bhadralok* society (if such a varied, individualistic, and fractious category of human beings may be called a society), they were subjected to group pressure and sometimes ridicule for their assimilation of English ways. Segments of Hindu *bhadralok* society were insisting upon conformity to Hindu norms of behavior and were asserting the primacy of Hindu values in Bengali life. These pressures were, in effect, a form of Hindu populism, and they seriously challenged the representativeness of Congress leadership and the right of congressmen to speak for the larger society. When forcibly exerted, these pressures must not only have undermined the self-confidence of Congress leaders; they must also have reduced their viable options in dealing with Muslims or other Hindus.

This essay examines the professional and private lives of Congress leaders in Bengal with the object of revealing the disintegrative effect of the separate demands imposed upon them by their multiple roles. It attempts to find out why and how they were experiencing and responding to the pressures of their professions, their society, and the needs of the Congress.

It is too easily assumed that the communalization of politics in Bengal stems directly from Hindu-Muslim conflict. Whereas in other north Indian provinces Hindus and Muslims had clashed over language policy, cow slaughter, and communal balance in government services, pre-1905 politics in the Bengali-speaking region was relatively free of these conflicts.

Those Muslims in Bengal who did complain publicly about disparities in the economic and political opportunities available to Hindus and Muslims were frequently non-Bengali Muslims of Calcutta, such as Nawab Abdul Latif and Amir Ali, whose connections with Bengali Muslims outside Calcutta seem to have been slight. Because few Bengali-speaking Muslims raised their voices before 1905, it is difficult to gauge Muslim opinion. For example, it is not certain that the views of Abdul Latif and Amir Ali were more representative of Bengali Muslim concerns before 1905 than were the views of influential Muslim Congress supporters in the Bihari-speaking districts of Bengal. In the prepartition years, two prominent lawyers and civic leaders with distinguished ancestry, Mazhar-ul Haq of Chapra and Bankipur and Sayyid Ali Imam of Patna supported the Congress without ceasing to work for Muslim interests. Mazhar-ul Haq, in fact, worked actively for the Congress *and* the Muslim League in Bihar after the latter was founded in 1906. That English officials preferred to regard Abdul Latif and Amir Ali as authoritative spokesmen for Muslim opinion is understandable but it is not evidence of their representativeness.

This essay's point of departure, then, is that politics in Bengal had not polarized along communal lines before 1905 despite the failure of the Congress to attract many Bengali Muslims. The 1905 partition crystallized a Hindu-Muslim division which hitherto had been more potential than articulated and organized. In stating this, there is apparent disagreement with John Broomfield. Broomfield has implied that in pre-1905 Bengal the *bhadralok* were worried about their relations with "the mass of the [Bengali] community, Hindu and Muslim." He goes on to say that:

> What we observe here is a point of critical significance: profound bhadralok
> uncertainty on the crucial issue of whether their society should be open or

closed. If we look carefully at the subjects of social and political discussion at the turn of the century we find that this was the fundamental issue underlying bhadralok debates. Should Bengali society be dominated by a caste elite, drawing its authority and its strength from the great tradition and organic unity of Hinduism, or should free access to the elite be provided for able individuals of all classes through an expansion of the utilitarian institutions that had been developed in the nineteenth century in contact with Europeans?[6]

Broomfield demonstrates convincingly that this became a fundamental issue after the 1905 partition. Perhaps it was inevitable that it should be so. But in suggesting that competition with Muslims and non-*bhadralok* castes was central to *bhadralok* concerns before then, it seems that he has telescoped separable developments. Prior to 1905, neither Muslims nor castes such as the Namasudras had mounted a serious challenge to *bhadralok* dominance in education, the professions, or, in most areas, even in the control of landed resources. Nor had efforts to help low-caste Hindus by Sasipada Banerji, Sivanath Sastri, or the Indian Association been on a scale large enough to arouse significant controversy. Insofar as the openness of society or competition for the material goods of life was central to internal *bhadralok* politics, resentment was expressed against the wealthy lawyers, zamindars, and Brahmos. Usually this resentment took the form of attacks upon the anglicization of educated Bengalis rather than direct criticism of the acquisition or use of their wealth. Broomfield does discuss the "considerable class feeling within *bhadralok* society."[7] This comes much closer to the central issue of pre-1905 *bhadralok* politics. Hindu populism was in part a leveling protest against the spectacular economic successes of elite members of the English-language professions.

This essay discusses the interaction of congressmen and Bengali society. It is an indirect approach to the question: Why was the Congress goal of building a national movement into which both Muslims and the larger Hindu society would be integrated pursued with so little vigor? The focus is on the Congress leaders in Bengal because, as unrepresentative as they were of many late nineteenth-century trends, they were a prime object of Hindu populist pressures, they did articulate the goal of communal harmony and national integration more clearly than any other group, they were the dominant Indians in the Legislative Council after 1892 and in the Calcutta Municipal Corporation, and they and their supporters did control most major Bengali newspapers. Although nineteen congressmen from Bengal (Bengal proper, Bihar, and Orissa) will be identified for statistical purposes, considerable illustrative information will be drawn from the lives of other congressmen and from the development of the legal profession in other parts of India.

WHO WERE THE LEADERS?

Who were the leaders of the Congress movement in Bengal? How does one establish who is and who is not a leader in a movement as loosely organized as the Congress was in its first twenty-five years? The Congress met once a year and did not have full-time workers between sessions. Only a handful of men from each province attended the annual sessions on a regular basis. To obtain a composite profile of the all-Indian Congress leadership, I compiled a list of delegates who between 1885 and 1914 spoke five or more times or who were appointed to three or more special Congress deputations and committees, such as those to visit England, consider the Permanent Settlement, and draft a Congress constitution.[8] The list contains eighty-six names. Because of the autocratic way Congress conducted its affairs, the list represents those individuals whom A. O. Hume, Pherozeshah Mehta, Surendranath Banerjea, and other members of the inner circle approved to speak and selected to perform important Congress tasks. Several key figures were missing from the list, including M. G. Ranade, Aurobindo Ghose, and Bipinchandra Pal. Despite these omissions, I felt the list was useful for the purpose of drawing a composite portrait of Congress leadership. Inclusion of the names of men whose period of leadership was brief or whose leadership was exercised behind the scenes would not have altered the portrait significantly.

The composite profile contained few surprises. Sixty of the eighty-six were in the legal profession. Not only were the majority in law but a sizeable proportion practiced in the High Courts, where incomes were often substantial and where forensic skills and full familiarity with the English language were needed. High achievement was not limited to the lawyers. The list contained twenty-three journalists, ten businessmen and bankers, and eleven educators, many of whom had attained distinction in one or more professions. The esteem for these men outside the Congress may be gauged by the fact that thirty-five of the eighty-six served in the Legislative Councils, each of which prior to 1909 contained fewer than ten elected members.

The provincial distribution was wide. Madras had twenty delegates, Bengal had nineteen, Bombay had eighteen, and the United Provinces and the Punjab had thirteen and seven, respectively. This distribution fails to reflect the dominance of Bombay leaders (A. O. Hume, M. G. Ranade, Pherozeshah Mehta, William Wedderburn, and Dadabhai Naoroji) in the conduct of Congress affairs in its first twenty years, but it does indicate the inner circle's desire for regional balance.

Brahmans outnumbered non-Brahman Hindus, thirty-eight to nineteen. There were also six Muslims, five Parsis, and five Englishmen.

The figures for Bengal's delegates follow the all-Indian pattern. Thirteen

of Bengal's nineteen delegates were lawyers.[9] Nine were Brahmans, one
was Muslim, one was Bihari. The Bengal delegates differed as a group
from others in that they owned zamindaris more often than did delegates
from other provinces. Eleven of the twenty-one zamindari-owners were
from Bengal. However, eight of the eleven were lawyers by profession and
none seems to have depended on land as his major source of income. The
Bengal list also lacked even a single prominent extremist, assuming that
Aswinikumar Dutt should be classified as a moderate. The all-India list,
on the other hand, contained B. G. Tilak, G. S. Khaparde, Lajpat Rai,
and G. Subramania Iyer. Finally, the Bengali delegates were more likely to
have been educated in England (six had been). This pattern was compatible with prior impressions that, as a group, Bengal's leaders were more
anglicized in lifestyle than leaders from other provinces.

Study in England was in fact a key factor in determining leadership
within the Congress. The nucleus of Indian leadership was drawn from a
group of nine men from Bombay and Calcutta who had formed interregional friendships in London. The future Congress leaders who were
together in London in the late 1860s were Pherozeshah Mehta, Badruddin
Tyabji, W. C. Bonnerjee, and Manomohan Ghose.[10] As those young
friends were finishing their studies, a second group who also became
Congress leaders began to arrive. W. C. Bonnerjee met Surendranath
Banerjea and Romeshchandra Dutt when they landed in 1868 to study for
the civil service.[11] Before Banerjea and Dutt returned to Calcutta, they
were joined by Lalmohan Ghose[12] and Anandamohan Bose.[13] All these
men seemed to have come under the influence of Dadabhai Naoroji and
his efforts to start an all-Indian political organization. Naoroji was an
older Parsi merchant who lived in London and acted as an informal
ambassador for the nationalist cause for half a century.

All these men except Dadabhai returned to successful careers in India.
Judging from their incomes, their London training was a major asset.
Mehta, Tyabji, Bonnerjee, and the Ghose brothers established exceedingly
prosperous law practices, earning as much as leading English barristers
and more than almost any other Indian lawyers. Anandamohan Bose
also practiced law with profit but gradually turned his attention to education, founding City School (later City College), where Surendranath
Banerjea taught. Neither Surendranath nor Romeshchandra Dutt practiced law, although both had received legal training and both had large
incomes. Surendranath taught, ran a college, and edited the *Bengalee*
after his explusion from the Indian Civil Service (ICS). And Romeshchandra remained in the ICS until 1897, when he joined the Congress.

Although most Congress leaders in Bengal were lawyers, their fathers
had been in "service" under the British, a zamindar, or a native state
more often than in the law. In most cases it seems that the sons earned

incomes which far exceeded those of their fathers. Illustrations of this disparity were found outside Bengal. Ranade's father earned Rs. 250 per month as private secretary to the Maharaja of Kolhapur while Ranade's own salary as High Court Justice was in the neighborhood of Rs. 4000 per month.[14] Gandhi's law income of over Rs. 6000 per month in South Africa must have been many times the amount his father earned as a minister in a small princely state.[15] Lala Lajpat Rai's father never earned more than Rs. 35 per month as a Persian teacher in a government school whereas Lajpat averaged more than Rs. 1000 per month as a vakil in Hissar between the ages of twenty-two and twenty-eight, before he joined the Chief Court bar at Lahore.[16]

Probably all the Congress leaders who had successful professional careers received help from Englishmen at important stages in their academic and occupational training. It is evident from the biographies of Indians born in the 1840s, as many early Congress leaders had been, that the ratio of English teachers to students in the schools was high and that teachers took a personal interest in the development of better students. They awarded these students scholarships, entertained them in their homes, advised them about their careers, and helped them go to England or the local university for further study.

English kindnesses did not stop with college, although they seem to have diminished considerably as Indians moved nearer to the point of direct competition with Englishmen. Many nationalists who went to London in the nineteenth century, before the number of Indians in England was large and before English-speaking Indians ceased to be a novelty, boarded with English families, continued to learn the ways of their rulers, and returned with positive feelings about the English as individuals. Romeshchandra Dutt, Surendranath Banerjea, Pherozeshah Mehta, and Gandhi are examples.

THE ENGLISH-SPEAKING PROFESSIONS

Whether they completed their schooling in England or in India, Indians graduating in the 1860s and 1870s were equipping themselves to move into professions still manned by Europeans. And part of their success depended upon having learned how to win the confidence, and how not to antagonize, European teachers, lawyers, and administrators. At least a minority of Englishmen in the legal profession, as in the schools, were willing to assist promising Indians. Possibly that assistance was often contingent on how English a young man's bearing and accent were. This may have been a factor in the decision of English lawyers to accept such men as W.C. Bonnerjee,[17] Bhupendranath Basu,[18] and C. Sankaran Nair[19] as apprentices.

Gaining access to the highest positions in the bar was a lonely and arduous process for most men who made it, with or without English help. Most Indians did not make it. The majority of those who enrolled in law classes either dropped out or failed the examinations, and many others who passed did not find employment in the major cities and had to look for work in the mofussil (the districts outside the major metropolitan areas). Legal education and apprenticeship suffered from lack of system. Few English professors of law seem to have given the close attention to the education of their students which teachers in the schools had. Law college students found that their courses were only marginally related to their examinations or future work. P. S. Sivaswami Iyer and V. Krishnaswami Iyer, subsequently prominent Congress lawyers, used to sign the register for their law class at Presidency College, Madras, and then spend their class time at the beach.[20] K. N. Katju confirmed that many students did not attend classes or read the assigned texts. He wrote that while preparing to take the High Court Pleader's Examination in 1906, "everyone used cribs and aids to scramble through no matter how poor his grounding in legal principles or how meagre his reading of those classics."[21] Law classes were crowded, teachers were poorly paid, sometimes young English lawyers were appointed to teach until they could find a private practice, and some law classes were operated chiefly for profit.[22]

After graduation, the more successful law students usually entered an apprenticeship in the High Court which was likely to be unsupervised and unstructured, regardless of whether they apprenticed with an English or an Indian lawyer. Apprentices attended court and observed the performances of the best known lawyers. Judging by the frequent references in memoirs and biographies, the High Court lawyers had a keen appreciation of the verbal aptitudes of their colleagues. This was reflected in speeches at the annual Congress sessions, for which some men spent weeks preparing, knowing that delegates valued highly an elaborately argued speech. Apart from attending cases in court, apprentices tried to make themselves useful by taking notes and preparing briefs for their lawyers. In general, though, apprentices were ignored and their education was largely a matter of self-help.[23] It may be that the haphazard and unprofessional character of nineteenth-century legal training in India contributed to the early failure of Congress to develop businesslike procedures and a permanent organization.[24]

Indian efforts to break the English monopoly of the highest positions in the bar took three forms. First, Indians qualified themselves as barristers and tried to attract clients who usually took their cases to English barristers. Pherozeshah Mehta made one of the earliest attempts in Bombay. He soon discovered that in spite of his London education he was unable to obtain many briefs:

The entire practice was more or less concentrated in the hands of a few eminent counsel, such as Anstey, Scoble, Green, Latham, White, Mariott and one or two others. It was a very difficult thing either to dislodge them from their position, or even to carry away a few crumbs from their richly-laden table. . . . The litigant public hung upon [those counsel], and took no notice of the knot of hapless juniors hungrily looking for briefs. . . . There were hardly any firms of Indian attorneys to give the young men a lift in the profession. A deal of patronage rested in the hands of managing clerks, whose smile was to be courted.[25]

Mehta complained publicly in 1873 that Indian barristers were not receiving a fair share of the legal business. The Bar Association of Bombay responded by demanding an explanation from Pherozeshah for this "breach of professional etiquette." Eventually he gave up hope of finding sufficient work in the High Court and instead concentrated his practice in the mofussil, where he prospered. Badruddin Tyabji, the third Congress president, was more fortunate in finding work in the Bombay High Court after he returned from England, largely because his brother had already staked out a large practice as solicitor. Tyabji's cases came mostly from Indians. He found that the English lawyers did not like having Indian rivals and that English solicitors gave "all the work of the Government, the Municipality, public works, railways, post offices, telegraphs and the great mercantile firms" to English barristers.[26] Even with friendly Indian solicitors and vakils who were willing to send clients to Indian barristers, it took years to overcome a widespread assumption among Indians that even a London-trained Indian was less likely than an Englishmen to win in the High Courts.[27] However, by the 1880s Indian barristers were making deep inroads into the practice of Englishmen.

The second direction of Indian efforts was toward alteration of the rules restricting practice before the High Courts. High Court vakils fought for the right to appear without a barrister on the Original Side. (The High Court had an Original side and an Appellate Side. It was the more lucrative practice on the Original Side which English barristers hoped to preserve for themselves.) Victory came first in the 1870s in Madras, where vakils formed their own association to press for changes in the rules. The English barristers fought back and were supported by Judge Bittleson, a former barrister, who said he could not support new regulations which would "take the bread out of the mouth of a Christian and put it in the mouth of a pagan." Eventually, the Vakils Association, applying pressure with arguments and a vote not to act as junior counsel to any European barrister, persuaded the High Court justices to equalize the vakils' status.[28] The Calcutta High Court vakils, under the leadership of Rash Behari Ghose, soon followed the example of the Madras Vakils Association and won similar changes in the rules of the Calcutta High Court.[29]

The third issue which concerned Indian lawyers was the appointment of Englishmen to government legal offices. Again, it was the Madras vakils who led the way. They agitated not only to have Indians appointed to government legal offices but also to have vakils considered along with barristers for these offices. They won their campaign when V. Bhashyam Aiyangar became the first vakil in India to be appointed an advocate general.[30] Up to that time, Europeans in Madras had held the offices of advocate general, government pleader, government solicitor, crown prosecutor, and administrator general.[31] By 1900, a number of Indians in each of the four High Courts had been appointed to government legal offices and High Court judgeships.

Thus by the end of the century Indian lawyers in Bengal and elsewhere had broken European monopolies. Institutional changes in court procedures had been accomplished by acting in concert through Indian bar institutions. Moreover, Indian lawyers had combined informally to redistribute legal business by channeling clients to fellow Indians. At times this cooperation had been highly effective, as it was in the case of J. A. H. Branson. Branson was the Calcutta barrister who made offensive remarks about Indians during the Ilbert Bill controversy. The subsequent Indian boycott was so effective that Branson was forced to return to England.[32] On occasion, collective pressure was exerted on Indian lawyers as well. C. Sankaran Nair, a beneficiary of several English friendships, was the only member of the Madras Vakils Association to vote against the resolution calling on Indians not to assist English barristers, and in consequence his practice suffered for a while.[33]

Yet cooperation in the Indian bar was limited and fitful. In contrast to the common partnerships found between English lawyers, Indian partnerships were said to be infrequent and unstable. The Indian bar did not provide many of the corporate experiences of teamwork and specialization which ordinarily characterize modern professions and which might have been utilized within the nationalist movement. One reason why the legal profession was highly individualistic was the "chronic oversupply" and the consequent competition which limited "solidarity and capacity for corporate action."[34] The great success of a small number of Indian lawyers is perhaps the result of the individualistic aspect of the profession, and the numbers of people who did not reach the top reveal its hazards. Able men such as Gandhi[35] and C. R. Das[36] were total failures in their first years of law practice in the 1890s. Muhammed Ali Jinnah spent three years in Bombay, after his return from England, "without a single brief."[37] These three men ultimately built up successful practices. But the wealthy Indian lawyers represented only the peak of a broad-based pyramid.

The main concern of this discussion has been the High Court bar, to which many Congress leaders belonged. However, lawyers who were unable to qualify for or find a practice in the High and Chief Courts in the provincial capitals generally went to the mofussil. P. S. Sivaswami Aiyar estimated that only thirty-two out of the eighty students in his Presidency College class in 1882–1883 passed the law examination; of these thirty-two, only about one-fifth went to the Madras High Court as apprentices.[38] Most of the others turned to mofussil practice. Mofussil practice could be highly profitable for an able individual, such as Pherozeshah Mehta, with the proper qualifications and contacts. The prospects in law were so attractive, and the occupational alternatives so limited, that 2898 or over eleven percent of Indian university students in 1906–1907 were studying law.[39]

Little has been written about the mofussil bar. English officials believed that the success of lawyers in being elected to the Provincial Legislative Council even when most of the voters were landholders was due partly to the network of contacts that lawyers established in the course of their practice, which made canvassing easy. It is likely that the bar association was the most visible and active voluntary association in many mofussil towns and that it was the place where mofussil men were most likely to exchange political ideas. Many mofussil pleaders occasionally attended Congress sessions and, together with schoolteachers, represented the Congress' chief link to the mofussil.

SOCIAL ISOLATION AND A NEW STATUS HIERARCHY

The struggle to reach the top levels of the raj's occupational structure in the mofussil and the larger cities had nationalist implications, especially when it brought down racial barriers. But most of all, the new professionals were helping themselves. Few used either their money or their professional expertise in the service of their country before 1905. Once they had reached the top, not surprisingly they made no attempt to dismantle or level the structure. The structure recognized and rewarded ability and diligence, and as the very success of the new professionals demonstrated, it presented no insurmountable barrier to Indian talent. For those men who wanted to join them, the new professionals recommended self-improvement: assiduous study, "never two words when one was enough, clearness of thought and diction,"[40] regular work habits, frequent exercise, and so on. Few of them were levelers. Despite English efforts to portray them as parvenus, most of them came from high-caste families. They had not been trying to bring down or displace other Indian elites so much as to open the modern professions to proven Indian talent. Most of them were adding individual professional achievement and wealth to a previous, ascriptively based, high social status.

These men were part of a new status hierarchy composed for the most part of families with more than one generation in English administrative and professional occupations. The new hierarchy was parallel to the traditional social order, but many members near the top of the new hierarchy occupied an indefinite place in traditional society because of their non-traditional life styles and careers. It may have been the indefiniteness of their position vis-à-vis the old order which helps explain their preoccupation with making money. Perhaps many of them felt they had lost respect in the eyes of traditional Hindus when they abandoned ancestral customs in favor of English education and habits. Perhaps they were trying to compensate for loss of status in the old order by achieving in the new.

In any case, the English-educated elite lived in a society in which some form of social hierarchy was taken for granted. Neither Indian custom nor Anglo-Indian social and official practices provided a serious challenge to assumptions that people were ranked in order of lesser and higher beings. Englishmen treated Indians as inferior and excluded them not only from high office but also from their private clubs, barber shops, city parks, and railroad cars. It was not uncommon for members of Indian elites to treat their inferiors in similar fashion. Henry Nevinson, the *Manchester Guardian* correspondent, wrote about the visit he made with Madhu Sudhan Das, the Uriya leader, upon a Bengali deputy magistrate during a famine in Orissa. The Bengali magistrate "had evidently determined not to fall below the standard of European dignity. Consequently he received us with his legs on the long arms of his deck-chair—an attitude which, I suppose, he observed as customary among English officials when they receive 'natives.' " Madhu Sudhan Das tried in vain to persuade the magistrate to listen to the widows outside the door who said their husbands had starved to death. After failing to arouse a sympathetic response from the magistrate about the villagers' problems, Madhu Sudhan and Henry Nevinson had no choice but to leave, "waving good-night to his boots" as they went.[41]

Before 1905, the desire to display status and wealth was part of the effort to become acceptable to English society and even to be superior to most of that society. Renunciation of wealth was not yet a common way of qualifying for political leadership. Vishnu Narayan Mandlik, a leading Bombay lawyer and politician until his death in 1889, once hired a separate train to get to a court case he was working on, and Pherozeshah Mehta "engaged a special saloon for himself" on his way to the Calcutta Congress of 1901.[42] Only a handful of nationalists were wealthy enough to live as lavishly as Mandlik and Mehta, but their lifestyle was shared to some degree by W. C. Bonnerjee, Romeshchandra Dutt, and other Bengali Congress leaders. It was common for Congress leaders to live in palatial houses, maintain many servants, use first-class travel accommodations, and, in general, live on a scale which set them apart from most other Indians. The luxurious lifestyle and the elitist attitudes it encouraged were visible in the operations of the Congress itself. They inhibited efforts to build a popular base and they became a source of dissatisfaction in and around the Congress.

Younger nationalists were most outspoken about the elitism and anglicization of the Congress leaders. Aurobindo Ghose in 1893 wrote contemptuously of the "Indian Unnational Congress":

> The Anglicized Babu sits in the high place and rules the earth for a season. It is he who perorates on the Congress, who frolics in the abysmal fatuity of interpellation on the Legislative Council, who mismanages civic affairs in the smile of the City Corporation. He is the man of the present, but he is not the man of the future.

The future rested with a new, rising generation who had not committed cultural suicide by entering "the Services and the Law."[43] Gandhi was critical too, although he was much less sweeping. He had recently lived in a "fine bungalow" outside Bombay and had "frequently felt a certain pride in being the only first-class passenger in my compartment" on the train.[44] But he reacted to the behavior of Congress leaders at the 1901 Calcutta session. He remarked that J. Ghosal, a Bengali Brahman merchant, zamindar, and member of the leadership's inner circle, had his bearer button his shirt.[45] Gandhi noticed that while some speakers were permitted to exceed their time by half an hour or more, he was cut off by the president's bell in less than five mintues.[46] He also commented on Gokhale's use of a horse carriage to travel about Calcutta and his frequent trips to the India Club to play billiards.[47] This sort of criticism was not limited to men who had lived outside India. The Maharashtrian terrorist Damodar Chapekar had only scorn for the behavior of another Congress leader, Manomohan Ghose "or some such other name which I do not remember. Though a Hindu by religion he dresses like a European from top to toe and shaves his moustache like a eunuch. . . . He had a European to drive his carriage, and had to pay him a salary of Rs. 500 a month."[48] Congress leaders' investment of energy and income in attempts to live like sahibs or maharajas diverted their attention from the Congress and led Lala Lajpat Rai to remark that only Naoroji and Gokhale permitted the movement to interfere with their income and way of life.[49]

Although complaints similar to those of Aurobindo, Lajpat Rai, Gandhi, and Chapekar increased, especially after the turn of the century, many nationalists did not share these views. To earn as large an income as a *burra sahib*, to speak English as well as an Englishman, to have as good taste as the Victorians who shopped on Tottenham Court Road—this was to demonstrate equality with Englishmen. This was important not only to that handful of men who assimilated British values and habits but also to a much larger number who could share these triumphs only vicariously. Until a substantial number of Indians demonstrated to themselves and their admirers individual achievements in law, government, education, and business equal to those of Europeans, personal careers would continue to absorb energies which otherwise might have been channeled into the Congress. Preoccupation with personal achievement may have been a necessary stage of nation-building because it contributed to Indian self-esteem and helped overcome the negative feelings about fellow Indians which English education and political subordination inculcated. Many people took pride in the election of Dadabhai Naoroji and M. M. Bhown-aggree to Parliament in 1892 and 1895, respectively, in Ranjit Sinhji's exploits in English cricket matches, in the promotion of the first Indian, Romeschandra Dutt, to the position of acting commissioner, and in the elevation of Indian lawyers to the High Courts. Nevertheless, as success in the ICS examinations, industry, and letters became common, a new generation of nationalists began to question the value of individual achievements to the Congress cause. Aurobindo Ghose, Lajpat Rai, and other younger men appealed for sacrifice and a selfless approach to politics. However, these men had little impact on the Congress before 1905. The older generation remained firmly in control of the Congress and continued to enjoy large incomes.

The efforts of Congress leaders to adapt to British Indian professional life did more than absorb their energies. It also led some to identify with the institutions of the raj in a way that isolated them from the bulk of the Indian population. Surendranath Banerjea was probably being sincere when he told a group of English passengers on his ship en route to the 1894 Madras Congress that "we have everything to lose, nothing to gain by the severance of our connection with England. We owe whatever position or prestige we have acquired to our English education and culture. If you were to leave the country, our English education and culture would be at a discount. We are not particularly anxious to commit political suicide."[50]

Not only would the advantages of English education be lost, but possibly also the physical security to the life and property of the English-educated elite. Anxiety about violence is difficult to document because to have discussed it publicly would have played into British hands. As it was, Englishmen enjoyed reminding Indians of the "anarchy" of the eighteenth and early nineteenth centuries. We may imagine the relish of Lord Welby, chairman of the Royal Commission on Indian Finances, suggesting to Dadabhai Naoroji in London that "the history of India is that the people have been continually slaughtering each other" and then proceeding to quote Sir Madhaya Rao's alleged statement to Lord Roberts to the effect that if the British were removed from India, "it would be like loosing the bars of the cages of the Zoological Gardens and letting out the animals, that very soon they would all be dead except the tiger—the tiger was, I believe, the warlike people of Northern India."[51] Few nationalists would have agreed with this observation. However, there is enough evidence about the experiences and attitudes of early Congress leaders to indicate that some distrusted the volatility of the lower classes or at least had so little contact with them that they really did not know what to expect. A fear or apprehension of popular violence seems to have been common among at least a minority of early Congress leaders, just as efforts to use it were common among the extremists of the next generation.

The carnage of the 1857 Mutiny was part of the memory of the first-generation Congress leaders. Pandit Ayodhyanath, Surendranath Banerjea, W. C. Bonnerjee, P. Ananda Charlu, Monomohan Ghose, Pherozeshah Mehta, and M. G. Ranade were born in the 1840s and were in schools run by Englishmen during or soon after the Mutiny. Whether any of them sympathized with the mutineers is not known. It is likely, though, that they were thoroughly exposed to a British view of the mutineers as cruel and rapacious barbarians. It is interesting how little empathy is revealed in Dinshaw Wacha's account of the execution of two mutineers in Bombay city. Wacha was a Parsi, a close associate of Pherozeshah Mehta, and Congress general secretary after Hume's resignation. He remembered coming out of his school in Bombay with his classmates and finding that the two mutineers had been tied across the mouths of cannon in the usual military fashion:

> So far as my recollection goes, the European troops, Infantry and Artillery, took up a position by way of a square. The Indian regiments were located within the squares. There was a thrill of excitement all round and our pulse throbbed faster and faster till at a given word of command the cannons were fired and the pinioned criminals were blown. The burnt flesh sent an unpleasant odour which we all could easily sniff. All was over.[52]

Similarly, Surendranath Banerjea wrote about "the lower classes of the rural population" of Bengal as if they were not his own countrymen. He described his investigation of the sale of country liquor in Hughli district in 1887. He had heard reports that drunkenness was spreading among the lower classes although he had apparently never before visited the liquor shop "within a stone's throw of my house." He goes on to say:

> I was not content with these reports. I visited a liquor shop at Haripal, and the sight I witnessed there was one that I shall never forget. I saw half a

dozen men and women lying dead drunk on the floor of the shop. Another band of about a dozen men and women, all belonging to the lower classes, in varying stages of drunkenness, began dancing around me in wild delirious excitement. I apprehended violence and I slowly and cautiously retraced my steps from the shop.

After this experience Surendranath campaigned to reform the drinking habits of poor people. For the first time in twelve years of public life since returning from England, he lectured in Bengali rather than in English. Although his campaign was within his own Hughli district, he described the rural areas as if they were alien. "It was indeed hard, rough work—tramping along trackless areas, living in malarial countries, and eating strange food."[53] It may be that Surendranath's isolation from rural and lower-class life in his own province was different only in degree from a contemporary, wealthy Londoner's separation from the people of English slums and farms. Yet the isolation was genuine and it was recognized as a major hindrance to the making of a nation.

In communal, grain, and plague riots, well-to-do Indians found they were often more vulnerable than Europeans to mass violence. During disturbances, they depended on English officials to restore order with police or sepoys. This was true of the communal riots in Bombay city in 1874 and 1893 and of the attacks on *bhadralok* by *goonda* and upcountry men in Calcutta in 1907. It was also true of the Muslim attacks on Hindus in East Bengal in 1907. Even when Europeans were the main targets of rioting, as in the 1897 Muslim riots in Calcutta and in the 1898 Muslim plague riots in Bombay, the effect on Congress leaders must have been to reinforce the impression of lower-class volatility.

The argument here is not that Congress leaders were often themselves the victims of violence. Rather it is that violence occasionally intruded into the normally peaceful cities where Congress leaders lived and worked, and reminded some of them of their common interest with the British in the emerging social and political order and of their separation from sections of Indian society. There was sufficient violence that British and Indian enemies of the Congress were able to play on fears among Western-educated Indians of sectional and lower-class violence. Lord Welby's remark about letting the animals out of the zoo has been mentioned; Sayyid Ahmad Khan taunted the Congress in a similar vein in his speech of December 1887. He suggested that if the demands of Congress were met, Bengalis would rule India:

Over all races, not only over Mahomedans but over Rajas of high position and the brave Rajputs who have not forgotten the swords of their ancestors, would be placed as ruler a Bengali who at sight of a table knife would crawl under a chair. (Uproarious cheers and laughter.) . . . Do you think that the Rajput and the fiery Pathan, who are not afraid of being hanged or of encountering the swords of the police or the bayonets of the army, could remain in peace under the Bengalis? (Cheers.)[54]

The *Pioneer* of Allahabad publicized this speech, the Pioneer Press published it in pamphlet form, and Sir John Strachey quoted from it approvingly in 1888, adding that "the most essential of all things to be learnt about India" was that without England to keep the peace between conflicting peoples, "anarchy and bloodshed would spread themselves over the land."[55]

Sayyid Ahmad referred specifically to Bengalis but the term *Bengali*, if it had not become a code word, had come to stand for a member of the new professional elite in the eyes of Indians and Englishmen who disliked the competitive society that was emerging. By encouraging talk about communal and interregional violence, the British were making their prophecies more likely to fulfill themselves. They were also contributing to the estrangement felt by some Western-educated Indians from their own society and to the desire of others to revive Hindu martial traditions.

A more significant cause of the Congress leaders' isolation from Indian society was the conflict over social reform within their own families, castes, and ancestral villages. Probably a majority of the nineteen most active Bengali delegates had violated major Hindu dietary, marriage, and travel restrictions. Anandamohan Bose, Aswinikumar Dutt, Nilratan Sarkar, and Guru Prasad Sen were Brahmos, Kalicharan Bannerji was a Christian, and W. C. Bonnerjee, Bhupendranath Basu, Romeshchandra Dutt, Lalmohan Ghose, and others had exhibited disrespect for orthodox values. One component of the reformed attitudes was the hostility of certain Congress leaders toward the religious practices of orthodox Hindus. Something of the reform spirit may be sensed from Romeshchandra Dutt's family's concern with what Bipinchandra called "the bogey of pantheism." As a child, Romeshchandra used to stand in the window with his brothers and sisters on *Bijaya* day and count the images being carried to the Hughli River for immersion. When the number of images decreased, they rejoiced; when the number rose again, they lamented.[56] Some reformed Hindus feared the social pressures and absorptive powers of Hindu orthodoxy and sought to fortify themselves, mentally and institutionally, against seduction by traditional forms of Hinduism. The Native Marriage Act of 1872 was an example of the effort to build defenses. It was passed in response to a campaign by Keshabchandra Sen to legalize the Brahmo marriage ritual, which expert legal opinion considered to violate Hindu law then in force. The 1872 Marriage Act in effect required Brahmo partners entering marriage under the new law to declare that they were not Hindus. Norendranath Sen's *Indian Mirror* commented that with the required disclaimer of being Hindu, "the Brahmo Samaj has thereby been saved, just in time, from falling into that vast and all-absorbing vortex of Hinduism, which by its treacherous tolerance has swallowed up almost all the reform movements in the country. . . . Such absorption is inevitable, unless our people guard their Church carefully against the danger."[157] But such openly hostile acts as declaring oneself a non-Hindu not only increased the distance between Brahmos and the larger society; it also added to the divisions between Brahmos. Many Brahmos wished not to offend the majority community.

The greatest pressures came from outside of the reformed circles. It was these external pressures which strained family unity, diverted leaders' energies and emotions from politics, and conveyed negative messages about the possibility of making common cause with other Hindu elite groups. Bengalis who went to England, in particular, felt orthodox society's strength. They faced possible excommunication or ostracism. Belonging to the Brahmo Samaj or to reformed families provided some insulation from social disapproval. There were also precautions a man might make to relieve his community's apprehensions. Ramaswami Mudaliar, for example, was said to have been received back in Madras and his home town of Salem "without a murmur" after campaigning in the 1885 general elections because he took a servant with him to cook his vegetarian meals.[58] But many men were less fortunate and, if not ostracized, were suspected of having taken forbidden food and of having been corrupted by the fleshpots of Europe. When Surendranath Banerjea, Romeshchandra Dutt, and Behari Lal Gupta prepared to go to England to study for the ICS, they had to keep their plans secret. The latter two sneaked out of their houses at night to avoid being stopped.[59] Enough men returned from England with changed habits or views to give credence to orthodox fears. For example, Motilal Nehru's elder brother, Bansi Lal Kaul, had carefully observed the commensal rituals of Kashmiri Brahmans until he went to London for Queen Victoria's Jubilee in 1897. But his trip to England "broke the shackles of a lifetime" and he returned with anglicized eating and other habits.[60]

A few men came back thoroughly alienated from Indian society. An extreme case was W. C. Bonnerjee, who wrote home from England in 1865:

> I have discarded all ideas of caste, I have come to hate all the demoralizing practices of our countrymen and I write this letter an entirely altered man —altered in appearance, altered in costume, altered in language, altered in habits, altered in ways of thought—in short altered and altered for the better too, in everything, I should say in all things, which have contributed towards making our nation the [most] hateful of all others in the world.[61]

In later years, Bonnerjee and his family spent much of their time in London, where he maintained a house. Three of his children converted to Christianity and some of his children spoke and thought in English rather than Bengali. Bonnerjee was referred to disparagingly as "a Sahib and a Christian" by other Bengalis.[62] His anglicization was exceptional in its completeness. Other leaders remained Indian in many aspects of their lives and were respected for it. Nevertheless, Bonnerjee's membership in the Congress high command was a measure of its character: he was the first man to be elected twice as Congress president in spite of the fact that his behavior closely resembled that of the rulers. His admiration for England and his doubts about Indian culture were shared in varying degrees by other Congress leaders. Surendranath Banerjea, Anandamohan Bose, Romeshchandra Dutt, and many others were also open to charges of "Sahibism."

Society's disapproval of those Indians who had crossed the *kali paani*, married widows, or otherwise violated Hindu customs was registered in domestic as well as public life. This attitude placed heavy burdens on reformed Hindus because, however anglicized they were, members of the new professional elite continued to value traditions of family loyalty and unity. It is difficult to find examples of parental disapproval or family division which did not cause distress. Sea voyages and new habits interfered with basic filial responsibilities. Performance of the *sradh* is a case in point. Conceivably the common desire to perform orthodox *sradh* for their parents was an effort to atone for the grief caused by their challenge to family traditions and to reestablish a measure of harmony with a society they had affronted. In any case, carrying out family rituals was sometimes difficult. Bipinchandra Pal found that when his father died, "as a Brahmo and an outcaste I could not even touch his dead body nor perform the last duties of a Hindu son to his father at the cremation ground. It was my step-mother who had to light his funeral pyre while I had to stand by."[63] Wealthier men than Pal were able to overcome some Brahman objections to participation in the *sradh*. Bonnerjee, for example, more of an apostate than Pal, spent "thousands of rupees" on his mother's *sradh* at Benaras. "Brahmans from various provinces were invited to come, and lands were given away to them."[64] However, few men had such means for easing Brahman consciences.

The income and prestige of the new professionals won a certain tolerance from orthodox society for their reformed behavior. Still more freedom was gained when reformers broke away from their family traditions and formed new social groups within which marriages occurred, such as the Brahmo, Prathana, and Arya Samajes, or new subcastes such as the Kashmiri Brahman Moti and Bishan Sabhas of Allahabad.[65] These groups were somewhat self-contained with their own priests and social life. Even Ranade, who did not break with his caste, maintained two Brahman priests in his home to officiate for his acquaintances whose reformed lives had caused them to be boycotted.[66] However, none of these new social cells was able to give full protection from society's disapproval.

As a Brahmo, Bipinchandra Pal could not find servants to work for him in his father's village.[67] W. C. Bonnerjee could not live in his family's ancestral house because he knew that "the servants would refuse to wash any dishes that he used."[68] Motilal Ghose's marriage arrangement was endangered by rumors in his village that he and his brothers were meat-eaters. His neighbors assumed this because Motilal was a Brahmo and because witnesses claimed a large bull had entered the Ghose house and had not come out.[69]

Chittaranjan Das' biographer says that he experienced "social obloquy and opprobrium" and "the indignation of the whole country" because he arranged his widowed stepmother's remarriage. Das was a Brahmo but he found himself in trouble with the Samaj on account of his "atheistic and bohemian views." Because of these views, the leading Brahmo ministers refused to officiate at his wedding in 1897.[70] Das was relatively well protected from society's pressures. The majority of reformed Hindus in the Congress did not have even the limited security of Brahmo Samaj communities.

INDIVIDUALISM AND FACTIONALISM

It might be anticipated that the pressures from orthodox society, the common interest in English education, and the special, ambivalent relationship with the English rulers would have strengthened the bonds among at least the reformed members of the educated classes. The political organizations founded in the second half of the nineteenth century, such as the Indian and British Indian Associations of Calcutta and the Congress itself, were products of those bonds. These organizations acted as watchdogs for the economic and political interests of educated zamindars, lawyers, journalists, and teachers in Bengal. But in fact, the first twenty-five years of the Indian National Congress witnessed little lasting cooperation between public leaders. One reason for this situation may have been that orthodox pressure had an unsettling effect upon university graduates, leading some to doubt their own values and in certain cases to withdraw from politics and other activities in which their convictions might be challenged. Others responded sympathetically to the counterpull of traditional allegiances and identities, seeing in them possibilities for a national or at least Hindu unity and revitalization as well as for personal identity. The late nineteenth century in Bengal seemed to be a time of political uncertainty, disarray, and regrouping.

There was also a factor seemingly independent of orthodox pressure which contributed to the isolation of Bengali congressmen, a factor which had no obvious relation to anglicization or orthodoxy but which made reformed Hindus less able to resist orthodox pressure. This factor was a pervasive factionalism that at times resembled anarchic individualism. It may have been in part a function of the overcrowding and competition within the colleges and professions. And it may have been a result of the novelty of voluntary forms of organization which required subordinating concern for traditional social boundaries and individual status to the interests of a broader social organism. Individualism, and the acquisitioners which often accompanied it, and factionalism bothered many congressmen.

Bipinchandra Pal was an exemplar both of that individualism and of the Hindu revival which sought to control individual behavior, and it is doubtful whether he ever reconciled in either his thinking or his behavior the conflict between individual autonomy and society's needs. In beginning the second volume of his autobiography, he wrote, perhaps with painful personal experience in mind, that "the individual is not an isolated unit but is part of a whole, composed of many other individuals." Individualism, he believed, was particularly strong in Bengal. "The key-note of the Bengal school of Hindu law, the Dayabhaga, is individualism, while the key-note of the Mitakshara school, which governs the rest of India, has been what may be called collectivism." Bipinchandra felt that individualism was Bengal's "instinct of personal freedom" and the concomitant "social freedom," a spirit which had been dulled by orthodox Hinduism.[71]

By temperament and conviction an upholder of freedom, Bipinchandra had difficulty fitting into organizations and accepting the authority of leaders. He moved from one organization to another, battling and then breaking with his superiors in each. For example, in 1890 he was chosen from among 119 applicants for the post of librarian and secretary of the Calcutta Public Library. The library's hours were 8:00 A.M. to 9:00 P.M. Pal kept irregular hours, sometimes arriving at 8:00 A.M. and sometimes at noon but apparently working what he considered to be a full day. Some members of the library's governing council who, according to Bipinchandra, lacked "training in the principles of representative institutions" began to object, and one "wrote caustic remarks" on the attendance register about Bipin's irregularity. Bipin, however, regarded the library's president as the only man who might direct him and he let it be known that if the council member continued to make impertinent remarks in the register, Bipin would "be compelled to turn him out. . . . This attitude of mine inevitably offended some of my masters and I found it necessary to give this post up." He then took a job with the Calcutta Municipal Corporation but soon left this also. He next began working as a lecturer and missionary for the Sadharan Brahmo Samaj. He started two journals, *Asha* and *Kaumudi,* and used them to criticize the way in which the Brahmo Samaj was conducted. He explained the problems thus: "The Democratic constitution of the Sadharan Brahmo Samaj had been threatening to create an official Brahmo bureaucracy which seriously hindered the growth of freedom of thought in the community and real spiritual life in its members."[72] Soon after Bipinchandra had challenged the authorities of the library and the Sadharan Brahmo Samaj, he came under the influence of Bijaykrishna Goswami. Whether this discipleship was related to the death of his wife, as he thought, or an urge to bring his independent spirit under control, he continued to chafe under what he regarded as the autocracy of leaders in the associations to which he belonged. He was one of the most outspoken critics of "the despotism" of Pherozeshah Mehta within the Congress, and he joined Tilak, Aurobindo, and Lajpat Rai in their demands that the Congress become democratic in its internal affairs.

No doubt Bipinchandra is an extreme example of that testy independence and restlessness which caused organizations to splinter and partnerships to come apart. But whether one examines politics, journalism, social reform movements, or family life in later nineteenth-century Bengal, there seems to have been a pronounced tendency toward factionalism. Many factions formed without significant disagreements over principles. Other factions, when they argued over principles, seemed actually to be engaged in personal competition motivated by jealousy and concern for individual prestige.

Certain congressmen seemed to relish conflict. Motilal Ghose of the *Amrita Bazar Patrika* was such a person. His personality was colorful and controversial but he seemed incapable of lasting cooperation with other nationalists. An account of Motilal's effort to be elected to the Calcutta Municipal Corporation in 1892 has been preserved; it suggests the intensity that intragroup rivalry could reach. The group in this case was the Kayasthas of Ward No. 1 in north Calcutta. Eight candidates had started the campaign, but by election day the field had been reduced to three: a wealthy zamindar (Pasupatinath Bose), a young, rising Congress lawyer (Bhupendranath Basu), and a Congress editor (Motilal). The following description of the campaign, written probably by Motilal himself, appeared in the *Amrita Bazar Patrika* shortly before the election:

The three candidates who have presented themselves this year [from Ward

No. 1] for the honour of a seat on the Municipal Board are all Kayasthas. Now these Kayasthas like others marry and give in marriage and thus form relationships. In Ward No. 1, therefore, the Kayasthas as a rule are related to each other.

When therefore [would-be] Commissioner No. 1 appears in the field his affectionate father-in-law as a matter of fact canvasses for him. The spectacle fires the relations of other candidates with emulation and they thus plunge themselves into the vortex of the whirlpool. The voters and candidates being all Kayasthas are related to each other. The voter who is the uncle-in-law of a candidate is the grand-father of another, and thus the candidates find themselves in the midst of voters, who are generally their relatives.

The usual rule for candidates in all countries is to base their appeals to voters upon their own merits. In Ward No. 1 it is based, with very few honourable exceptions, upon relationship. One candidate pleads to a voter: "Is not my brother your son-in law?" and thus secures the support of a voter. This voter is immediately after besieged by another candidate, who tries to convince him that the brother of a son-in-law can never have so much claim as the brother of a maternal uncle, which relation he bears to him. When such is the way the votes are canvassed for, it is no wonder that the candidates and voters should all lose their proper senses.

It was very calm in the beginning. At that time the candidates met and shook hands like friends. This was succeeded by squibs, lampoons and satires. And now it is foul abuse—abuse which fouls even the mouth of a fisherwoman.

It was very dull in the very beginning, when the candidates and their friends bowed to each other whenever they met, formally and politely. It was very exciting and exhilarating when lampoons and satires were hurled upon rivals. Now that abuses have been resorted to the matter has become more nauseating than putrid human flesh.[73]

The campaigning and canvassing became increasingly tense and unfriendly. The day before the election, Pasupatinath Bose had his English lawyer apply for a ruling from the High Court to remove Motilal's name from the ballot on the grounds that Motilal's family, but not Motilal himself, was the registered rate-payer. Justice Trevelyan rejected the application. On election day, *goonda* appeared in order to intimidate voters. "Voters were physically restrained from voting." Mounted police were finally called to restore order.[74]

Motilal often feuded with Surendranath Banerjea and his supporters (Krishnakumar Mitra and Pandit Kaliprasanna Kavyakisharad). The bad feeling between Motilal and Surendranath was so great in 1896 that some doubted whether the Congress could be held in Calcutta that year.[75] In 1898–1899, the rivalry erupted in three defamation suits between Pandit Kaliprasanna and Motilal.[76]

Surendranath Banerjea was year after year the heart of the Congress movement in Bengal. He had a reputation for flexibility and lack of dogmatism and upon occasion he acted as a conciliator between Congress rivals. His newspaper, the *Bengalee,* rarely engaged in personal attacks. Yet Surendranath had poor relations with many fellow congressmen besides Motilal Ghose. It was well known that W. C. Bonnerjee's dislike for Surendranath prevented them from cooperating in the early Congress. Neither Anandamohan Bose nor Lalmohan Ghose gave Surendranath much support in keeping the Congress alive in Bengal. Anandamohan is a special puzzle. Although he had been a close associate of Surendranath in City College and as secretary of the Indian Association, he stayed away from him for nine years after 1887.[77] After the 1905 partition there were also bad feelings between Aurobindo and Bipinchandra Pal on the one side and Surendranath on the other.

This factionalism needs explanation. Here we can observe simply that there seems to have been frequent fragmentation of organizations and partnerships. It seems likely that many nationalists avoided strong commitment to political organizations because of the divisiveness. Given a choice between abstention and the messiness of factional politics, many men preferred the former. As a result politics was atomized as well as fractious. Congress leaders, unable to work together even within the Congress, were rarely in a position to strike back or give mutual support when attacked by orthodox society.

HINDU POPULISM

Two all-Indian controversies in the early 1890s revealed with striking clarity the strength of orthodox groups when aroused. The first was that over the Age of Consent Bill. In a sense the bill was an extension of the Brahmos' Native Marriage Act of 1872 because it raised the age limit for the whole of Hindu society whereas the 1872 act applied only to Brahmos. The Age of Consent Bill also received some of its strongest support from Bengali Brahmos. However, the opposition to the bill was probably more determined in Bengal than elsewhere. More marriages stood to be affected in Bengal where, according to the census of 1881, 14 percent of Hindu girls had been married before the age of ten, compared to 10 percent in Bombay and 4.5 percent in Madras.[78] The militant Hindu newspaper *Bangabasi* led the attack on the bill, which it said was part of England's attempt to destroy the Hindu religion. The *Bangabasi* compared the English to Muslim temple-destroyers such as Aurangzib and Kalapahar, and it regretted that "we are unable to rebel although we are not of those who say it would be improper to do so." In its attack on the bill and in its subsequent trial for sedition, the *Bangabasi* was supported by many non-Brahmo congressmen whom it had recently been denouncing. The *Bangabasi* had criticized the Congress and its supporters for their exclusiveness, for their ignorance and avoidance of the Bengali language, and for their hypocrisy in preaching nationalism while using English goods and adulterating Hindu culture and morality with foreign borrowings.[79] Probably the attacks by the *Bangabasi,* which had a circulation of twenty to thirty thousand, were a factor in the decision of reformed congressmen such as W. C. Bonnerjee and Motilal Ghose to oppose the bill. In the end, few late-nineteenth-century issues stirred educated Bengali society as deeply as did the Age of Consent Bill. And few emphasized as dramatically the vulnerability of those Bengalis who welcomed government interference in Hindu religious and social practices. One angry youth even tried to shoot Bipinchandra Pal after the latter disrupted a meeting summoned to protest the bill.[80] This incident, like the window-breaking and stone-throwing attack on the police following Surendranath Banerjea's 1883 conviction in the Saligram idol case,[81] may have been less a defense of orthodoxy than a nationalist protest against disrespect for and interference with Hindu usages in general. But the anglicized character of the Congress leadership in Bengal made this distinction a fine one at times.

The other sign of a resurgence of Hinduism was the spread of the cow-protection movement in the late 1880s and early 1890s. The movement peaked in 1893 with the outbreak of Hindu-Muslim riots in such widely separated places as Rangoon, the North-West Frontier Province and Oudh, Junagadh, and Bombay city. Most of the riots followed Hindu efforts to rescue cattle intended for sacrifice during Bakr Id. More than one hundred persons died in the riots, and in the district of Azamgarh alone, over eight hundred persons were arrested.

The cow protection movement was weak or nonexistent in most Bengali-speaking districts. Unlike in other provinces, no prominent Bengali Congress leader seems to have been directly connected with the movement. Nevertheless, Raja Sashi Sekharaswar Roy of Tahirpore, Bengal, had embarrassed the leadership in 1887 by trying to move a resolution in the Congress calling for a government ban on cow slaughter.[82] This attempt was resisted by men who were intent upon making the Congress attractive to Muslims. Two prominent patrons of the Congress movement in Bengal, the maharajas of Darbhanga and Dumroan, openly supported the cow protection movement.[83] And representatives from different parts of India, including Bengal, attended a meeting of the Gauraksha Sabha in the Congress pavilion following the Nagpur Congress session of 1891.[84] There is no doubt that the Congress leadership's failure to dissociate the organization fully from the cow protection movement was a factor in the decline in Muslim participation in the Congress. Whereas Muslims constituted 14.1 percent of Congress delegates (about 112 per year) before the 1893 riots, in the following thirteen years they made up only 7.1 percent (about 58 per year).[85]

Because the movement had gained little momentum within Bengali-speaking parts of the Bengal province, it was a much less direct indication to Bengali leaders of the latent power of the Hindu reaction than the Age of Consent Bill controversy had been. But no Bengali congressman could have been unaware of the riots and the spread of the cow protection movement, especially in Bihar, the eastern North-West Frontier Province and Oudh, and the Central Provinces, which preceded them. During the decade following the riots, Bengali congressmen did not, it seems, revive their early efforts to attract Muslims to the Congress. It is difficult to ascertain what Bengali leaders thought about the Muslim abstention from the Congress, since the issue was rarely discussed in public; presumably recruitment of Bengali Muslims was regarded as having few prospects for success. The Muslim abstention in turn may have left certain Bengali nationalists feeling freer to Hinduize their politics. However, Hinduization of political rhetoric, symbolism, and organizational forms became widespread among Bengali congressmen only after the partition.

Conclusion

This essay began with the observation that few Muslims made more than a casual contribution to nationalist political organizations in Bengali-speaking districts in the late nineteenth century. Although 23.4 million of British India's 49.5 million Muslims lived in Bengal province, according to the 1891 census, there is little evidence of Muslim participation in provincial conferences, the Indian Association, or the British Indian Association in the 1880s and 1890s. Surendranath Banerjea had persuaded Amir Ali and the Central Mahomedan Association to participate in the National Conference in Calcutta in 1885. But after that, Congress' emphasis upon representative government and competitive examinations and the lack of concerted Hindu overtures to Muslims deterred most prominent Bengali Muslims from joining. Abul Kasim, the pleader and zamindar from Burdwan, was the only continuously active Bengali Muslim in the Congress prior to 1905.

The absence of Muslims is reflected in the biographies included in *Freedom Movement in Bengal, 1818–1904: Who's Who,* published by the Government of West Bengal in 1968. Although it was prepared under an advisory committee consisting of N. K. Sinha, S. B. Chaudhuri, P. C. Gupta, and Amales Tripathi, the only Muslim among the 148 individuals is Nawab Abdul Latif.[86] Matiur Rahman has explained the separation of Muslims from nationalist politics as a consequence of the Hindu character of such activities as the *Hindoo Patriot,* the Hindu Mela, and the Shivaji festival.[87] However, he has not produced evidence that those activities were motivated by anti-Muslim bias or, more importantly, that Bengali Muslims perceived those activities as unfriendly or threatening. Perhaps they did. A more pertinent reason for Bengali Muslim abstention from the Congress may be that Congress activities in prepartition Bengal were confined largely to Calcutta, that the most active and influential Muslim civic leaders in Calcutta were non-Bengalis, that few Bengali Muslims in Calcutta belonged to the same educational and economic strata as congressmen, and that the source of separation was therefore as much regional as communal. In any case, Bengali Congress leaders during the 1885–1905 period were, as a group, men who, while having few Bengali Muslim social or professional associates, seemed to be free of communal prejudices and seemed to feel more antipathy toward militant sections of Hindu society than toward Muslims. University-educated Bengali Hindus, in and outside the Congress, were preoccupied with *bhadralok* deficiencies and divisions. Relations with non-*bhadralok* Hindus and Muslims were a matter of secondary concern prior to the partition. It was the Hindu *patua* of Kalighat, for example, who turned out inexpensive drawings which satirized the anglicized babus for the decay of family life, the sexual immorality, the drinking, and the reversal of sex roles that were assumed to have spread with the aping of European behavior.[88] The main thrust of the social criticism of popular Hindu writers such as Indranath Bandyopadhyaya, Rajanikanta Gupta, and Bankimchandra was directed against their own society, rarely against Muslims. The sudden communalization of politics that followed the 1905 partition would have been hard to predict several years earlier. *Bhadralok* society was still sharply divided. While nationalists were searching for means of integrating Hindu society and overcoming perceived social deficiencies, such as elitism, factionalism, and lack of courage, the means chosen were diverse. Which Indian past, which tradition, which hero was appropriate? The answers were many. The neo-Vaishnavism of Ramakrishna, Bijaykrishna Goswami, Aswinikumar Dutt, Motilal Ghose, and Bipinchandra Pal had little in common with the *lathi* play and hero worship of Saraladevi Ghosal's *biastami* days or the student *samiti* or Surendranath Banerjea's advocacy of an Akbar festival.

The final point is that many leaders of neo-Hinduism at the turn of the century had been raised in a manner which had isolated them from orthodox society and had made them vulnerable to the scorn and sanctions of traditional Hindus. Therefore, increasingly the reaction against anglicization came from fellow congressmen, ex-Brahmos, and English-returned Bengalis. Bipinchandra Pal, Aurobindo, Rabindranath Tagore, Vivekananda, and Brahmabhandhav Upadhyaya had in varying degrees found themselves outside traditions of Hindu *bhadralok* society. No doubt their return through neo-Hinduism received stimuli from political motives. But for many who made the transition there was a deeper aesthetic and spiritual meaning derived from the basic act of self-discovery and consolidating a fragmented identity. Aurobindo described the release or return he seemed to be seeking from the constraints of his anglicizàtion in the 1890s when he discussed the mid-century Bengali renaissance:

> The calm, docile, pious, dutiful Hindu ideal was pushed aside with impatient energy, and the Bengali, released from the iron restraint which had lain like a frost on his warm blood and sensuous feeling, escaped joyously into the open air of an almost Pagan freedom. The ancient Hindu cherished a profound sense of the nothingness and vanity of life; the young Bengali felt vividly its joy, warmth and sensuousness.[89]

Nationalists' preoccupation with the integration of high-caste society and the redefinition of Hinduism inhibited the creation of a multicommunity movement. But this preoccupation was overwhelmingly the result of tensions within high-caste circles, and only to a minor degree the result of conflict with Muslims or with nonelite Hindu castes.

NOTES

1.   A delegate list for 1907 was not preserved but ten Muslims were listed as delegates in 1908 and five in 1909. Syed Razi Wasti, *Lord Minto and the Indian Nationalist Movement, 1905–1910* (Oxford: Oxford University Press, 1964), appendix I.

2.   Matiur Rahman, *From Consultation to Confrontation: A Study of the Muslim League in British Indian Politics, 1906–1912*(London:Verry, 1970), pp. 156–59.

3.   Anil Seal, *The Emergence of Indian Nationalism: Competition and Collaboration in the Later Nineteenth Century* (Cambridge: Cambridge University Press, 1968), p. 331; and Government of Bombay, *Source Material for a History of the Freedom Movement in India*, vol. II (Bombay, 1958), p. 69.

4.   Including Seal's, Wasti's, and Rahman's.

5.   Rahman, *Consultation to Confrontation*, p. 208ff.

6.   John Broomfield, *Elite Conflict in a Plural Society: Twentieth-Century Bengal* (Berkeley: University of California Press, 1968), p. 15.

7.   Ibid., p. 32.

8.   The list was compiled from the indexes in Annie Besant, *How India Wrought for Freedom: The Story of the National Congress Told from Official Records* (Madras, 1915). Caste and occupations were derived from the delegate lists in the annual I.N.C. Reports and from Bimanbehari Majumdar and Bhakat Prasad Mazumdar, *Congress and Congressmen in the Pre-Gandhian Era, 1885–1917* (Calcutta, 1967), part II.

9.   The Bengal delegates were Abdul Kasim, Ambicacharan Mazumdar, Aswinikumar Dutt, Baikunthanath Sen, W. C. Bonnerji, Bhupendranath Basu,

Anandamohan Bose, Asutosh Chaudhuri, Jitendranath Choudhuri, J. Ghosal, Guru Prasad Sen, Kalicharan Bannerji, Lalmohan Ghose, Nilratan Sarkar, Romeshchandra Dutt, Surendranath Banerjea, Jogeshchandra Chaudhuri, Saligram Singh, and Kaliprasanna Kavyabisharad.

10. Husain B. Tyabji, *Badruddin Tyabji: A Biography* (Bombay, 1952), p. 22.

11. Surendranath Banerjea, *A Nation in Making: Being the Reminiscences of Fifty Years of Public Life* (Oxford, 1927), p. 10.

12. Ibid., p. 15.

13. H. C. Sarkar, *A Life of Ananda Mohan Bose* (Calcutta, 1910), p. 54.

14. Ranade rose to the High Court through government service, not through the legal profession. Ramabai Ranade, *Ranade: His Wife's Reminiscences* (Delhi, 1963), p. 42.

15. Louis Fischer, *The Life of Mahatma Gandhi* (New York: Macmillan, 1962), p. 67.

16. *Lajpat Rai: Autobiographical Writings*, ed. Vijaya Chandra Joshi (Delhi, 1965), pp. 15–16, 42.

17. Sadhona Bonnerjee, *Life of W. C. Bonnerjee: First President of the Indian National Congress* (Calcutta? 1944?), p. 10.

18. *Who's Who in India* (Lucknow, 1911), part VIII, p. 121.

19. K. P. S. Menon, *C. Sankaran Nair* (Delhi, 1967), p. 17.

20. K.A. Nilakanta Sastri, ed.; *A Great Liberal: Speeches and writings of Sir P. S. Sivaswami Aiyar* (Madras, 1965), p. 227.

21. Samuel Schmitthener, "A Sketch of the Development of the Legal Profession in India," *Law and Society Review*, vol. III, no. 2 and 3 (November 1968–February 1969), pp. 363–364. Most of the references and arguments in this analysis of the legal profession were suggested by Schmitthener's excellent article.

22. Ibid.

23. See Sastri, *A Great Liberal*, pp. 228–229.

24. However, the nineteenth-century Indian bar was not unique in its lack of professionalism. See Robert H. Wiebe, *The Search for Order, 1877–1920* (New York: Hill & Wang, 1967), p. 116–117, on the late professionalization of the American bar.

25. H. P. Mody, *Sir Pherozeshah Mehta*, pp. 27–28, 33, 37. Schmitthener identified the three types of Indian efforts to break the English legal monopoly.

26. Tyabji, *Badruddin Tyabji*, pp. 28–29.

27. M. C. Setalvad, *Bhulabhai Desai* (New Delhi, 1968), p. 11.

28. Menon, *C. Sankaran Nair*, pp. 17–18.

29. Sastri, *A Great Liberal*, p. 213.

30. Aiyangar, unlike most of the lawyers mentioned in this section, was hostile to the Congress. C. P. Ramaswami Aiyar, *Biographical Vistas: Sketches of Some Eminent Indians* (Madras, 1966), p. 132.

31. Sastri, *A Great Liberal*, p. 233.

32. Schmitthener, "Sketch", p. 377.

33. Menon, *C. Sankaran Nair*, p. 18.

34. Marc Galanter, "Introduction: The Study of the Indian Legal Profession," *Law and Society Review*, vol. VIII, no. 2 and 3 (November 1968–February 1969), p. 208.

35. Fischer, *Life of Gandhi*, p. 46.

36. Hemendranath Das Gupta, *Deshbandhu Chittaranjan Das* (Delhi, 1960), p. 24.

37.   Matlubul Hasan Saiyed, *Mohammad Ali Jinnah (A Political Study)*, 2nd ed. (Lahore, 1953), pp. 5–7.

38.   Sastri, *A Great Liberal*, p. 228.

39.   Galanter, "Introduction," p. 213.

40.   These are the words used by Dadabhai Naoroji to describe what he learned from Watts' *Improvement of the Mind* while a student at Elphinstone Institution. R. P. Masani, *Dadabhai Naoroji* (Delhi, 1960), p. 11. The didactic, self-improving attitude is obvious in Surendranath Banerjea's *A Nation in the Making*.

41.   Henry W. Nevinson, *The New Spirit in India* (London, 1908), pp. 148–149.

42.   M. K. Gandhi, *An Autobiography or the Story of My Experiments With Truth*, 2nd ed. (Ahmedabad, 1948), pp. 272–273, 283.

43.   Sri Aurobindo, *Bankim Chandra Chatterji* (Pondicherry, 1954), pp. 24, 44.

44.   Quoted from *An Autobiography* by Erik H. Erikson, *Gandhi's Truth: On the Origins of Militant Nonviolence* (New York: Norton, 1969), p. 190.

45.   Gandhi's attitude toward this seems to have been ambiguous, for he saw it as an opportunity to do service. *An Autobiography*, p. 278: "I volunteered to do the bearer's duty, and I loved to do it, as my regard for elders was always great."

46.   Ibid., p. 281.

47.   Ibid., pp. 283, 287.

48.   "Autobiography of Damodar Hari Chapekar," in Government of Bombay, *Source Material of the Freedom Movement in India*, vol. II, *1885–1920* (Bombay, 1958), pp. 983–984.

49.   Lajpat Rai, *Young India: An Interpretation and a History of the Nationalist Movement from Within* (New York: B. W. Huebsch, 1916), p. 146.

50.   Daniel Argov, *Moderates and Extremists in the Indian National Movement, 1883–1920* (Bombay, 1967), p. 56.

51.   R. P. Masani, *Dadabhai Naoroji*, pp. 126–127. Lord Roberts published that remark in his *Forty-one Years in India: From Subaltern to Commander-in-Chief* (London, 1897), II: 388–389.

52.   D. E. Wacha, *Shells from the Sands of Bombay*, p. 67, quoted in Government of Bombay, *Source Material*, I: 296.

53.   Banerjea, *Nation in Making*, pp. 89–90.

54.   Speech of 28 December 1887, *Sir Syed Ahmed on the Present State of Indian Politics* (Allahabad, 1888).

55.   *India: Its Administration and Progress* (London, 1888), pp. 499–501.

56.   *Modern Review*, vol. VIII, no. 37 (January 1910), p. 105.

57.   Charles H. Heimsath, *Indian Nationalism and Hindu Social Reform* (Princeton: Princeton University Press, 1964), pp. 93–95.

58.   Mudaliar was a vakil who served on the Public Service Commission and turned down an offer to be president of the Congress. G. Paramaswaran Pillai, *Representative Indians*, 2nd ed. (London, 1902), pp. 214–216.

59.   J. N. Gupta, *Life and Work of Romesh Chander Dutt* (London, 1911), p. 17.

60.   B. R. Nanda, *The Nehrus: Motilal and Jawaharlal* (London, 1962), pp. 37–38.

61.   Bonnerjee, *Life of W. C. Bonnerjee*, pp. 14–15.

62.   Ibid., p. 99ff.

63.   Bipin Chandra Pal, *Memories of My Life and Times (1886–1900)*, vol. II (Calcutta: Yugayatri Prakashak Ltd., 1951), p. 2.

64.   Bonnerjee, *Life of W. C. Bonnerjee*, p. 101.

65. Nanda, *The Nehrus*, p. 67.
66. Ranade, *Ranade: His Wife*, p. 138.
67. Pal, *Life and Times*, p. 4.
68. Bonnerjee, *Life of W. C. Bonnerjee*, p. 100.
69. Paramananda Dutt, *Memoirs of Moti Lal Ghose* (Calcutta, 1935), p. 21.
70. Prithwis Chandra Ray, *Life and Times of C. R. Das: The Story of Bengal's Self-Expression* (London, 1925), pp. 18, 25.
71. Pal, *Life and Times*, pp. i-viii.
72. Ibid., p. 128.
73. Dutt, *Memoirs of Moti Lal Ghose*, p. 81.
74. Ibid., p. 82.
75. Ibid., p. 86.
76. Ibid., p. 115.
77. Majumdar and Mazumdar, *Congress and Congressmen*, p. 103.
78. Heimsath, *Indian Nationalism*, p. 153.
79. Shyamananda Banerjee, *National Awakening and the Bangabasi* (Calcutta, 1968), p. 130ff.; Nirmal Sinha, ed., *Freedom Movement in Bengal, 1818–1904: Who's Who*, pp. 405–408; and Dutt, *Memoirs of Moti Lal Ghose*, pp. 72–77.
80. Pal, *Life and Times*, pp. 117–118.
81. Banerjea, *Nation in Making*, p. 71.
82. Ibid., p. 100. The raja was elected to the Bengal Legislative Council in the first elections under the 1892 act.
83. The Maharaj of Darbhanga probably contributed more funds to the pre-1900 Congress than any other individual in India.
84. Note on the agitation against cow-killing by D. F. McCracken, Offg. Gen. Supt., Thagi and Dakaiti Department, 9 August 1893. December 1893, Prog. No. 210, India Home Prog., Public.
85. The Muslim attendance figures are based on appendix I in Wasti, *Lord Minto*, p. 221.
86. These figures do not include the special sections on the heroes of the Santal Rebellion and the Indigo Disturbances. The volume was edited by Nirmal Sinha.
87. Rahman, *Consultation to Confrontation*, p. 1.
88. W. G. Archer, *Bazaar Paintings of Calcutta: The Style of Kalighat* (London, 1953), pp. 12–13.
89. Aurobindo, *Bankim Chandra Chatterji*, p. 9.

A Public Policy Profile on Rural Development in Bengal

NICOLAAS LUYKX
East-West Center

INTRODUCTION

It was not until relatively recent times that there have been significant public policies proposed or implemented specifically for the development of the rural areas of Bengal. Many of these have been undertaken with indifference, lack of commitment, or in the face of serious controversy.

The British East India Company came into prominence in Bengal during the latter half of the eighteenth century and dominated its history for a full hundred years. Following the disasters of the mid-nineteenth century, the liberal conscience of Victorian England stimulated efforts to mitigate the harshness of natural calamity and exploitation by commercial interest. These actions were motivated largely by a sense of compassion and propriety. Despite the growth of rural infrastructure, social services, and local administration, little genuine development took place in the next hundred years. The turmoil of partition and independence, the density of population, and the extent of poverty, disease, ignorance, and hardship were hardly evidence of improvement in the lot of the average villager. For the most part, rural people persisted in a subordinate role within a pervasive patron-client system that, despite its fundamental humanitarian bias, provided little scope for the client's advance to peerage.

It is a thesis of this essay that rural development is a matter of restructuring life in rural areas. This includes the expansion of opportunity for economic, political, social, and cultural fulfillment. It also includes the improvement of the capacity of individuals and groups to shape and utilize these opportunities. Further, it includes the emergence of a set of norms conducive to such changes.

178

In drawing the picture of rural development policy in Bengal, I reach back briefly to the arrival of the British East India Company and the course of events up to 1947. Thereafter, I take up the principal postindependence programs implemented in West Bengal and East Bengal. Space requirements force this presentation into the form of a sketch or profile, but the concluding picture will be an outline of what I feel to be the crucial issues facing rural development in Bengal.

But first a few words about the region are in order.

"Bengal" has been variously defined throughout history. The Bengal Presidency over which the British East India Company acquired revenue rights in 1765 included Assam, Bihar, and Orissa. The greatest extent of the Bengal Presidency was in 1810, when it reached as far as Delhi and to the Punjab. Assam was pared away in 1874, and East and West Bengal were temporarily separated during the period 1905–1911. Bihar and Orissa were not separated until 1912, but the ultimate diminution came with partition in 1947. The State of West Bengal at that point was one-seventh the size of the area known as Bengal a century earlier.[1]

By 1956 West Bengal had added territories bringing its size up to its present dimension of 33,927 square miles. In 1961 the population of West Bengal was estimated at 34.9 million, indicating an average population density of 1029 per square mile at that time. In 1961 the population of East Bengal (then, East Pakistan) was estimated at 55.3 million in an area of 55,126 square miles, resulting in an average population density of 1002 per square mile. In the decade since that time populations have grown still further, although recent disruptions due to war make the current situation difficult to interpret.

Bengal is a delta laid down at the confluence of some of the world's largest rivers. The Ganges and Brahmaputra meet at about the middle of the region (see frontispiece) and are joined by the Meghna at a point south of Dacca to the east. Other significant rivers, such as the Damodar, come in from surrounding areas. The Damodar comes from Bihar and joins the Hooghly south of Calcutta before emptying into the sea. Riverbeds have shifted continuously throughout history, and the mouths of the Ganges pour into the Bay of Bengal over a waterfront more than two hundred miles in breadth. Although the rivers flood along their courses and deposit silt which sustains much of Bengal's agriculture, the biggest influence on agriculture is the alternation of wet and dry seasons characteristic of the monsoon.

In Bengal the monsoon rains begin in May and end, for all practical purposes, in early October. During March and April there are intermittent nor'wester storms that strike suddenly, usually with brief heavy downpours. The period from November and extending into March is virtually without significant natural rainfall, and is a time of serious unemployment for most farmers. Temperatures in Bengal are conducive to farming throughout the year.

In East Bengal rice and jute are the two principal crops. The major rice season (*Amon*) is dependent on the monsoon rains, and it is during this season that the vast majority (about eighty-three percent) of the country's rice output is produced.[2] Approximately the same proportion holds true for West Bengal.[3] Jute is a much more important crop in the east than it is in the west. In East Bengal about a million tons are produced annually; in West Bengal the figure is closer to forty thousand tons.[4] Other crops of importance throughout Bengal are wheat and barley, beans, potatoes, sugarcane, pulses and oilseeds, and a number of spices.

With high population density the average farm is quite small. In East Bengal the average farm is reported as 3.5 acres, with over half the farms in holdings of 2.5 acres or less. Only 0.4 percent of the holdings are over 25 acres.[5]

Data for five villages in the Burdwan district in West Bengal indicate that forty-one percent of the landholdings were less than three acres. However, over half the families in these villages were without land and participated in agriculture either as laborers or as sharecroppers.[6]

The Company and Permanent Settlement

When the British East India Company began its operations in Bengal in the latter half on the seventeenth century, its position was tenuous and costly. By a series of steps the Company sought to establish itself and to obtain revenues with which to support its expanded operations. In 1698 it obtained the revenue collection rights to three towns adjacent to the original settlement and, having inserted itself into the revenue system of the Mogul Emperor Aurangzeb as a zamindar, proceeded to expand its control.[7] After a colorful series of intrigues, skirmishes, and battles among European, Mogul, and indigenous Indian authorities, tensions resolved themselves with the Company emerging as the diwan, or revenue collector, for all of Bengal including Bihar and Orissa.

As immense as was the power to which the Company acceded, it was no simple task to administer the revenue system. The British continued to operate through intermediaries until suspicions of revenue leakages and a genuine need to know the revenue capacity of the territory led them to take a direct hand in fulfilling the role of diwan. It was some twenty years, however, before a seemingly feasible method of revenue collection was worked out. It proved unsatisfactory.

In 1793, the collection of revenue was turned over to zamindars who were obliged to remit to the diwan (the East India Company) a permanently settled cash fee. One-tenth of this amount was the zamindar's commission, plus some minor additional revenues. This system promised the British a dependable revenue base without the administrative headaches. It is also argued that the system catered to the social tastes of the directors of the Company and the governor general, Lord Cornwallis.[8] The zamindars, who were previously only revenue collectors, now became a propertied class not unlike the English landed gentry.

The Permanent Settlement also insulated the British from the knowledge of actual conditions in rural Bengal. The rights of the zamindars were ensured so long as they transmitted the revenues on time. Village records were nonexistent, and the insecurity of tenant cultivators of the zamindari led to a gathering unrest. Cultivators were tenants at will and could be turned out without recourse.

The first attempt at ensuring the rights of at least a segment of the tenant cultivators came with the Rent Act of 1859. This act formally guaranteed the security of tenure of tenants who had been on the land continuously for at least twelve years. Although a commendable step, these guarantees really applied to only a small proportion of all cultivators. And even those with occupancy rights found themselves harassed and hounded by zamindars at other points of vulnerability.[9] A subsequent Tenancy Act in Bengal was passed in 1885 with the objective of controlling rent and preventing indiscriminate ejection of cultivators. However, this field of legal protection was simultaneously bounded by custom and traditional practice. In evaluating changes it is hard to measure the cost of deteriorating patronage benefits in the face of enhanced formal security. This is especially true when tenant cultivators are poorly informed as to their legal rights and cannot pay for the fight to have these rights enforced.

Virtually from the outset of the Permanent Settlement there had been doubts about its effectiveness in promoting rural stability and development. For the sake of administrative convenience, the governing authority had abdicated its responsibilities for rural development, blinded itself to rural conditions, and systematically failed to realize the actual revenue potential of the land.[10] Subinfeudation meant that several intermediaries (sometimes, dozens) stood between the actual cultivator and the zamindar.

In East Bengal it was not until May 1951 that the Permanent Settlement was abolished. At that time it was replaced by the East Bengal State Acquisition and Tenancy Act of the previous year.[11] Under its terms the cultivator was confirmed as proprietor and was to pay his taxes directly to the government. Government soon discovered that its administrative vigor on the revenue side had gone soft. The administration has since been under considerable pressure to organize, staff, and rationalize a function it had left in the hands of others for a century and a half.

The Influence of Famine on Rural Policy

From the earliest days, variations in agricultural output per person have led to recurring periods of local scarcity and privation. Even under today's conditions, a failure in the monsoon can lead to acute food shortages and the associated rise in prices of choice food grains beyond the reach of the ordinary consumer. Recent illustrations may be found in the succession of bad crop years in India in the late 1960s.

Famine conditions are those of extreme food shortage and severe human suffering. Records differ when reported by different sources, but up to the middle of the nineteenth century one source estimates an average of one major famine every fifty years.[12] These famines were usually confined to local areas and were primarily the result of climatic variations.

With the development of a rail network in India during the latter half of the nineteenth century and the growth in the grain trade (including export), local prices could reach famine levels well beyond the extent explainable solely by the degree of shortfall in local production, if any. As always, famines have been a combination of food shortage and lack of purchasing power among those who suffer most. A picture of profiteers, hoarding stores of grain against a speculative rise in prices, is part of the record of every scarcity over the past hundred years.

Government has shown relatively little ability to cope with this phenomenon because it attempted direct symptomatic melioration rather than an attack on root causes. Famine relief was usually some combination of food-for-work policies, direct food distribution, and control of prices and the movement of goods. However commendable as an alternative to doing nothing, such policies attacked only the evidence of problems but not their causes. Hence, the problems have tended to recur.

It was at a very late juncture that government implemented effective public policy for organizing, training, and guiding cultivators and other small operators.

In the middle of the nineteenth century there was no department of agriculture. Although a recommendation for its establishment was included in the report of the Famine Commission of 1866,[13] it was not until after the famine of 1878 that the central administration in British India combined the idea of a central department of agriculture with the formation of similar departments in each province. Instructions were then issued to that effect.

Therefore, in 1885, Bengal established a modest department of agriculture. It was only subsequent to the famine at the turn of the century that the foundations of a regular agricultural service were laid. Nevertheless, despite the efforts to build a research and extension organization, expenditures on the Agriculture Department of Bengal up to independence did not compare favorably with those in other states of British India.[14]

The Agriculture Department's research program began in 1908 during the temporary division of Bengal. In 1911, the first rice-improvement program on the Indian subcontinent was established, with a headquarters at Dacca. Despite all this, the government's work in agriculture never rose to meet the province's needs. This failure led to a history of successive, and to date only partially successful, attempts at meeting these needs by alternative means.

The first agricultural schools in Bengal were established in 1922, in West Bengal at Chinsura and in East Bengal at Dacca. However, these attracted few students, largely because of the unfavorable employment conditions at the lower levels of agricultural work.[15] An institute for higher education in agriculture, the first in Bengal, was founded in affiliation with Dacca University in 1941. In twenty-five years of operation it provided some 350 graduates and 30 postgraduates.

WEST BENGAL AFTER INDEPENDENCE
Panchayats

In both East and West Bengal the rural areas had been under Union Boards up through the period of partition and independence. In West Bengal they continued up to the late 1950s when village panchayat elections were held. At that time an *anchal* (area) panchayat displaced the Union Boards.[16] In an area as politicized as West Bengal, the system of *Panchayati Raj* (a national policy emphasizing local self-determination) would have been a vehicle of convenience for the more volatile, attention-getting politics of partisan and factional strife.

When *Panchayati Raj* was announced as a national policy in 1961, West Bengal was specifically excluded because it was said to lack a panchayat tradition. Between 1958 and 1961, panchayats had been established in 96 of the 193 community development blocks, but a fear was expressed that effective democratic institutions at the local level would not be allowed to flourish.[17]

The issue is largely unresolved because evidence of continuing instability and political extremism in West Bengal favors action by the forces of centralization. Not only does the state grasp at powers it might otherwise share with rural leaders, but also the central government, alarmed at political violence, may impose central rule as it did in March 1970.[18]

Intensive Agricultural Districts Program (IADP)

Although the initial thrust in rural development following independence had been in the realm of community development, it became clear during the course of the Second Five-Year Plan (1957–1961) that targets set for food production during the period would not be met. Sensing an emergency in the making, the government of India invited a team of specialists under Ford Foundation auspices to review the situation and make recommendations for its improvement. The team's report[19] inspired the noted Package Program, which was introduced into single districts in seven states. The "package" in question meant the simultaneous introduction not only of good seeds but of fertilizer, pesticides, farm implements, and other production inputs as well.

Burdwan district in West Bengal was included under the program during its second year (1962). Significant advances were made between 1962 and 1969 in increasing the irrigation potential during the principal growing seasons and in raising the proportion of land under double-cropping from seven to twenty percent.[20] However, because the new varieties, particularly the noted IR-8, were less well adapted to the cloudy, sodden conditions of the *Amon* season (the principal growing season fed by monsoon rainfall) than they were to the sunny, dry season (if irrigation were available), other factors in the package held greater promise than did the seeds.

Increased fertilizer application, even on the better local varieties, seemed to hold the greatest promise during the wet season.[21] Other obstacles stood in the way of a more widespread impact of IADP in Burdwan district. Among these were the uneven topography which made the cultivation of dwarf varieties of rice hazardous at times of flooding. Also, farms were highly fragmented and generally of uneconomic size. With a condition of high rates of land rental, it is reported that few cultivators had the means or felt incentives to invest in the Green Revolution.[22] Cooperatives have provided little assistance in the district to the majority of agricultural workers, those with three acres of land or less, because their economic condition is so unstable that the only source of credit generally open to them is through private moneylenders.[23] The weight of the evidence suggests that the Green Revolution is a rich man's plum: only those with over three acres of irrigated land, owned and operated, reported increases in rice yields and greater diversification of production.[24]

Even the political parties shunned the rural poor, at least up until the mid-1960s. And even then the Marxist parties stood to gain more political ground by promoting disaffection among the rural population than by prosecuting its cause.

Damodar Valley Corporation (DVC)

The valley of the Damodar River in West Bengal has a history of frequent flooding. The river was seriously implicated in the disastrous famine of 1943 when its waters breached the rail line that might have brought significant relief to the starving province. Because of the problems of flooding, the need for irrigation to serve agriculture, and the need for hydroelectric power to serve a growing industrial region, plans were laid in the years before partition. The valley was to be developed along lines analogous to those of the Tennessee Valley Authority of the United States. The upper valley, in Bihar, is rich in mineral resources and stood to gain as an industrial region from the development of hydroelectric power plants. The lower valley, in West Bengal, is an agricultural plain with considerable potential if flooding could be brought under control and significant irrigation facilities provided.

The disturbed political, administrative, and developmental situation at the time of partition was such that a positive program like that of the Damodar Valley Corporation (DVC) was accepted with few reservations by the legislatures at the center and in the states of Bihar and West Bengal. Flood control, irrigation and water supply, and the production and distribution of electricity were to be the principal functions of DVC.[25] An integrated series of dams was constructed to meet the multiple objectives of the project. During the rainy season the dams diverted excess water into their catchment areas for release during the dry season. The irrigation achievements in Bengal were only about two-thirds of the anticipated command area, due largely to the failure of Bengal government to provide connecting channels between the main canals and the farmers' fields.[26] Eventually, the DVC did construct some of these field channels. However, these operated in such a way that the water was largely unregulated and varied perversely in direct proportion to the pace of natural rainfall.[27]

Nonetheless, Bengal benefited greatly from the DVC because it received virtually all the advantages of flood control and most of those from irrigation. The dams were built in Bihar, where the hardships of relocation from the proposed catchment areas had to be borne by the population of that state. An ingenious set of formulas involving heavy central contributions was worked out in order to make the scheme attractive to the legislatures of both Bihar and Bengal.[28]

The inherent autonomy of the DVC, however, went down hard in both Bengal and Bihar. Most of this animosity was jealousy at seeing an independent power operating within state territory. Coupled with this was the awkwardness in each state government's having to ask and give concessions relating to the interests of a bordering state and the central government.[29]

In a course of events strikingly similar to the diminution of the powers of TVA and the rise of those of the participating states in the United States, Bengal and Bihar began to provide many of the services originally set up as the responsibilities of the DVC, especially the generation and distribution of electric power. What had been an attractive proposal during the turbulent times of independence turned into a source of annoyance and embarrassment to state leaders as conditions stabilized and each state acquired the effective powers to assert itself in relation to the center and its neighbor. Much of this assertiveness can be laid at the door of the West Bengal State Congress party.[30]

Calcutta Metropolitan Planning Organization (CMPO)

Despite its assertiveness in the case of the semiautonomous Damodar Valley Corporation, the State of West Bengal has, in effect, declared itself incapable of coping with the city of Calcutta. It turned to outside sources in the central government and international aid-giving agencies for the technical skills and financial support of a major regional planning effort.[31]

The allocations under the Third Five-Year Plan, the U.S. Food for Peace program, the Ford Foundation, and other organizations were substantial but the net results have been few. Certain critics feel, with some justification, that the government of West Bengal and the Calcutta Metropolitan Corporation are not taking the job of urban planning seriously enough to implement their principal recommendations.[32]

In many respects Calcutta is a national phenomenon whose problems extend well beyond those of West Bengal. The former prime minister, Jawaharlal Nehru, pointed out in 1961 that "Calcutta is the biggest city in the country. Its problems are national problems—quite apart from problems from West Bengal, and it is necessary that something special should be done."[33] The hinterland extends hundreds of miles to the west, into an industrial region that has been characterized as the Ruhr of India. Despite the far-reaching influence of the surrounding region on the city, and vice versa, there is nothing in the Basic Development Plan for the period 1966–1986 that recognizes the need for concommitant agricultural and rural development in the region.

EAST BENGAL AFTER INDEPENDENCE

Village Agricultural and Industrial Development (V-AID)

In the unsettled conditions of postpartition East Pakistan, rural development responsibilities were in the hands of the separately established departments of government. These included agencies dealing with agriculture, animal husbandry, forestry, fisheries, cooperation, marketing, health, and so forth.[34] Each had a hierarchical organization, uncoordinated with the hierarchies of any of the others. The problem was compounded by the paucity of technically trained personnel, who had opted for Pakistan following partition. Those personnel who were in the service of these agencies almost to a man lacked effective knowledge and experience of meaningful rural development work.

Because of these difficulties, the government of Pakistan endeavored to build a rural development extension service that, in a single agency, would serve the needs of all the nation-building departments. As a model, the government reached back to the same precedents on which India's Community Development Program had been established. Building on those precedents and on the contemporary experience of India's Community Development Programs and the United States extension programs, Pakistan launched its own effort in June 1952—the Village Agricultural and Industrial Development program (V-AID).

In 1938 a Rural Reconstruction Department had been established in Bengal, following on pioneering rural development efforts elsewhere in undivided India during the 1920s and 1930s.[35] However, the inappropriateness of having a development establishment separate from the nation-building departments was recognized by the Bengal Administration Enquiry Committee of 1944–1945. Upon the recommendations of this committee, known also as the Rowlands Committee, rural development responsibilities were to be assigned specifically to the technical and administrative branches of the civil service and integrated into local government activities.[36] Despite the principles emphasized at the time of the disbanding of the Rural Reconstruction Department just prior to partition, much the same kind of organization was reestablished in V-AID— largely because of the combined inability and unwillingness of the existing administrative machinery to meet the training and technical service needs for village development during the early days of independence.

Multipurpose village workers were trained at one of three original (later expanded) training institutes in East Pakistan. They were then assigned to the bottom rung of the V-AID organization. At these levels V-AID utilized specially constituted, locally elected councils of elders to legitimize and institutionalize local development efforts.[37] A hierarchy of advisory councils with units at each administrative echelon brought representatives of the technical departments into contact with the V-AID effort. The agency itself was organized into a separate hierarchy whose chief administrator was located at the Central Ministry of Economic Affairs. The chief administrator of V-AID in East Pakistan reported to the Provincial Commissioner of the Division of Planning.

To train the middle and higher ranks of V-AID personnel, an academy was established in East (as well as in West) Pakistan. This academy, located at Comilla, began operations in 1959, at a time when V-AID was on the threshold of dissolution.

Despite the application of a great deal of dedicated professional talent whose emotions and technical skills became wedded to the cause of rural development based on community development principles such as "self-help," "felt needs," and "local coordination," V-AID foundered on the realities of the bureaucratic powers it sought to bypass. The technical departments were subordinated in the programs. The chief officers of the administrative districts of the civil government were involved only as members of advisory committees, and the formal rural local government bodies were not even in the picture. This de facto confrontation flared into the open as the Agriculture Department became overtly competitive and as other supporters of integrated rural development (including the Comilla Academy) set off in more promising, if only slightly less turbulent, directions.[38]

In short order, V-AID was banned from working within the jurisdiction of the Directorate of Agriculture. A year later it was abolished altogether. The organization was gone but the problems remained:

> When V-AID failed in its attempt at coordination the province was left with serious problems: mutually exclusive departments trying to operate separate and sometimes conflicting programs in the mofussil; a civil administration unconnected with, and often unconcerned about, development programs; and a system of local self-government badly weakened.[39]

Agricultural Development Corporation (ADC)

Government decided on new endeavors to correct these problems. Despite its bureaucratic "victory" over V-AID, the Agriculture Department was still regarded as incapable of meeting the considerable needs for increasing agricultural production. The report of the Food and Agriculture Commission, released in November 1960, specifically stated that the department lacked the knowledge and facilities to do the job.[40] Despite the ill-fortune that the government of Pakistan seemed to be having with attempts to bypass entrenched and ineffective units of government, it did not give up. The success it experienced with the creation in 1959 of the engineering-oriented Water and Power Development Authority (WAPDA)[41] led it to attempt the establishment of a semiautonomous Agricultural Development Corporation (ADC). The primary responsibility of ADC was to procure and distribute agricultural production inputs (such as seeds, fertilizers, pesticides, and credit) and to extend knowledge through various information and training activities.

For many reasons the ADC was slow to organize. Not the least of the problems was the unwillingness of the Agriculture Department to yield to the recommendations of the Food and Agriculture Commission. Instead the department continued to expand its programs in the rural areas.

Basic Democracies and the Rural Works Program

After slightly more than a decade of independence in Pakistan, martial law was proclaimed by Mohammed Ayub Khan in a bloodless coup in October 1958. The effort was principally to restore order and direction to a nation whose political scene was approaching chaos and whose economic scene was stagnating. A year later Ayub Khan promulgated the broadly innovative "Basic Democracies Order," which reorganized local government. Not only was a new form of electoral college[42] organized under this order, but the system potentially became an instrument for greater local involvement in national affairs and for bringing public services closer to the rural areas and the towns.

Within the districts of East Bengal three tiers of local government were established. At the lowest level were the Union Councils. At the next higher jurisdiction, covering an administrative area of approximately one hundred square miles and a population of 150,000 to 200,000, were the Thana Councils. At each of the then seventeen districts were the District Councils. The Union Council bore a close resemblance to the Union Board set up under the Bengal Village Self-Government Act of 1919.[43] The members were elected within electoral wards from population clusters of about 10,000 persons (later raised to 12,500). The members of the Union Council elected their own chairman. Although the Union Council had a long list of optional functions and an income based on land revenue, it did not in fact progress much beyond the precedents of the Union Board in the decades prior to independence and fell short of meeting contemporary local government needs.[44]

Much the same could be said of the District Council, whose membership was composed of officials and representatives elected from the body of Union Council chairmen in the district. The council's revenue base was largely a share of the land revenue, although additional taxes could be levied. With an extended list of optional functions the District Council was provided with a fairly full scope. However, in 1963 it was reported that the new District Councils were suffering under the same weaknesses—lack of planning, inefficient administration, and a shortage of funds—which had plagued the old District Boards.[45]

The same could not be said of the Thana Council, especially after it became the object of intensive experimentation and development as a pilot project in the rural administration experiment of the Academy for Rural Development at Comilla. The Thana Council was an innovation without precedent at that hierarchical level. Originally established as the locus of a police station providing access to most rural areas within a walk of a few hours, the thana level of jurisdiction provided an opportunity to deliver other public services at a point closer to the rural people and to do so in a coordinated manner.[46] The district level had been the previous concentrated location of public services closest to the rural people. As increasing numbers of officers of the various nation-building departments were assigned to the thana level, they were organized into a thana office building constructed with funds under the Rural Works Program. At this location they could be more easily contacted by farmers and coordinated by thana-level supervisory administrators. The basic functions of the Thana Council were envisioned as planning and coordination.[47]

Unlike the Union and District Councils, there were no separate revenue sources available to the Thana Council other than grants from higher levels. This was fitting because the council, per se, had no executive functions beyond those which its members could exercise in their regular roles as government officers or as chairmen of the Union Councils within the thana.

The chairman of the Thana Council was the subdivisional officer (SDO), a young man near the beginning of his career in the higher civil service, the Civil Service of Pakistan (CSP). The SDO was at the same time chairman of all the Thana Councils within his subdivision and was thus available only intermittently. The day-to-day affairs of the Thana Council were in the hands of the circle officer, an appointed official in the provincial civil service, the East Pakistan Civil Service (EPCS). The appointed members of the Thana Council were thana-level government officers representing the administrative and technical cadres of the various government departments. The elected members were the chairmen of the Union Councils within the thana.

Several levels of administrative status and jurisdiction were represented at a fully attended Thana Council meeting, as were several levels of social station and background. This fact, coupled with the proximity to both rural people and government services, made it a natural object for experimentation. One challenge was to devise ways in which to make the Thana Council a cohesive functioning unit. Another was to fit the aptitudes of the council to development needs.

Government officers were not accustomed to coordinating with each other, much less with elected rural leaders. The early meetings of the pilot Thana Council in Comilla were marked by erratic attendance and confusion over roles and status.[48] A need for training and for a functional raison d'être had to be filled. Intrinsically the members of the council were not rural development planners, and their entire experience was contrary to the norm of coordinated and cooperative rural involvement.

One role that did seem to come more easily to the local council than any other was the management of rural public works projects at low cost. This

discovery came at a time when the U.S. Food for Peace program had
provided surplus food grain to Pakistan. The leader of the Harvard Development Advisory Service Team in Pakistan suggested that a rural
works program be attempted in East Pakistan on a pilot basis in Comilla
Thana.[49] The pilot project adapted a rural planning device from Malaysia
—the Red Book, which was a series of map worksheets and detailed
instructions. The elected and appointed members of the Thana Council
worked under the guidance of the circle officer, who had been through a
special training course at the Academy for Rural Development. They
prepared base maps of the existing drainage canal and road network and
a series of annual plan maps that were designed to meet the priority needs
for drainage canals, culverts, ridges, and village roads over a period of
five or more years. Because similar plans were being concurrently laid for
rural works adapted to the jurisdiction of the Union Council and the
District Council, extended coordination of plans was undertaken between
hierarchical levels. Technical engineering opinions were provided under a
mandate to the Water and Power Development Authority (WAPDA).
The methods for identifying projects, for assigning them priorities, for
collating Thana Council and Union Council projects, for securing technical opinions from such agencies as WAPDA, for training local project
committees (chaired by Union Council members) to supervise local labor
hired during the dry season, for using Food for Peace wheat in partial
payment of wages (a practice displaced in later years by wage payments
using proceeds from government sales of the wheat), for measuring physical accomplishments, for keeping records and accounts, and for establishing working relationships between government officers and council members—all were incorporated into a manual of procedures. This manual
became the basis for the training program and operational guidance of
the Rural Works Program as it was expanded from its pilot phase to all of
East Pakistan and subsequently to the whole country. Not only did the
Rural Works Program provide a rural infrastructure;[50] it also gave local
officials and elected leaders experience and confidence in managing public
affairs in coordination with other units of local government and with the
available technical public services.[51]

The Comilla Pilot Project in Rural Cooperatives

An alternative approach to rural cooperatives was experimented with on a
significant scale in Comilla Thana by the Academy for Rural Development beginning in 1960.[52] Although variously stated in various sources,
the objectives of the project eventually worked out to be:

1. The *organization* of economically dispersed small holders, share-

croppers, and laborers who were vulnerable in their dealings with commercial traders, moneylenders, landlords, and employers.

2. The *training* of rural people in technical vocational skills, problem-
solving, management procedure, hygiene, literacy, and related develop-
mentally relevant knowledge, attitudes, and skills which were unavailable
from traditional sources in village society.

3. The provision of *supportive services* especially for the promotion of
productivity and income. These included organizational and production
planning assistance, access to credit and other production inputs, to
technical information, and to stable markets.

4. The constructive guidance through *discipline*, both in the form of
positive inducements such as access to the services mentioned above, and
to a certain extent in the form of negative sanctions. These controls con-
serve scarce resources and provide mutual protection against individual
vagaries.[53]

The project's intent was to give rural people the capacity to participate
in shaping their own futures and to enter into collaborative relations with
government and other institutions in effecting developments that were
beyond the capacity of government alone.

The Comilla pilot project in rural cooperatives comprised a system of
village-level cooperative societies integrated under a central cooperative
association which acted as a servicing headquarters for all the cooperatives
within the hundred or so square miles of the thana. The basic unit was the
village-based cooperative, which was integrated into the cooperative system. Although each cooperative was formed voluntarily by a group of
local farmers, they obligated themselves to follow a program of activities
that took full advantage of the services provided through the central
cooperative association.

A primary society had about forty members who selected their own
leaders. The membership was expected to meet weekly under the coordination of the manager to discuss financial management, technical training
in agriculture, and other matters. Each member was also expected to
purchase at least one ten-rupee share in the central association each year
and to make a small savings account deposit every week (the minimum
amount was decided by each local society—usually a quarter of a rupee or
more). Each week the manager of the cooperative society visited the
central association's headquarters to deposit these funds and have them
recorded. While there he attended training classes on seasonally important agricultural topics. Another member of the village cooperative,
selected to be the "model farmer," attended regular training sessions held
at conveniently located centers in the rural areas. These two officers of the

primary society acted as de facto agents in their home villages, leading training sessions at each weekly meeting and using their own landholdings as demonstrations.

Credit, power pump irrigation, tractor cultivation, the supply of improved varieties of seeds, fertilizers, and pesticides, and the processing and marketing of farm products were among the services provided by the central association. The members of the local cooperatives were expected to make the fullest possible use of these services. The amount which could be borrowed by members of a local cooperative depended on the total savings of the group together with the amount they held as shares in the central association, and qualified by an appraisal of the functional viability and vigor of the cooperative. The loans were allocated within the society by the managing committee according to a general production plan in which the purpose of each member's loan was stated. The financial arrangement for savings and loans constituted a rural banking system.

In time, nonagricultural cooperatives were organized in Comilla Thana among local craftsmen, cycle rickshaw operators, and others (many of whom were landless laborers). As the membership of these groups increased it became necessary for two intervening "federations" to be organized between the primary cooperatives and the central association: one for agricultural cooperatives and one for nonagricultural (special) cooperatives. Each federation maintained accountants and inspectors who acted as tutors and overseers of the progress of the societies, the accuracy of their records, and the progress of individual members. These inspectors kept a lookout for weaknesses and breakdowns in the system. Difficulties which the inspectors could not resolve on the spot during their field visits were referred to the appropriate federation for corrective action. The federations could, if necessary, exert pressure for compliance by withholding essential services or, as a last resort, they could sell collateral assets to recover defaulted loans—although this was rarely necessary.

The development of the cooperative project was tied in with the academy's pilot project in rural administration. The rural cooperative system was envisioned as an integral element in the Thana Training and Development Center. The support was mutual, since the cooperatives bolstered the government's rural development activities and the local officials served as trainers at the weekly classes for managers and others.

The expansion of the pilot project beyond the initial experimental area of Comilla Thana took place in several stages. In mid-1963, three thana projects were set up, one in each of three other divisions of the Province of East Pakistan. These were located adjacent to training institutes operated by the Department of Basic Democracies and Local Government. Key staff members underwent a six months' course of training at Comilla. These principal staff members, once they were posted, continued to coordinate through a specially designated supervisory officer located at Comilla and through attendance at monthly coordination conferences.[54] Following a pattern similar to the three earlier expansion thanas, the Comilla model was readapted in 1965 in seven other thanas of Comilla district.[55] Because the Comilla project was a pilot operation, the expansion projects were administered by the Directorate of Agriculture and later by the Agricultural Development Corporation. Collaborative arrangements existed between these agencies and the Comilla Academy, especially with respect to training and coordination.

Although numerous difficulties were encountered in attempting to implement these expansions of the original model, there was considerable progress. As of June 1968, there were 339 primary cooperative societies in Comilla Thana, of which 78 were nonagricultural.[56] As of June 1967, less than two percent of the loans made between 1961 and 1967 were overdue.[57] In mid-1968 there were 673 primary agricultural societies in the three expansion thanas launched in mid-1963, with a loan repayment rate of ninety-two percent.[58] In the seven thanas elsewhere in Comilla district into which the Comilla-type cooperative model had been expanded in 1966, a total of 948 primary societies had been established and a loan repayment rate of eighty-two percent was reported.[59]

Thana Irrigation Plan (TIP)

At this time expanison was methodically continuing into the remaining thirteen thanas of Comilla district, as well as into other areas on a modified basis. However, questions were also being raised regarding the pace of rural transformation. The Comilla-type cooperative system was a relatively sophisticated complex requiring considerable time to establish and institutionalize a viable network of agricultural and nonagricultural societies linked to a central servicing headquarters and to the agencies of the civil administration.

As an alternative to pursuing the strategy of first building up fairly sophisticated system of cooperative societies to spread agricultural modernization and technological change, a reverse procedure was suggested. It was proposed to utilize the method of planning through the Thana Councils that had been successfully worked out under the Rural Works Program as a device for planning the installation for power pump facilities and irrigation channels on a broad scale. Irrigation was seen as the chief technological requirement for rapid agricultural change under monsoon conditions which included a long dry season. Pump and motor sets were to be integrated with special local farmer organizations that could be set up as irrigation groups. Their relatively simple structure made the irrigation groups more amenable to rapid expansion. This program was accepted by government and formalized as the Expanded Works Program —Thana Irrigation Plan (TIP), with a target of installing forty thousand pumps in the province over a five-year period.

In addition to the complex of supporting institutions provided locally through the planning and coordination of the Thana Council, administrative support at the highest level was secured through a provincial coordinating committee that included the chief administrators of the Department of Local Government, the Agricultural Directorate, the Water and Power Development Authority, and the Agricultural Development Corporation. Agricultural credit was introduced into the irrigation program with the support of the Agricultural Development Bank, the Provincial Cooperative Bank, and the medium of Tacavi loans under the revenue administration. The sequence of activities was leading ultimately to the integration of other services into the program.

The growing perception of the comprehensive nature of rural development needs, and the existence of encouraging demonstrations of other integrated programs, led in 1969 to the placement of a formal proposal before the Pakistan Planning Commission to establish multifaceted rural development cooperative projects in all the thanas of East Bengal along lines adapted from the Comilla experiment.

It was at approximately this time that natural calamity and civil unrest swept the province. However, it did not fail the notice of the administrators of martial law that the areas where the projects were established had gone through the period with greater stability, on the whole, than had most other areas. Progress was suspended because of the worsening political situation. War broke out in March 1971, making constructive action impossible.

REFLECTIONS ON RURAL PUBLIC POLICY

Rural development policy in Bengal must cope with some concerns that are unique to the region and with others that are broadly shared with other densely populated agrarian areas. The density of population, the low levels of education, the incidence of disease, the vulnerability to a dramatic climate, and the shallow governmental capacity in the nation-building public services are problems experienced in many other parts of the world. But the specific ways in which these problems appear in Bengal are, of course, unique. Also unique is the mystique of being a "Bengali," a member of a large linguistic, cultural, and historical entity that is perceived internally and externally as distinct from other areas. Despite these complicating factors, and many others, public policy for rural development will have to deal with at least six basic issues.

First, the rural scene is a "system" of broad relationships that, at least in concept, need to be perceived as integrated. Such a perspective indicates the need to gather information, select goals, mobilize resources and interests around these goals, and plan a foundation of nationhood that can be shared. This approach highlights a need for integrated local and central planning. The administrative services of government must also be integrated with private, commercial, and social interests. Dynamic stability and leadership at the highest levels are essential.

Second, investments in flood control, irrigation, transportation, electric power, public buildings, and other facilities will need to be made with foresight and determination well beyond the demand for short-term economic benefits.

Third, investments in agricultural research and extension (including crop and animal husbandry, rural credit and banking, special education, and the like) will have to be made so as to take advantage of international developments and to involve the relevant elements in the rural areas.

Fourth, rural governing instutitions will have to be developed according to the goals that have been selected. Rural planning and public facilities bodies will be necessary to manage local irrigation, marketing, banking, credit, education, and public works in collaboration with institutions at higher levels.

Fifth, revenue and other fiscal institutions—including competent assessment and collection agencies as well as policy- and law-making institutions—will have to be developed to build a system of resource mobilization and allocation. Poverty and low productivity mask the rich resource base of Bengal, which could be developed.

Sixth, a flexible approach needs to be fostered in the reformation or design of rural policies and institutions. The pilot projects at Comilla and elsewhere offer hard evidence to government that standing practice can be modified.

The tasks faced by any government are immense, and the governments in Bengal have been deeply involved in these tasks with the help of, and in spite of, their domestic and international well-wishers and critics. Although inevitably flavored with utopian sentiment, the cases I have discussed offer lessons that should not go unnoticed.

NOTES

1.   Marcus F. Franda, "West Bengal," in *State Politics in India*, ed. Myron Weiner (Princeton: Princeton University Press, 1968), n. 1, p. 247.

2.   Haroun er Rashid, *East Pakistan. A Systematic Regional Geography and its Development Planning Aspects*, 2nd ed.(Lahore,Pakistan: Sh. Ghulam & Sons, 1967), pp. 151–153.

3.   West Bengal State Statistical Bureau, *Report on Sample Survey for Estimation of Acreage and Yield Rates, 1959–60* (Alipore, West Bengal: West Bengal

Government press, 1965), part 1, table 10, p. 27; part 2, table 10, p. 21.

4.   Rashid, op. cit., p. 207; West Bengal State Statistical Bureau, op. cit., part 1, table 10.1, p. 28.

5.   United States Agency for International Development/Mission to Pakistan, *Statistical Fact Book: Selected Economic and Social Data on Pakistan* (Islamabad, Pakistan: USAID Mission, 1968), table 6.14.

6.   Francine R. Frankel, *India's Green Revolution: Economic Gains and Political Costs* (Princeton: Princeton University Press, 1971), tables 9 and 10, pp. 165, 166.

7.   Hugh Tinker, *South Asia: A Short History* (New York: Praeger, 1966), pp. 107–110.

8.   Elliot Tepper, *Changing Patterns of Administration in Rural East Pakistan* (East Lansing: Asian Studies Center, Michigan State University, August 1966), p. 5.

9.   B. M. Bhatia, *Famines in India* (London: Asia Publishing House, 1963), pp. 130–131.

10.   Tepper, op. cit., pp. 7–8.

11.   Ibid., p. 10.

12.   Bhatia, op. cit., p. 7.

13.   Tepper, op. cit., p. 13.

14.   Ibid., p. 17.

15.   Kalimuddin Ahmed, *Agriculture in East Pakistan* (Dacca, East Pakistan: Ahmed Brothers Publications, 1965), pp. 332–333.

16.   Ralph W. Nicholas and Tarashis Mukhopadhyay, "Politics and Law in Two West Bengal Villages," *Bulletin of the Anthropological Survey of India*, vol. XI, no. 1, p. 34.

17.   Ibid., p. 36.

18.   Frankel, op. cit., pp. 188–189.

19.   Ford Foundation, *Report on India's Food Crisis and Steps to Meet It* (New Delhi: Government of India, Ministry of Food and Agriculture and Ministry of Community Development and Cooperation, 1959).

20.   Frankel, op. cit., p. 160.

21.   Ibid., p. 163.

22.   Ibid., pp. 163–169.

23.   Ibid., pp. 170–172.

24.   Ibid., pp. 173–175.

25.   K. S. S. Raju, "The Damodar Valley Corporation" (unpublished manuscript, March 1970), p. 9.

26.   Ibid., p. 20.

27.   Frankel, op. cit., p. 158.

28.   Marcus F. Franda, *West Bengal and the Federalizing Process in India* (Princeton: Princeton University Press, 1968), pp. 72–74.

29.   Ibid., pp. 89–95.

30.   Ibid., p. 127.

31.   Franda, "West Bengal," pp. 315–316.

32.   Calcutta Metropolitan Planning Organization. *Basic Development Plan: Calcutta Metropolitan District 1966–68* (Calcutta: Government of West Bengal, Development and Planning Department, CMPO, 1966), preface; see also Franda, "West Bengal," fn. 110, p. 316.

33.   As quoted in Calcutta Metropolitan Planning Organization, op, cit., preface.

34.   Government of Pakistan, *A Report on Agricultural Extension Work in the U.S.A. and Reorganization of Extension Service in Pakistan* (Karachi: Government of Pakistan Press, 1952), p. 26.

35.   The noted work of F. L. Brayne in Gurgaon district (Punjab) while he was deputy commissioner, of Spencer Hatch in South Travancore, of Rabindronath Tagore at Shriniketan, and of Malcom Darling, although impermanent, was influential on much of the work taken up by governments at a later date.

36.   Tepper, op. cit., p. 104.

37.   Jack D. Mezirow, *Dynamics of Community Development* (New York: The Scarecrow Press, 1963), pp. 56–63.

38.   See Mezirow, op. cit., pp. 133–135; Tepper, op. cit., pp. 19–20; and Akhter Hameed Khan, "The Pakistan Academy for Rural Development, Comilla" (text of a presentation delivered at the Massachusetts Institute of Technology, July 1964, and printed in *Rural Development in East Pakistan: Speeches of Akhter Hameed Khan* (East Lansing: Asian Studies Center, Michigan State University, 1964), pp. 21–51.

39.   Tepper, op. cit., p. 105.

40.   As cited in Tepper, op, cit., p. 21.

41.   Nicolaas Luykx, "Organizing for More Effective Labor Utilization in Rural East Pakistan," in *Some Issues Emerging from Recent Breakthroughs in Food Production*, ed. Kenneth L. Turk (Ithaca: New York State College of Agriculture, 1971), pp. 154–155.

42.   Karl von Vorys, *Political Development in Pakistan* (Princeton: Princeton University Press, 1965), pp. 197, 272–273, passim.

43.   Tepper, op. cit., p. 106.

44.   A. T. R. Rahman, *Basic Democracies at the Grass Roots: A Study of Three Union Councils in Kotwali (Comilla) Thana* (Comilla, East Pakistan: Pakistan Academy for Rural Development, 1962), p. 15; and Tepper, op. cit., p. 108.

45.   Richard O. Niehoff and George M. Platt, "Local Government in East Pakistan" (unpublished manuscript), cited in Tepper, op. cit., p. 110.

46.   A. K. M. Mohsen, *The Comilla Rural Administration Experiement: History and Annual Report 1962–63* (Comilla, East Pakistan: Pakistan Academy for Rural Development, October 1963), pp. 51–64.

47.   Akhter Hameed Khan, "Note Prepared for Mr. Azfar, Chief Secretary, Government of East Pakistan, May 1959," as reproduced in Moshen, op. cit., appendix C-1, pp. 88–89.

48.   Mohsen, op. cit., pp. 18–24.

49.   Khan, "The Pakistan Academy," pp. 49–51.

50.   John W. Thomas, "Rural Public Works in East Pakistan's Development" (Cambridge, Mass.: Development Advisory Service, Center for International Affairs, Harvard University, Economic Development Report No. 112, 1968).

51.   Tepper, op. cit., p. 119.

52.   The progress of this experiment has been widely reported on. Primary sources are in the annual reports of the cooperative project published by the Academy for Rural Development beginning in 1961; additional data are collected in Arthur F. Raper and others, *Rural Development in Action: The Comprehensive Experiment at Comilla, East Pakistan* (Ithaca: Cornell University Press, 1971).

53.   Nicolaas Luykx, "Rural Governing Institutions," in *Institutions in Agricultural Development*, ed. Melvin G. Blase (Ames: Iowa State University Press, 1971), pp. 195–203.
54.   Raper, op. cit., pp. 235–236.
55.   Ibid., pp. 238–239.
56.   Ibid., table D, p. 308.
57.   Ibid., p. 74.
58.   Ibid., p. 236.
59.   Ibid., p. 241.

A Bibliographic Essay on Bengal
Studies in The United States

DAVID KOPF
University of Minnesota

In May 1972, at the Eighth Annual Bengal Studies Conference in Toronto, some fifty scholars participated in seven panels dealing with a variety of topics ranging from Brahmo contact with Unitarianism in the nineteenth century to current priorities in Bangladesh. As with every other conference since the earliest one at Michigan State in 1965, ideas were hotly discussed, and even mediocre papers with vaguely formed issues evoked sharp controversy, while clarity and academic detachment remained the two scholarly virtues conspicuously absent during the proceedings. And, as always, each American participant succumbed to that indefinable, indefensible, and indefatigable spirit or mystique of Bengal which in the face of chronic disaster—from the partition of 1905 to the bloody birth of Bangladesh—has produced a rapturous ambivalence between love and hate, optimism and pessimism, loyalty and alienation.

To understand the progress of Bengal studies in the United States during the last decade, one must somehow account for that zealous and irrational appreciation of Bengal by American academics who are generally conservative in bestowing affection, rational by profession, and relatively dull in choice of lifestyle. The Bengal known to American scholars who have lived and researched there over the last decade is without doubt the most politically unstable and the most violent state in South Asia, the most troubled socially, and the least progressive economically. The great Bengali urban metropolis of Calcutta (where most of the Americans under consideration have lived for a year or more) has the distinction among Indian cities of having been treated by the world press in a consistently derogatory manner as the "city of dreadful night."[1] Calcutta's image and prospects were perhaps best summed up by a sympathetic *New York Times* correspondent a few years ago in an article entitled "Can India Survive Calcutta?"[2]

Nevertheless, with few exceptions, most of the graduate students who were trained as Bengal specialists between 1958 and 1964 have persisted in their chosen field. Edward Dimock, who inspired the majority of them in a seminar on the cultural and literary history of Bengal at Chicago, has attributed the enthusiasm for Bengali culture to the attraction of the language, to Bengal's "long and lush . . . literary tradition," to Bengal's "tremendous fund of source material," and to Bengal's rich and diversified history.[3] Moreover, Dimock contended that American scholars with area studies background and with competence in a modern South Asian language had become impatient with "simplistic thinking" about the "macrocosm" of India and were instead probing deeply into the "microcosm" of regional cultures.[4] In Dimock's words, "we must begin to examine in necessarily minute detail the single strands which make up the complex fabric of India."[5] Each region of the subcontinent has unique aspects which are in "themselves fascinating and highly individual, and as such worthy of study and understanding."[6] Parochialism, however, is not the objective of the American student of Bengal: "it is through the unit that we are attempting to approach the totality."[7]

Part of the emotional commitment to Bengal, therefore, is to be explained as a consequence of an area studies training and an emphasis on regional languages and cultures. Bengal happened to be selected as the first experiment to justify the hypothesis and one can only imagine the excitment of the pioneers whose articles and monographs opened a virtual new world. In an editorial preface to the second volume of the Bengal studies proceedings, I noted that:

> In May, 1966, the University of Missouri played host to the second annual conference on Bengal Studies which had convened to discuss "Bengal Regionalism: Origins and Conceptual Problems." There was much confusion and uncertainty about the validity of intensive regional studies in those days and we were often criticized by well-meaning scholars who were doing precisely the same thing for Punjab, Maharashtra, and the Dravidian South. Though most of us were quick to defend the regional approach, we were conceptually unsure of ourselves. Evidently we were not alone that year in trying to avoid a crisis of scholarly identity between India and Bengal, Maharashtra, or the Punjab. A month earlier, Robert I. Crane had assembled South Asian notables of every region and discipline at Duke University to inquire into "Regions and Regionalism in South Asian Studies."[8]

ACADEMIC PROFILE OF THE BENGAL SPECIALIST

This essay deals with a selection of the published work of fourteen scholars—thirteen Americans and one acculturated New Zealander—who in the estimation of their peers have made solid contributions to Bengal studies. Who are these persons? Where were they educated and what was their intellectual orientation to South Asia? What are their disciplines and their general characteristics as scholars of Bengal studies? Interestingly, the two senior scholars who published earliest on Bengal, Edward Dimock and Stephen Hay, were Harvard Ph.D.'s. Dimock worked in the Department of Sanskrit and Indic Studies, whereas Hay was a product of the Department of History with a specialized interest in East Asia.

In the late 1950s both these men joined the University of Chicago during the period of formative growth of the university's South Asia Center. At the initiative of Myron Weiner, a political scientist specializing on India, the Bengali language was first offered at the university. The early interest in Bengal by Dimock, Hay, and Weiner explains why Chicago produced so many graduate students committed to that region of South Asia. And of those students, the majority were in history, a discipline which traditionally favored intensive area concentration. Thus among Hay's students up to 1964 were included Philip Calkins, Leonard Gordon (on leave from Harvard), Warren Gunderson, Ronald Inden, Barrie Morrision, and myself. Weiner's student of Bengal was Marcus Franda while Ralph Nicholas from anthropology was the first graduate from that department with the same regional specialization.

At the University of Pennsylvania under Norman Brown's direction, South Asia Regional Studies was established as a department offering degrees to doctoral candidates with a concentration in one of several disciplines. Rachel Van M. Baumer received her doctoral degree from this program after having studied Bengali literature with the late T. W. Clark. Blair Kling developed his interest in modern Bengali history there while studying with Holden Furber, dean of South Asian historians in America. John McLane and John Broomfield, the former an American and the latter a New Zealander, are both historians who were area-trained abroad. McLane is a graduate of British universities whereas Broomfield studied at Australian National University.

Among the pioneers of Bengal studies over the last decade, historians predominate. Of the fourteen, ten are trained historians while two others are strongly influenced by history in their work. This stress has made most of the Bengal scholars conscious of the temporal dimension, of processes and stages of growth and decline, of the need to view Bengali society and culture dynamically rather than statically. Most conferences and seminars on Bengal have been organized chronologically around major historical periods, and one of the leading questions that invariably emerges at such gatherings deals with the problem of change and continuity in Bengali culture.

On the other hand, a great emphasis on the little tradition of Bengal as against the great tradition of India, the relativistic bias of some anthropologists at Chicago, and the inevitable consequences of regional identity have modified the characteristic historicity of the group by stressing the inner structure of the culture more than the irruptive external forces and movements impinging on it. Those Bengal scholars who have sought a key to the unique culture of the region have tended to treat historical changes as irrelevant happenings which hardly touch the hard core of the closed system.

Nonetheless, the Bengal specialist has not gone to ideological extremes in his work. Other influences and considerations have operated in the field. If, for example, historians predominate among Bengal specialists, it is the modernists who predominate among historians. This tendency may be explained as a result of a happy coalescence of interests between advocates of regionalism in South Asia and representatives of the Department of Health, Education, and Welfare anxious to extend fellowships to students achieving linguistic competence in the crucial languages of Asia. The National Defense Education Act center idea favored Bengali or Marathi or Hindi because they were the living languages of the Indian people. It is probably safe to generalize that agencies willing and able to send Americans to India or Pakistan favored proposals on problems that were of contemporary interest or at least modern in the sense of tracing the origins of present-day concerns. Therefore, it should come as no surprise that though only Nicholas and Franda among the fourteen are social scientists per se, the majority of historians are greatly influenced by social science methods and techniques.

Thus it can be said that the Bengal specialist is subject to a number of influences: historical perspective, cultural relativism, social science, and present-day concerns. Nor is it possible to establish for him any neat category between the social sciences and humanities. As area specialist exposed to both approaches and as historians who by the nature of their craft must belong to both camps, Bengal scholars have thus far proved a mixed bag indeed.

An Analysis of Bengal Scholarship in America

Probably the first work of consequence by an American scholar of Bengal appeared in 1963 with the publication of Edward Dimock's translation of Bengali tales from court and village in a volume entitled *The Thief of Love*. Dimock had three purposes in bringing out the volume: to justify the regional approach to South Asia by showing "that there is a good deal of enjoyment as well as enlightment to be had from study of the regional literatures of South Asia"[9]; to illuminate the medieval period of

India, "that period from the thirteenth through the eighteenth centuries"[10]; and to meet a need clearly felt at the University of Chicago: "there are precious few translations from the literature of the medieval period of any South Asian language."[11]

Dimock's volume, as he described it, was a pioneer effort to open up a new world or perhaps rediscover it. "When we considered India at all," he wrote, "most people of my generation, growing up in the thirties and forties, thought of it in terms of the British Empire."[12] It was not the real India that people conjured up in their minds but a series of images generated by popular literature and the cinema. Said Dimock, "India was a British land, and her culture, represented to us in movie versions of Kipling stories, was that of Britain, re-enacted in a tropical and foreign land."[13] The second set of images Dimock sought to counter was that of the nineteenth-century Orientalist scholar who conceived India largely in terms of the Sanskritic-oriented culture or great tradition of the Indian macrocosm. It was Dimock's conviction that by moving away from the British and Orientalist perceptions of India and by moving into the popular cultures and popular languages of the regions, a new and richer dimension of understanding about India could be achieved.

Dimock's partiality for medieval Bengali language and literature and his emphasis on the interaction of the classical great tradition (Aryan) with the regional traditions (Dravidian) had important implications which later Bengal scholars did not always accept. Dimock argued in his introduction that Bengali stood to Sanskrit rather much as Italian did to Latin. Surely if the objective of the scholar were to explore Italian history and culture, he would prefer to work with Italian sources rather than Latin. But then Dimock's analogy took a certain twist when he referred to a Bengali literary tradition that has been "unbroken from the ninth or tenth century Buddhist esoteric texts called *caryā-padas*, to the present."[14] The first difficulty was Dimock's overly close identification between the regional language of Bengal spoken today and its linguistic and literary phase of development during the middle ages. The second difficulty was that he did not carry the analogy between Bengali and European languages far enough in the historical perspective of change and continuity. Is the language of the Italian people today the language of the pre-Renaissance period? Do the English people today speak in the idiom of Chaucer? As for Bengal, is the literature of the Bengali people today really the same as the literature of the pre-Muslim period? Is the Bengali of Caṇḍidāsa the same Bengali of Rabindranath Tagore? Dimock's stress on origins and the unbroken continuity of a tradition thus turned the quest inward in the direction of a closed inner core of the Bengali culture which, it was believed, remained pure and immune from revolution, invasion, and conquest—and from the processes of modernization which had been transforming Western literary traditions for centuries since the Renaissance.

Not surprising, therefore, is the fact that Dimock chose as his last translation chronologically in *The Thief of Love* Bharatchandra's *Vidyā-Sundara*, composed sometime before 1760. The British began to dominate Bengal about then: the victory at Plassey was in 1756; the selection of Calcutta as capital was in 1772; the development of a new Bengali prose style was dated from 1800 with the establishment of the College of Fort William; and the reform work of Rammohun Roy, "father of modern India," has generally been set at about 1815. From then on, a radically new Bengali language and literature emerged through textbook translations, journalism, novels, short stories, poetry, and drama. The writers were among the newly risen Western-educated intelligentsia whose creative outburst and ideological pursuits on behalf of modernism and a new cultural identity have come to be known as the Bengal renaissance.

In 1965, sandwiched between articles in *Changing Japanese Attitudes Toward Modernization*, there appeared a lone piece on Indian modernization by Stephen Hay: "Western and Indigenous Elements in Modern Indian Thought: The Case of Rammohun Roy." With Hay, among Americans interested in Bengal, Dimock's quest backward in time to understand continuity was shifted to the future to understand change. And instead of Dimock's preoccupation with the sources of the inner culture, Hay addressed himself to the study of Bengal in interaction with the Western world. "All through the non-Western world in recent centuries," wrote Hay, "the pace of change has been vastly accelerated by contact and conflict with the expanding society and culture of the modern West."[15] Hay too conceived of himself as a pioneer, not merely of discovering new facts about Bengal but of contributing new ideas to the evolving conceptual scheme on the problem of Asian modernity in the context of cultural encounter and accommodation with the West. He said: "Our problem, then, is to create and refine a conceptual framework for the study of change in non-Western civilizations, within which indigenous and Western, traditional and modern elements can be analyzed and meaningfully related to each other."[16]

Hay's choice of Bengal as his region of inquiry apparently did not stem from any strong commitment to the language and culture. "Nowhere in India were Western influences stronger, and Indian responses more vigorous, than in the region where the British planted their capital: Bengal."[17] This was Hay's justification for selection of venue. It was Hay, while depicting the new class of upper-caste "Hindu gentry" responding favorably to the "cultural traditions of their new rulers," who first coined the term *bhadralok*[18] as a conceptual device for comprehending the Bengali elite under British colonialism and imperialism.

Rammohun Roy, born in 1772, twelve years after Bharatchandra's death, was chosen by Hay because he was the "first Indian intellectual seriously to study the civilization of the West."[19] Moreover, Rammohun expressed in his writings "the fundamental ideas on the nature and relationship of Indian and Western society and culture whose implications have been worked out by a succession of later thinkers and reformers, and are still being worked out today."[20] Therefore, by studying Rammohun one could learn something significant not merely about Bengal but also about "the nature and relationship of indigenous and Western, traditional and modern elements in nineteenth and twentieth century Indian thought."[21]

The importance of this article by Hay and of his general approach to the history of Bengal is that it cleared away many of the Eurocentric attitudes about modernity in South Asia and opened new vistas for dealing with the general problem in a more objective, scientific, and sophisticated manner. In point of fact, Hay never offered anything new about Rammohun or about the Bengal of Rammohun's time. In the article, available information on Rammohun was used to advance an idea and to promote interest in a valuable line of questions. Through Rammohun, for example, Hay finally worked out a definition of modernization: "a continuing process of improvement directed toward the achievement of this-worldly enlightenment and well-being through the sustained and systematic application of reason."[22] Hay's conclusion that Rammohun was a modernizer of his own tradition rather than a westernizer was no less important in implication than his conclusion that the impact of British intrusion in Bengal did in fact constitute a watershed between tradition and modernity in South Asia:

> Westerners . . . brought to South Asia traditions of modernization which have transformed the views of Hindu and Muslim intellectuals toward their own traditions, making it impossible for them to return to their pre-modern, or traditionalist, orthodoxies. It is only a question of time until creative individuals come forward to continue the work pioneered by Rammohun Roy of selecting, reinterpreting, and integrating traditions from many civilizations, within the framework neither of traditionalism, nor of revivalism, but of continuing cultural modernization.[29]

In 1966 two rather different books on Bengal were published: Edward Dimock's *The Place of the Hidden Moon*, and *The Blue Mutiny* by Blair Kling. Both had been doctoral dissertations, Dimock's dealing with erotic mysticism in the Vaiṣṇava-Sahajiyā cult of Bengal and Kling's dealing with the Indigo Disturbances in Bengal between 1859 and 1862. In terms of the problem of continuity and change in Bengal, Dimock was clearly reinforcing his earlier work by steeping himself in the literary and religious tradition of Vaiṣṇavism as expressed in the sixteenth century during the era of Caitanya and his disciples. Kling, on the other hand, dealt directly and effectively with changing agrarian patterns as a result of British intrusion and responses to it by Bengali cultivators, zemindars, and the urbanized intelligentsia of Calcutta.

Dimock's sources for *The Place of the Hidden Moon* were mostly Bengali and Sanskrit texts which he employed laboriously and expertly as building blocks in constructing as it were the architecture of Bengali culture. To be sure, Dimock established a comparative bridge between leading themes of Bengali Vaiṣṇavism and similar themes in the European medieval tradition—as, for example, the existence among Christian and Hindu poets of an apparent parodox between the spiritual "sacred" and the carnal "profane."[24] The attempt to reconcile love of spirit and love of flesh as two warring intellectual or religious principles was, in Dimock's opinion, not a cultural peculiarity but "a human peculiarity" (neither East nor West).[25] This applied to the "two essential phases or characteristics of love, union and separation," which were human and not cultural.[26] Wrote Dimock:

> In Bernard's image, the soul "desires" to be united with the Christ, and this statement emphasizes that the two are separate. It is this aspect of the image which is most usual to Christian, and I might add to orthodox Vaiṣṇava, poets, although the pain of separation always suggests the joy of union. For love in separation is pure love, spiritual love.[27]

These comparative assessments, especially the subsequent subtleties about love and marriage in the two great traditions of religious poetry, are extremely sensitive and useful both in comparative mysticism and in comparative medieval religious systems. But Dimock's purpose in all this, it seems to me, was not to break down discrete systems as a universalist but to win recognition and equality for a Bengali tradition by showing its functional equivalent in the hallowed heritage of the Western tradition. Thus Dimock argued effectively that the Vaiṣṇava-Sahajiyā combination of sacred and profane love is neither uniquely the manifestation of a non-Christian heathen faith nor to be "passed off as the product of a primitive mentality."[28]

Dimock's monograph represented one of the most sensitive and inspired attempts to resurrect a medieval tradition of India done in the twentieth century. It was also a masterful attempt to rectify a false image of both Sahajiyās and Vaiṣṇavas allegedly using religion as a pretext for orgies of self-gratification. Dimock, for instance, made an early and careful distinction between *kāma* and *prema* (carnal and spiritual love, respectively) as applied to the Rādhā-Kṛṣṇa theme in Bengali poetry:

> True love is prema, the love that Rādhā and the Gopīs had for Kṛṣṇa, the love that the true worshipper emulates, which, when he has realized himself as Kṛṣṇa and his partner as Rādhā, he could not help emulating. In his attitude and in his worship there can be no trace of kāma, of carnal desire, of desire for the satisfaction of the self; kāma, unless it is transformed into true love, prema, leads not to joy, but to misery and hell.[29]

The world Blair Kling created in absorbing narrative style in *The Blue Mutiny* was totally different from Dimock's medieval age centering about the great reformer Caitanya. Reading Kling's book dispels doubts that British intrusion materially changed Bengali life and society. Kling's was the first monograph by an American that dealt in large part with the rural history of Bengal under the British. In it he traced the rise of the indigo plantation system from 1802 through its golden age as a profit-making business (1834–1847) to its decline and collapse in the 1850s and 1860s. One segment of the book contains the story of nonofficial European planters, a story that is often ignored in the history of the colonial experience. The fact that by 1860 these planters had bought two-thirds of the land in Nadia district suggests how powerful they had become. *The Blue Mutiny* also tells the story of the zemindars, or native landowners, who competed with the Europeans. Above all it tells the story of the cultivators of indigo, their trials and tribulations, their leaders during the rebellion. Finally it tells the story of sympathetic Europeans and the Calcutta intelligentsia who joined forces against violence, coercion, and exploitation in the plantations.

Kling argued that the Indigo Rebellion was an important event in Bengali history for at least three reasons: first, the Government of India Act XI (1859) led to a full investigation of plantation abuses and provided legal options for the oppressed peasant and enabled the cultivator to "grasp the concept of lawful rights" with the result that they became "enthusiastic supporters of the legal process"[30]; second, it provided the Calcutta intelligentsia with the experience of "applied techniques of political agitation" which they would later use in the nationalist struggle; and third, it helped give "rise among the intelligentsia to an idealization of the rustics."[31] Besides opening a field in Bengal studies on resistance movements, Kling's important contribution was in his objective treatment of the facts—which made some Indian zemindars look as evil as did Europeans when portrayed by nationalists, and made European officials and magistrates appear much less imperious and unconcerned than when depicted by their own countrymen during the Victorian era. Kling's strict adherence to facts raises the question: Would Indians have done any differently in the position of the planters?

In 1967, the Asian Studies Center of Michigan State University published the first set of papers of the Bengal Studies Group which had met two years earlier in East Lansing. The subject of the conference was "Bengal: Literature and History." Following the direction Bengal studies were taking in America, the papers were divided by Dimock, the editor, into the medieval period and the period of the nineteenth century and after. The writers had been asked to use literary sources for the study of Bengal's cultural history.

The medieval papers included Dimock's study "The Ideal Man in Society in Vaiṣṇava and Vaiṣṇava-Sahajiyā Literature," a translation of "Two Autobiographical Accounts from Middle Bengali Literature" by Wayne Kilpatrick, and a study of "The Hindu Chiefdom in Middle Bengali Literature" by Ronald Inden. Inden's piece is of special interest because this was his earliest product as a student of social history and as a follower of Dimock seeking the true Bengal in the middle ages. From Bengali sources entirely, Inden masterfully reconstructed the "inner" political history of Bengal in the seventeenth century. The term *inner* is used advisedly here because Inden went beyond the usual level of Mogul imperial or regional Muslim dynastic history to the level of actual control by a number of independent and semi-independent rajas or zemindars.

According to Inden, though the Moguls conquered Bengal, problems of communication and transport compelled them to delegate actual power to the local chiefs. But to Inden, concerned less with such "passive external factors" and more with the culture pattern and Bengali value system, the real question was this: What were the "more 'active' internal factors relating to political organization and activity within the chiefdom itself that from the point of view of the inhabitants living inside the chiefdom made it a permanent political institution?"[32] Inden answered his question by setting the organization and functions of the chief's political system (*rājya*) against a close study of the structural components which made up the chiefdom. Thus there was the political system itself, the territory or *deśa*, and the hierarchy of social groups or *samāja*. All these components were pulled together in a complex economic network based largely on agriculture—paddy cultivation—as the main source of wealth. The social system comprised the caste groups who according to Inden were dominated by the same three upper-caste groups of contemporary Bengal: "the Brāhman-priests, pandits, and preservers of Hindu tradition; the Baidyas-physicians; and the Kāyasthas-officials and landholders."[33] Inden, then, from a medieval text, listed the lower specialist castes.

Inden's leading conclusion, perhaps, was that the whole system was held together by sets of patron-client relationships at the apex of which stood the raja himself as the "most powerful leader and patron in the chiefdom."[34] Wrote Inden, "he provided them with protection and a number of other services, while they paid the revenue and provided local support."[35] Moreover, these relationships were arranged in hierarchies as with "villagers, headmen, and chiefs" and "officials and armed retainers."[36] It was through the patron-client relationship that the raja and his government "performed their political, economic, and religious functions within the local society."[37] Consequently, the main thrust of Inden's argument was this: "The local Hindu chiefdom was not, therefore, just a creation of external factors; its political organization played an important role in shaping and maintaining local Hindu society. For both of these reasons, the local Hindu chiefdom was a permanent feature of the social structure of Bengal."[38]

The papers for the modern period, with one exception perhaps, differed from the medievalist approach by giving equal stress to the external factor of British intrusion and the internal factor of Bengali response. As one of Stephen Hay's two students contributing to the volume, I wrote "The Dimensions of Literature as an Analytical Tool for the Study of Bengal, 1800–1830." Taking the generation of intelligentsia of whom Rammohun Roy was the most conspicuous member, I examined their literary productions from differing perspectives in order to reconstruct the main historical outline of the period in which they lived. In the process, I had discovered, like Kling, that it was impossible to discuss Bengal under the British without focusing as much on the Englishmen who interacted closely with the Bengalis as on the Bengalis themselves. Thus, contrary to Inden who saw no point in discussing Moguls in Bengal, I actually emphasized the role of a group of English Orientalists who, by acting as windows to the West for Bengalis, influenced aspects of the internal culture.

In the article, I examined the cultural dimension first and found that much of the Orientalist literature reflected cultural attitudes toward Bengalis which underwent a definite change from negative to positive as a result of a sympathetic cultural orientation and training program which young civil servants received at the College of Fort William (established 1800). Bengalis in turn responded well to Englishmen who took an interest in their own culture. In the historical dimension Orientalist literature, because of its "bias for classicism in which the essence of Hindu civilization was believed to be contained in a golden age,"[39] profoundly influenced Hindu nationalism by reinforcing pride in a people about the virtues and wonder that was their pre-Muslim past. Examples of the earliest modern historical writings by Bengalis are interesting today for the expressions of a worldview delicately balanced between tradition and modernity. In the socioeconomic dimension, it was the grouping of intelligentsia that I addressed myself to in an effort to generalize about caste and class considerations of these writers of the new Bengali prose literature. I found that most of them were of the same three upper castes present in Inden's medieval chiefdom, though now modified in thought and behavior by Western education and a career in the professions. As for the final or existential dimension, I focused on the psychological aspects of the intelligentsia's groping for a new identity in the modern world:

> The Bengali intellectual of the early 1800s found himself insecure psychologically not only because he was in the center of a spatial encounter between two cultures, but also because he found himself centered lengthwise in a newly discovered historical dimension. The Orientalists infused him with their image of an Indian golden age while the Serampore missionaries transmitted a Protestant's view of the medieval dark ages. Both left the Bengali with a faith in the perfectibility of all mankind. On the one hand, the intelligentsia viewed itself as representative of an exhausted culture and on the other, as representative of a culture organically disrupted by historical circumstances but capable of revitalization. It is not surprising, then, that Bengalis themselves should interpret their nineteenth-century heritage as a renaissance.[40]

Warren Gunderson, Stephen Hay's other student, dealt with the subsequent generation of intelligentsia in a paper entitled "Modernization and Cultural Change: The Self-Image and World View of the Bengal Intelligentsia as Found in the Writings of the Mid-Nineteenth Century, 1830–1870." Like Hay, Gunderson saw modernization as a significant process in nineteenth-century Bengal; and like Hay in his article on Rammohun, he rejected the typological theories of modernity which all too neatly dichotomize traditional from modern societies. Gunderson's own position was that the intelligentsia is important to study because "in non-Western societies undergoing modernization, the western-educated individual plays a crucial role"[41]; "that Bengali intellectuals responded to the challenge of a new cultural situation in ways which were rational and realistic"[42]; and that "they developed an outlook which favored cultural change and modernization and which gave legitimacy and respectability to their own positions."[43]

Gunderson's attempt to depict the character of the age at mid-century is one of the best examples yet of intellectual history among American scholars of Bengal. He used the literature of the intelligentsia to unify their innermost feelings and thoughts as the expression of an era. He found that as a result of momentous economic, social, and technological change in Bengal under the British, "progress, advancement, improvement: these became the watchword of the age."[44] The advanced guard of the age of progress was the middle-class intellectuals whom Gunderson defined as "an umbrella under which the urban-dwelling, educated Bengali, regardless of income, status, or aspirations, could find shelter."[45]

Gunderson's main conclusions about modernization among the Bengali middle class followed Hay's own and represented a growing realization among Americans that modernization was not necessarily synonymous with westernization. This notion is apparent in Gunderson's statement that "Bengali intellectuals showed an ability to borrow selectively and to incorporate new forms and ideas, without ceasing to be Bengalis."[46] Thus, along with Hay and others, Gunderson was prepared to argue that an attachment to cultural forms by Bengalis wishing to maintain their own identity did not necessarily label them as exponents of "orthodoxy or traditionalism."

The third paper on modern Bengal was by T. W. Clark's student, Rachel Van M. Baumer, who had written her dissertation on the many facets of Bankimcandra Chatterji's thought and had chosen for her topic in this volume "Communal Attitudes in the Nineteenth and Twentieth Centuries." Instead of the focus on acculturation as a result of British-Bengali interaction, she directed her attention to Hindu-Muslim relations as reflected in the writings of Bengali Hindus. This paper had particular merit because of the excellence of the translations and the lucid, well-structured narrative style.

Baumer's method was to trace Hindu attitudes to Muslims in three separate works by three separate authors writing at three different times during the modern period. In my opinion, this method enabled her to write the most effective paper of any in terms of carrying out the objectives of the volume: to fuse literature and history by using literature historically. She looked at Ram Ram Basu's *Rājā Pratāpādityacaritra,* written for the College of Fort William in 1801; she examined *Sītārām,* a later novel by Bankimcandra published in 1887; and she analyzed Saratcandra Chatterji's *Maheś,* which appeared in 1921. Baumer discovered that in the early 1800s Basu, when writing this history of a Bengali raja in sixteenth-century Jessore district, was completely oblivious to "Hindu-Muslim tension."[47] In fact, "the word Muslim rarely occurs in the text."[48] But in Bankimcandra, Hindu nationalism had evolved a hostile attitude not yet so much against the British overlord as against Muslims. According to Baumer, cultural differences between Hindus and Muslims were to Bankim "fundamental and irreconcilable."[49] In Saratcandra there seems to have been a reaction against Bankim's kind of communal attitude and an appeal "to [Saratcandra's] own community for a return to reason for peace and harmony in everyday life with men of the other community."[50]

Baumer's article was extremely revealing and pertinent in the light of recent events which brought about the bloody birth of Bangladesh. But in the context of Bengal studies in America, her article represented the first effort to work with modern Bengali literature in contrast to Dimock's work with the medieval. The result was to open up a new world of Bengali fiction which could be studied aesthetically or as sources for social and cultural history.

The year 1868 proved to be a harvest year for Bengal studies—at least among the modernists who were beginning to show the fruits of their labor in history, anthropology, and political science. This was the year John Broomfield published his prize-winning *Elite Conflict in a Plural Society*; Leonard Gordon brought out his "Portrait of a Bengal Revolutionary" on M. N. Roy in the *Journal of Asian Studies*; Ralph Nicholas summed up years of research on the Bengal village in "Structures of Politics in the Villages of Southern Asia" in the Singer-Cohn volume *Structure and Change in Indian Society;* and Marcus Franda published his *West Bengal and the Federalizing Process in India*. The regional approach to South Asia which the Bengal specialists had pioneered was producing results.

Broomfield, trained in area studies in Australia, demonstrated in his work that parallel interests had developed between Australia and America with regard to approaches to the history of Bengal. Hay, Inden, and others at Chicago had already recognized a certain unity of self-interest among the long-prevailing upper castes of Bengal who obviously had adapted themselves rather well under the British and constituted a regional elite during the era of colonialism and imperialism. It was precisely here that Broomfield found his primary area of interest, which he eventually developed into the concept of the Bengali *bhadralok:*

> At the beginning of the twentieth century Bengali rural and urban society differed in many fundamental respects, yet they shared a common dominant elite. In city, town, and village there was one group of Bengalis who claimed and were accorded recognition as superior in social status to the mass of their fellows. These were the *bhadralok,* literally the "respectable people," the "gentlemen." They were distinguished by many aspects of their behavior—their deportment, their speech, their dress, their style of housing, their eating habits, their occupations, and their associations— and quite as fundamentally by their cultural values and their sense of social propriety.[51]

As a student of Bengali sociopolitical history in the British period, Broomfield framed his monograph on the *bhadralok* in the context of British-Bengali interaction and focused on the institution of the Bengal Legislative Council. Broomfield assessed leading political events in Bengal from 1912 to 1927, addressing himself for the most part to communal relations between Hindus and Muslims from the end of the first Bengal partition of 1905 to the rise in power of a Muslim *bhadralok* in Bengal legislative politics. No book by a Bengal specialist so skillfully combined the traditional historian's exciting narrative with the problem-centered approach of the social scientist.

What Broomfield has contributed, therefore, is a kind of sociology of Bengal politics in historical perspective. The drama that unfolded under British rule and administration was that of groupings in a pluralist society maneuvering to promote their self-interest in competition with one another. Like Kling's book, Broomfield's constituted a major breakthrough in the older British Empire historiography of India, which was essentially concerned with British diffusion rather than with British-Indian interaction. It was not the British who really interested Broomfield but Bengali elites who had no other choice but to confront the British while at the same time playing another more crucial role within their own culture and in competition with one another. This kind of sociological analysis, restricted to one region, also enabled Broomfield to shatter the older generalizations about the liberal moderate nationalists. He humanized them by demonstrating how their ideological commitment was culturally and socially determined.

Politics was also Gordon's primary concern in his article on M. N. Roy as young Bengali revolutionary. But, contrary to Broomfield, it was not sociology so much as cultural anthropology which shaped Gordon's view of "modern" Bengal. The influence of Dimock, Inden, and Chicago anthropologists was clearly discernable in this valuable article on the unique features of the Bengal revolutionary. Gordon is perhaps the first Bengal specialist of the modernist school to have been captivated by the notion that there are eternal Bengali traits and relationships, or an unbroken continuity of culture, offering the key, as it were, to understanding Bengali participation in all historical forces and movements.

Although M. N. Roy was a revolutionary nationalist advocating independence against the British, Gordon felt it unnecessary to refer to any Englishman at all in Bengal except perhaps those whose names turned up in CID files. Instead, Gordon's young man Narendranath (Roy's real name) began his revolutionary career in the peculiarly Bengali way: he was really part of a faction (*dal*) rather than part of a larger movement; moreover, the leader of the faction was not an idealistic revolutionary with charisma but a cross between an elder brother (*dādā*) and a spiritual preceptor (*guru*), and the group of revolutionaries (most of them very young) were really the leader's student-disciples (*chelā*), who considered one another as coreligionists (*gurubhāi*). Gordon has presented some statistics on these factions, and gleaned from the Sedition Committee

Reports (compiled between 1907 and 1917), which seem to indicate that most members of the revolutionary factions were between sixteen and twenty-five years of age and that ninety percent of them were of the three upper castes (Broomfield's *bhadralok*). Also significantly, Bengali, to Gordon, was the warm attachment which developed between disciples and leader within the faction, an attachment far more important than ideology and which meant in effect that with the death of the *dādā* the *dal* itself disintegrated.

Ralph Nicholas, who had studied two West Bengal villages in 1960–1961 and has published a number of articles on them since, was the first Bengal specialist in anthropology. In 1968, when his important article in the Singer-Cohn volume appeared, he had turned to the new subdivision of social anthropology called "political anthropology."[52] The fact that Nicholas found himself the only American anthropologist of Bengal, that he had entered a hybrid field where a great many conceptual problems remained unsolved, meant that he had to create (or at least generalize upon) a model of a village political structure while still digesting a wealth of ethnographic data. He met the challenge more than adequately.

Nicholas defined political activity in terms of power and conflict rather than in terms of administrative authority and action. As he himself put it, "I am talking about the conflict over power, not about administration, government, or the direction of public policy in South Asian villages."[53] The question he turned to was social cleavage as it typified political conflict in villages. His ethnographic accounts of the two villages suggest two different types of cleavage: the vertical, which divides structurally equivalent political groups "characteristic of the ideal unstratified society,"[54] and the horizontal, which divides "super- and subordinate groups from one another" and is "caracteristic of the ideal stratified society."[55] Vertical cleavages seem to be manifested mostly as factions, "and within certain castes, in the form of divisions between segments of patrilineal descent groups."[56] Horizontal cleavages, on the other hand, were found in South Asia between castes and "between ruling autocrats and their subjects."[57]

Nicholas did not freeze his data into a model nor did he suggest anywhere that existing patterns of one or the other variety were not alterable in contemporary India by modernizing processes. He found the village situation remarkably fluid, suggesting perhaps that internal, culturally determined factors were not sufficient in themselves to explain the social and political dynamics of village life. Nicholas, as a historic-minded anthropologist, was quite aware that the historical forces were not merely passive external factors in village society but were processes which could radically alter existing norms and styles. In his final conclusion he states:

Of the changes which have been brought about in rural India by social and economic reform the effects or potential effects of two seem most important. Universal adult franchise generally has a great impact upon the political system of villages in which the dominant caste is a minority of the population. Land reforms, when they become effective, will bring major changes in the political systems of villages in which control over land has been concentrated in a small number of hands.[58]

As Nicholas was the first Bengal anthropologist, Marcus Franda was the first political scientist. Franda, an area-trained specialist, wrote his first book on the political integration of a culture region in which he had ample opportunity to fuse his scientific understanding of the federalizing process with his acquired sympathy for the state culture of Bengal. What emerged was a study of political culture in which a conflict of issues between the center and state on such concerns as irrigation, land reform, and party government represented the clash between national policy decisions and the realities of local conditions.

By selecting Bengal, Franda had chosen the one region of India which has felt least comfortable in its constitutional role simply as one of many states, continually asserting its autonomy both politically and culturally. He explained this problem initially with a historical account of Bengal, which until 1874 included East and West Bengal, Orissa, Bihar, and Assam and was the most populous region in all South Asia. Then, at independence in 1947, Bengal was reduced to one-seventh the size of Greater Bengal a century ago.[59] The fact that Calcutta was capital of British India until 1911, and that Bengalis held most of the privileged positions under imperialism, goes far to explain historically the reason for the twentieth-century Bengali image of crisis, agitation, and rebellion.

Among Franda's discoveries was that on the highest level of center-state interaction (as evidenced, for example, by the appointment of the States Reorganization Committee by Nehru in 1953) the national policy has been a "middle ground between the alternative paths of coercion and complete surrender to provincial sentiments."[60] As for explaining the Bengali attitude to the center, Franda's data seem to indicate a high degree of responsiveness by regional politicians to local interests which often clash with national policies and programs. As an illustration he cited an aspect of the Domodar Valley Corporation controversy between local cultivators and the federal government. The Bengalis argued that local improvement was more crucial than completing the second stage of the DVC project. Thus argued Franda: "The West Bengal Congress Party has a reputation for being susceptible to pressure from people who are considered 'key men', and for being capable of resisting ideological orientations, and it is on this basis that it has effectively organized the state."[61]

This is Franda's most significant conclusion about the effectiveness of Bengali regional demands against the center: "the cohesion and strength of state party units (at least where the dominant party is in power in the state) and the degree to which the populace can be mobilized for political action—play a large part in determining the nature of center-state problems in India."[62] Besides Franda's obvious contribution of placing the problem of regions and regionalism in a political context, he has also been the first among Bengal modernists to examine the problem of interaction in the post-British period. The older British subject–British overlord relationship has now been replaced by that of the Bengali politician–Indian national perspective.

The year 1969 witnessed the publication of a monograph on the Bengal renaissance by myself, two more volumes of papers from earlier conferences on identity and urbanism, and Rachel Van M. Baumer's article on literary tradition and modernity in Sankar's novels. My book on the Bengal renaissance followed Broomfield's as the second Bengal monograph in America to be awarded the Watumull Prize.

The Bengal renaissance, a vital component of the Bengali self-image for a century or more and a perennial theme in South Asian historiography, was a sensitive area of scholarship by virtue of having been appropriated as cultural baggage in the ideology of Indian nationalism. This renaissance has been variously interpreted as the search for identity in the modern world, nation-building, linguistic modernization, the flowering of the Bengali literary genius, the socioreligious purification of Hinduism, and the finest hour of creative achievement by the *bhadralok*. More often than not the origins of that renaissance have been traced back to the arrival in Calcutta in 1815 of Rammohun Roy, a charismatic hero of the Bengali people. From his attitudes and the subsequently evolving institutions associated with his name have been derived all that is modern and progressive about twentieth-century India; from his courageous assault against the citadel of contemporary corrupt Hindu society while at the same time maintaining his cultural integrity against Western critics, he established the prototype of the present-day dynamic Indian who feels no conflict between his heritage and his quest for modernity.

These and other such hypotheses formed the basis of my research on how the renaissance actually got started. As an area-trained specialist with social science exposure, I felt uncomfortable with the Rammohun Roy interpretation partly because of the inadequacy of the Great Man theory as a explanation and partly because of the obvious nationalist bias in minimizing the role of the English, whom I surmised served equally well as a catalyst. I was equally dissatisfied with the British view of the birth of the Bengal renaissance, which placed too much emphasis on

Macaulay's Minute of 1835 as a catalyst. Westernizers argued that Macaulay's minute committed the government to a policy of favoring English education as against the Orientalist policy of obstructing the flow of progress by having sponsored education in the languages of the Indian people.

What I discovered chiefly was that the Bengal renaissance originated through interaction between a group of linguistically competent and culturally sympathetic Britishers known as Orientalists and a group of partially westernized, professional Bengali intermediaries called the intelligentsia. Rammohun was surely a leading figure but he was essentially just one of a new grouping of intelligentsia whose contribution to the renaissance had to be evaluated collectively. As for the Orientalists, my conclusion was that they were neither averse to change, since they did encourage the English language as a means for "native" improvement, nor was their support of the indigenous "oriental" languages so much intended as an obstacle to modern ideas as it was a calculated effort to convey new learning into the spoken, vernacular languages of the people.

By intensively studying the College of Fort William, a pivotal Orientalist training institution for English civil servants established in Calcutta in 1800, I was able to describe fully how Europeans underwent deep changes as a result of becoming intellectually and psychologically acculturated to India. This kind of acculturation produced the progressive Orientalist with a syncretistic modernizing program centered around the assumption that the new wine of nineteenth-century civilization could be poured into the old bottles of Indian institutions and practices with dynamic results. The Orientalist cultural policy for India was therefore not an antithesis to Macaulay's westernizing policy but an alternative. This is why I concluded the book by affirming that the Orientalists played a major role in the birth of Indian renaissance and modernity:

As portrayed in this book, the Orientalists bear little resemblance to the dismal image that has been theirs since the Victorian era. The Orientalists served as avenues linking the regional elite with the dynamic civilization of contemporary Europe. They contributed to the formation of a new Indian middle class and assisted in the professionalization of the Bengali intelligentsia. They started schools, systematized languages, brought printing and publishing to India, and encouraged the proliferation of books, journals, newspapers, and other media of communication. Their impact was urban and secular. They built the first modern scientific laboratories in India, and taught European medicine. They were neither static classicists nor averse to the idea of progress; and they both historicized the Indian past and stimulated a consciousness of history in the Indian intellectual. It was they who transmitted a new sense of identity to Bengalis that enlarged what Robert Bellah has called "the capacity for rational goal setting," an instrumental process in the development of a modern outlook.[63]

I also edited in that year, 1969, the second volume of the Bengal Studies Conference papers entitled *Bengal Regional Identity*. One of the exciting new fields of Bengali history reported on at the conference was that of the delta region of Bengal from classical times to the rise of Muslim dominance. Barrie Morrison, who had developed an interest in Bengali history and archaeology in the ancient and early middle periods, wrote on "Region and Sub-region in Pre-Muslim Bengal." Through an analysis of seventy-one inscribed copper plates found in various parts of East and West Bengal and covering the period between A.D. 433 and 1285, Morrison addressed himself to the question of whether or not there was a Bengal.

What Morrison did find of great significance (and which he would elaborate upon in his published monograph a year later) were the four principal political divisions within the area now designated as the delta of Bengal. These political subdivisions of the Bengal region were Varendra, "lying north of the floodplain of the modern Ganges, west of the Jamuna and east of the Mahananda Rivers"[64]; the Bhagirathi-Hugli area on both banks of the river, encompassing the modern districts of 24 Parganas and Midnapore; the Samatata area comprising the Sylhet-Comilla-Chittagong area east of the Surma and Meghna Rivers; and "the modern Dacca and Faridpur districts which lie at the present confluence of the Padma and Meghna Rivers."[65] A detailed study of the four major administrative areas demonstrated "varying political relations with each other and with great variation in the kinds of religious donations made."[66] Thus concluded Morrison: "These variations are sufficient to demonstrate that the inscriptions do not provide any evidence of the existence of a Bengal regional identity before the coming of the Muslims."[67]

Perhaps the most important and challenging implication of Morrison's research appears in the epilogue to the article where he discussed Bengal cultural identity in the middle period. For years, Dimock and others had cherished a conviction that a Bengal culture pattern had existed in the delta from the ninth century—perhaps earlier—with its distinctive language, literature, religion, social system, and political order. But Morrison argued that "it seems probable that the institutions which would make possible the emergence of a 'regional identity' did not come into existence before the thirteenth century or even the nineteenth century."[68] The early inhabitants of the delta were a "linguistically and culturally diverse population."[69] Among these "heterogeneous people" there was "little evidence of the existence of major political institutions which would bring

them together and provide a focus for any sense of regional identity."[70]
After discussing a few hypotheses, Morrison convincingly concluded that:

> When the opportunities for the expression of their perception were found
> under conditions of patronage and peace, such as obtained under the
> Mughals and the British, the Bengalis produced a rich and varied array of
> cultural achievements—in literature, sculpture, scholarship, and fine handi-
> crafts. It was through the act of expressing themselves that the population
> of the Delta began to distinguish themselves as Bengalis and acquire a sense
> of identity. The expression of this culture left such a brilliant and lasting
> impression upon Bengalis and the rest of the world that we occupy our-
> selves trying to understand the origin and content of this culture.[71]

Dimock's contribution to the volume, "Muslim Vaiṣṇava Poets of
Bengal," represented his first to deal with the Bengali Muslim in relation
to the Bengali Hindu in the middle period, aiming most probably to find
the culture pattern and identity in a syncretism between the two. After
all, as Dimock noted, "Hindus and Muslims live and have lived for centuries side by side, sharing pastoral and other festivals; and . . . many
similarities of the devotional Sufi doctrines to those of the Hindu *bhakti*
make it but a short step from one religion to the other."[72] In fact, Dimock
was now seriously considering "syncretistic cults" in Bengal:

> We might look briefly at the area of poetry, and within that area, the poetry
> within the Vaiṣṇava tradition—a tradition usually considered strictly Hin-
> du. It cannot be said that the Muslim Vaiṣṇava poets of Bengal represent a
> major syncretistic movement, or even that they represent more than a mi-
> nor example of interaction between the two major traditions. On the other
> hand, instances of Muslims writing poetry on Rādhā-Kṛṣṇa, Caitanya, or
> other Vaiṣṇava themes are not isolated and unique ones.[73]

Thus the poetry of the Vaiṣṇava tradition links the two communities
into a larger Bengali regional culture. A story like Jayadeva's love of
Rādhā for Kṛṣṇa in the *Gītagovinda* helped break down orthodox Islam
and Hinduism in the delta by creating a prototype for the distinctively
Bengali love story. Dimock's selection was superb, as were his comparative references between Sufi and Vaiṣṇava poets treating similar themes.
And perhaps most moving of all were his final remarks in which the theme
of universalism counterbalances the "parochial" quest for a Bengali
regional identity. From the *Ain-i-akbari* by Abu'l Fazl, Dimock referred
to Akbar's policy of trying to eliminate hostility between Hindus and
Muslims with the hope "that the thorn of strife and hatred be caused to
bloom into a garden of peace."[74] Concluded Dimock:

> Our poets, judging from the language of their poetry, were not educated

men; they were, perhaps, wise and religious men. We know nothing about them except their poems, and that they, like many Hindus, felt that truth need not be named, that it is not the possession of any single tradition or sect. Among some at least, the thorn of strife and hatred may have bloomed into a garden of poetry and peace.[75]

Ralph Nicholas developed the same syncretistic idea as Dimock in "Vaiṣṇavism and Islam in Rural Bengal," but as an anthropologist observing present conditions in the Bengali village. Thus it was quite natural indeed for Nicholas to hypothesize that the distinctiveness of Bengali Vaiṣṇavism and Bengali Islam "is a product of some unique features of Bengali rural society, and that religious distinctiveness has, in its turn, contributed to Bengal's regional identity."[76] To Nicholas one of the fundamental reasons why Bengal is so distinctive as a culture is because it is highly distinctive physically. His description of Bengal as the greatest delta on earth (fifty thousand square miles), of the continuously changing course of Bengal's major rivers, and of the frontier-type settlement in rural Bengal (which has followed the best agricultural land eastward and southward where the rivers were most active) constituted one of the most succinct geographical introductions to Bengal that exists anywhere. When one adds Nicholas' observation that Bengal's ethnic homogeneity, so conspicuously non-Aryan, is probably due to the fact that throughout classical times it was "beyond the pale of Aryan civilization" and thus was never "profoundly affected by Hindu conceptions of 'proper' social organization,"[77] then the sources of Bengali heterodoxy or uniqueness are easily grasped.

One effective way that Nicholas as a social anthropologist demonstrated the "significant similarities" between Vaiṣṇavas and Muslims as Bengalis was to present "parallel sets of religious roles."[78] Thus in the countryside there is a similarity between the mendicant Hindu and Muslim (called *bairāgī* and *fakir,* respectively). There is also the role of the *gurumurshid* pair defined in relation to the disciple (*celā-murid*). Both the Hindu *guru* and the Muslim *murshid* function to "initiate the *celā* or *murid* into the mystical knowledge of profound religious experience or religious ecstasy."[79] If they are saintly enough in life, these religious teachers may in death be treated as saints, and their tombs become sacred areas for devotees. As Nicholas reported, "there is probably no village in Bengal that does not have the tomb of a *pīr* (*dargā*), the tomb of a *gosvāi* (*samādhi*), or both."[80]

Of major importance in the article was the theoretical portion in the conclusion wherein Nicholas reviewed leading concepts of "culture area" (cultural uniqueness) in anthropology with the end of accepting one or the other to fit the Bengal case. For example, as he himself did to some extent in the paper, one might show the "unique properties of [Bengal's] language and literature, its culture and social structure, its history, and even such elemental characteristics as its physical geography and the biological peculiarities of its inhabitants."[81] But Nicholas was apparently beginning to favor an idea which Dimock had pursued for years—to direct one's questions to the "symbolic systems that lie at the center of belief and practice in these religions."[82] Nicholas was moving toward Lévi-Strauss, one of many anthropologists who argue that "cultures and societies are systems, the components of which function together for the maintenance of the whole."[83] But Lévi-Strauss had gone even farther: "Each system has a key that reveals the ideal form of all sets of relations within it."[84] Though Nicholas accepted the idea of rural Bengal as a system, he was not prepared then to name a "key to all its parts."[85] In fact, he ended his article with a series of questions rather than with generalizations, conceding implicitly that Bengal studies were after all in their infancy.

Among the modernists dealing exclusively with urban elites, Rachel Van M. Baumer, Blair Kling, and Leonard Gordon offered exceedingly fresh papers, demonstrating the strides being taken by Bengal specialists in America. Baumer's article in particular, "Bankimcandra's View of the Role of Bengal in Indian Civilization," generated a kind of intimate rapport between scholar and subject which could only be possible through a deep understanding of the language and an even deeper understanding of the society and culture. Baumer's article demonstrated the wide world of difference experienced when one crossed over the line between Dimock's medieval and Nicholas' village Bengal to the milieu of the Bengal *bhadralok* and intelligentsia.

As Baumer's excellent translations indicated, Bankimcandra was a fairly well educated man with a sophisticated sense of humor and satire, as much at home with sustained intellectual prose in the pages of the *Baṅgadarśan* as he was with creative fiction in the form of short stories and serialized novels. His was a familiar type in the nineteenth-century world: the nervous, ambivalent intellectual holding onto tradition while sinking deeper and deeper into the quicksand of impending modernization. But somewhat more precisely, he was a pioneer of the third-world intelligentsia who stood not merely between tradition and modernity but between Afro-Asia and the West groping through their culture's past to discover an identity.

In Baumer's article this process was illuminated exactly. Bankimcandra's progressive or modernist outlook was evidenced, according to Baumer, in the didactic motivation for writing these articles "designed to instruct Bengalis in the ways necessary for the future restoration of greatness."[86] Though Bankimcandra was Western-educated and held down a

European position in the civil service, his blueprint for Bengali or Indian revitalization did not include a repudiation of one's national heritage while undergoing radical westernization. On the contrary, he urged reviewing one's own past, where a discovery of the real India would reawaken pride in one's culture and a new sense of identity:

> The past held inspiration and lessons for the future; the problems of the present needed recognition and solution in preparation for the future; the future could be as great as Bengalis, working together, wished to make it. Thus history became a tool in the promotion of nationalism, introspection the mental exercise for the restoration of moral fibre, and awakened pride the emotion from which would derive the inspiration to action.[87]

But as Baumer has shown all too well, Bankimcandra's own reading of the Bengali past within the larger framework of Indian civilization was not all that consistent nor was his own quest for an identity ever fully resolved intellectually. In the first place, though Bankimcandra prided himself as a Bengali he was also a proud Brahman with a Brahman's exaggerated esteem for the golden age of Aryan civilization—a civilization to which Bengal was peripheral. Thus we find Bankimcandra performing subtle mental gymnastics to prove the Aryan purity of Bengali Brahmans and the non-Aryan impurity of the Bengali Sudras who converted en masse to Islam. All the while, as Baumer demonstrated, Bankimcandra attempted to proclaim "that Bengalis were one with other Aryan-descended Indians who shared the glory of that "ancient Aryan race, who were the greatest of all races on earth and our forefathers."[88]

This search for an identity was, as Baumer developed it, a three-stage process composed of the discovery of a golden age, the discovery of a dark age, and the ideology of future recovery contingent largely on a correct historical assessment of one's golden and dark ages. Why did India decline? Because "in his view, Brahmans became greedy and tyrannical, Ksatriyas, weak and luxury-seeking, and Sudras, passive and unprotesting."[89] He asked, what have we become? And he answered, "Bengalis lack physical strength, Hindus lack virility, while India lacks social cohesion and unity of purpose."[90] The way to future recovery was, according to Bankim:

> The nation whose historical recollections of former greatness remain tries to keep that greatness, or if lost, to restore it again. Blenheim and Waterloo are results of the memories of Crecy and Agincourt. Even though Italy fell, she has risen again. Today the Bengalis want to become great—alas! where is the historical memory of Bengalis?[91]

In Blair Kling's article "Entrepreneurship and Regional Identity in Bengal," though he treated the same *bhadralok* class to which Bankimcandra belonged, the problem of identity is seen from a somewhat different perspective. Turning more and more to a study of the modern economic history of Bengal, Kling found himself faced with the question of why Bengalis preferred "to earn meager salaries as teachers, civil servants, accountants and clerks," while leaving "the major industries and most of the banking, commerce and real estate in the hands of non-Bengalis."[92] In short, as the atypical entrepreneurial Prafulla Chandra Ray once said while admonishing his fellow *bhadralok*, "the Bengali has got many noble qualities . . . in one essential aspect, however, he has proved a dismal failure, namely in the art of earning his livelihood."[93]

P. C. Ray's indictment of his fellow Bengalis as lacking the spirit of enterprise has become part of the stereotype of the contemporary Bengali whom non-Bengalis of South Asia tend to ridicule. Fortunately, Kling as a historian has handled the problem in a historical context rather than in one anthropological. Thus he seemed less concerned with the alleged deficiency of entrepreneurship as reflective of an enduring value system but more concerned with favorable and unfavorable economic conditions over a long span of time and dealing principally with Bengali-British interaction. To be sure Kling was well aware that "on the one hand, the vast majority of middle class Bengalis are the descendants of Brahmans and Kayasthas who have traditionally held both business occupations and the indigenous business castes of Bengal in contempt."[94] But one could not ignore the fact that, on the other hand, "under British influence Bengalis have aspired to a value system that associated trade with elitist status."[95]

Kling found that between 1750 and 1850 the intellectual and administrative castes of Bengal did associate with the British in merchant activities "without losing self-respect."[96] But starting in the period of 1828–1848 during unusually severe economic turbulence, Bengalis began to turn away from business. In addition to economic depression, which broke out again and again, there was another factor which helps explain Bengali abdication from enterprise: "During the first half of the nineteenth century, business ethics were still unformed, and firms with long established reputations were defrauded by their British partners, leaving their Indian partners liable for debts. As a result, in the 1850s many Bengali capitalists retreated from commerce."[97]

Kling has ably demonstrated how throughout the nineteenth century some Bengalis, aware of the importance of a spirit of enterprise, continually prodded their countrymen to change their values by imbibing a new puritan ethic. But in 1918, despite the entrepreneurial aspect of the Swadeshi movement, an Industrial Commission report "attributed the failure of Swadeshi industries in Bengal to the lack of enterprise and business sense among Bengalis."[98] The response by Bengalis was that "the government itself thwarted entrepreneurship in Bengal."[99] Kling's own feeling at this stage in his research is summed up in the following:

> Thus, in an important way the regional identity of the Bengali is a function of his economic situation. But the interrelationship between economics and regional identity is a complex one. The Bengali attitudes toward business that set him apart from the non-Bengalis differ widely among Bengali castes. These attitudes derive from traditional values, from new values acquired through association with the British, and from recent historical experience in the course of which Bengali entrepreneurship was subjected to one frustration after another.[100]

If the papers in that volume on identity displayed anything in common about Bengalis, it was surely their tendency throughout history to be different from their South Asian neighbors. If Dimock and Nicholas were accurate in their depiction and analysis from medieval to present-day rural society, it was more important for Hindus and Muslims to be Bengali than to be Hindus or Muslims. Baumer's Bankimcandra went through amazing intellectual contortions to reconcile his Bengali identity with his Brahman-Aryan identity, while Kling's effort to make sense out of the Bengali aversion to a spirit of enterprise only accentuates the difference of style and attitude between the complex Bengali and his fellow Indians.

Leonard Gordon's article, "Bengal's Gandhi: A Study in Modern Indian Regionalism, Politics, and Though," adds still another case study of Bengali heterodoxy in still another dimension of twentieth-century nationalist politics. Although Gandhi emerged throughout north India as the charismatic hero of the liberation struggle, in Bengal some of the most prominent nationalist leaders treated him with contempt. In fact, one of Gordon's chief aims was "to try to explain why the very name 'Gandhi' is anathema to many Bengalis."[101]

Gordon used the image of Gandhi in Bengal as a central focus for writing the intellectual history of Bengali politics. Thus one of the best features of the study is Gordon's analysis of the ideology of such men as Subhas Chandra Bose, Rabindranath Tagore, and M. N. Roy. This is not to say that Gordon has not stressed crucial events in the struggle for power; but he has probed deeper into the issues underlying these events and even deeper behind the issues to the strong ideological commitments. Bose, for example, in his book *The Indian Struggle* (1934), "saw himself on the side of reason, science, and modern values against the most deplorable traits of enfeebled India which Gandhi was exploiting."[102] Tagore, another who "admired Gandhi's gift for awakening the rural masses to self-help and political consciousness," turned against Gandhi because he objected to the "blind obedience he felt the movement entailed," to "panaceas like spinning, and to the xenophobia he detected in Gandhi's message."[103] Gordon summarized Tagore's ideological position in the following way: "Tagore wanted to retain the gains of Western education, science, medicine, technology and lay the ground for the meeting of all cultures on a basis of mutual exchange. He feared that Gandhism, particularly in practice, would end in India in turning in upon herself and bringing about her own destruction rather than gaining her long-sought freedom."[104]

But as in Gordon's other article on M. N. Roy as a youthful revolutionary, there was an attempt to link ideology and politics to Bengali culture per se or at least to some of the conspicuous values of the culture. Here was perhaps Gordon's most significant contribution to date: the attempt to relate the Bengali's negative response to Gandhi to the Sakta tradition of the upper-caste Hindu *bhadralok*. Up to this point in Bengal studies, and probably as a result of Dimock's influence, Vaiṣṇavism was the religious tradition among Bengalis almost universally emphasized. But Gordon, fully aware of the Bengali terrorist use of the mother goddess image in politics, now extended the Sakta religious tradition as a general, culturally determined hypothesis to explain *bhadralok* revulsion to Gandhi and to Gandhism. As Sakta followers of Durga or Kali, the *bhadralok* associated themselves "with traditions of violence, . . . carried out animal sacrifices," and had a "tradition of private murder for revenge."[105] Referring in particular to Subhas Bose, Aurobindo Ghosh, and M. N. Roy, Gordon wrote:

> These three men would have agreed that in order to regain the lost strength, power and autonomy, all means were permissible. This would fit with their *Śākta* background (no matter how secular they became later in life) and with Bengali traditions of violence mentioned earlier. They would have agreed with Nirad Chaudhuri that Gandhi's way was "the morality of the *servus*." Gandhi's politics did not appeal to them except so far as it was effective in launching a militant nationalist movement.[106]

The second volume of Bengal studies to appear that year was *Urban Bengal*, edited by Richard Park. According to the editor the conference was "less concerned with the administrative and technological consequences of urbanization in Bengal and more with the social and political repercussions that flowed from urban centers."[107] Park seemed most intrigued about the papers dealing with premodern Bengal (seventeenth and eighteenth centuries), and he noted that attempts to depict the "traditional" Bengali city and then hypothesize about it were much appreciated by the conference as a whole.

One of the medieval papers was a joint effort by Inden and Dimock entitled "The City in Pre-British Bengal" and based on a poetic school of folk literature known as the *mangala-kavya*. Though originally prompted to use this literature as history, they eventually chose to view the descriptions of cities in it as idealized representations rather than as conventionally accurate pictures. A source such as Mukundarāma's *Caṇḍi-Maṅgala,* for example, was used by Inden and Dimock not so much to reconstruct a Bengali city of the early middle ages as to extract from its accurate particulars and "fanciful descriptions" reflections of Bengali cultural values.[108]

It is therefore clear, although not altogether surprising, that we are moving here in the direction of anthropology using history for anthropological reasons rather than of history using literature for historical ends. The quotation from Vansina's *Oral Tradition: A Study in Historical Methodology* justifying oral tradition as "more likely to be accurate than those which are conscious (written)"[109] is puzzling because Dimock and Inden were apparently not concerned with accuracy but with the "realistic ideal" of the Bengali town.[110] Mukundarāma's description of Gujarata was to them "the projection of material reality on a divine canvas. It is both physical and metaphysical."[111] This kind of analysis is more valuable to the field of anthropological philosophy, which thrives on the study of myth, than to the discipline of history, which however liberally interpreted still pursues its basic goal of demythologizing man's past and historicizing it. In the following conclusion by Dimock and Inden, the anthropological import of their study becomes apparent as they use the Bengali city as a key to unlock the unique Bengali society and culture:

> All of this leads us to an interesting conclusion about the Bengali Hindu's conception of the ideal society. The ideal unit in Bengali society according to Mukundarāma is not the Bengal region as a whole; nor is it Bengal as represented in a simple village or in its regional capital. The ideal unit of Bengali society is considered to be the local chiefdom with its capital; and the highest social ideal that a man can attain is to become rājā and master of his local chiefdom and to live at the pinnacle of the complex urban life which goes on in the chiefdom's capital town. . . . The entire social structure of Bengal is encapsulated in the ideal local chiefdom and its capital.[112]

The article by Philip Calkins, "The Role of Murshidabad as a Regional and Subregional Center in Bengal," is a more conventional piece of urban history in the sense that Murshidabad represents only itself and its function during a given period. Calkin's concern was with Mogul Bengal and with a Mogul city, Murshidabad, capital of the province from 1704 to 1772. Although he accepts 1800 as the year when "Murshidabad had lost much of its importance as a commercial and administrative center,"[113] Calkins was reluctant to accept 1700 as the point of origin for its importance: the city was already important as a commercial center before it was selected as provincial capital.

Calkins' article is extremely valuable because he has carried on where Barrie Morrison left off in matching political units with cultural subregions during the Delhi Sultanate period (1200–1576) and Mogul period (1576–1757). Calkins not only established a correlation between Morrison's earlier subregions and the locations of political centers for the Muslim period but broadened the correlation to include economic centers as well. Calkins has one important reservation about his hypothesis—the large-scale sea trade that began to expand in the seventeenth century altered the configuration of the other subregions, placing greater economic emphasis on the Bhagirathi-Hugli subregion. "In one sense," said Calkins, "the significance of the location of Murshidabad is bound up with this expansion of European trade."[114] Witness the fact that "Murshidabad was chosen [as provincial capital] because it already was an important place (commercially) in 1700."[115]

One of the most original segments of the article was Calkins' account of the city of Maksusabad, which he contends was the name for the first town of Murshidabad. By the 1660s it was evidently headquarters for the district or *pargana*, and "the officers stationed there had jurisdiction over the growing center of European factories at Kassimbazar."[116] This kind of valuable historical reconstruction establishes Calkins as a gifted Bengal scholar genuinely interested in history. Using such sources as *Bengal Gazetteers*, European traveler reports, and diaries, Calkins amassed impressive evidence that "from the middle of the seventeenth century, then, Makhsusabad was situated at the crossroads of the major commercial route from southeast Bengal into North India, and on the route down the Bhagirathi-Hugli, and on to Europe or the Far East."[117] Not only was Murshidabad thus center of an economic as well as a political network. According to Calkins, "although the political and administrative role of the city has been emphasized in historical accounts, I suspect that the commercial city was of greater importance to the surrounding area."[118]

The papers on modern urban Bengal may not have been as original as those dealing with the medieval period, but they were equally good as scholarship and perhaps a little more daring conceptually. In "The Urbanized Intelligentsia of Calcutta and their Asian Counterparts in the Nineteenth Century," I made both a summary of my findings on the origin of a modernizing intelligentsia in Bengal and an attempt to test my generalizations about Bengal against other cases of Asian intelligentsia responding to varying kinds and degrees of Western intrusion. This article constituted the first venture among the Bengal group to compare any aspect of Bengal's culture and history with the outside world. If in the same volume Dimock and Inden were moving into Bengal ostensibly in search of a key to the discrete culture, I proceeded outward among the remainder of the human race, placing my new information on the Bengali-English encounter in the larger perspective of Asia's encounter with the West.

One of my conclusions in *British Orientalism and the Bengal Renaissance* was that the so-called nationalist wing of the Western-educated intelligentsia in Calcutta, which was relatively tradition-oriented and most concerned about maintaining an Indian identity, was as dynamic and progressive an elite as the westernized wing, which was inclined to disavow its heritage and tradition and to take on anglicized ways. In the same way that Orientalists offered a modernizing alternative to the westernization program of the Anglicists, so I argued, the protonationalist intelligentsia of the renaissance period offered a modernizing alternative to the xenophilia proposed by the westernized intelligentsia. The specific questions I raised were these: "Was it necessary to adopt the English language, religion, social system and political structure in order to modernize? Or was modernity less the forms and trappings of a given European cultural configuration and more a complex of universal processes that could be made to function in the same way when integrated into any existing tradition?"[119]

I defended the Bengali intellectuals who identified with "the tradition," arguing that in the first place "the tradition as a systematic arrangement of culture traits was the invention of sympathetic 'acculturated' Englishmen in interaction with Bengalis" and that this "so-called tradition was most frequently used dynamically as a means to promote change rather than apologetically as an end in itself."[120] In fact, I went on to say that "traditional reformers were as much antithetical to status quo Hinduism as were the extreme westernizers."[121] The question I now raised in the article was "how unique was the experience of the Calcutta intelligentsia in nineteenth-century Asia?"[122] My objective was "to compare and contrast the tradition-oriented modernizing intelligentsia in Calcutta with apparently comparable movements in Istanbul, Peking, and Hong Kong."[123] My method was to analyze their similarities and differences in four categories: patterns of Western intrusion, the social organization of a modernizing intellectual class, the modernizing activities of this new elite, and the development of their modernizing ideologies.

I found that, despite differences in patterns of Western intrusion (such as being directly ruled by Europeans as in Calcutta and Hong Kong or indirectly affected by European penetration as in Istanbul and Peking), a modernizing intelligentsia did develop in all cases and that it was divided along tradition-identifying and Western-identifying lines. This kind of comparative analysis showed a remarkable parallel—especially on the ideological plane—between Rammohun Roy in Bengal seeking to update Hinduism, Namuk Kemal among the Young Ottomans seeking to update Islam, and K'ang Yu-wei among the mandarin reformers seeking to reinterpret Confucianism along modern lines. A main conclusion was that:

> Faced with the tremendous power of the West on the one hand, and his own culture's impotence on the other, the modern professional intellectual of Asia invented cross-cultural blueprints designed to revitalize his own traditions. These blueprints, though they reveal much about the value systems of unique cultures in transformation, tell us just as much about the universality of this ideological function vis-à-vis Western intrusion. In other words, if on the one level, the intelligentsia employed the symbols of their own culture's value system, on another level the process of intellectual response seems to have been remarkably the same all over the non-Western world.[134]

John McLane's article, "Calcutta and the Mofussilization of Bengali Politics," was also about the Calcutta elite but not so much on their function as intelligentsia as on their function as politicians moving into the Bengali countryside after 1905 to mobilize rural support for the nationalist cause. McLane's acceptance and usage of the concept *bhadralok* was much like Broomfield's, and indeed the article was framed around the kinds of questions raised by Broomfield in his *Elite Conflict in a Plural Society*. Specifically, McLane took a single district—Bakarganj—to "illustrate the process of politicization in its most successful and exceptional form under the leadership of Aswini Kumar Dutt, Bengal's proto-Gandhi."[125] This attempt to mobilize the mofussil had many other manifestations besides recruiting peasantry. The Gandhian aspect led to a "glorification of the simple rural life, village uplift work, and revival of village industries."[126]

Underlying these events between 1905 and 1907, McLane argued, was a "critical dualism . . . within Bengali society itself, between the *bhadralok* and the non-*bhadralok*."[127] Besides being of the upper castes, the *bhadralok* were distinguished by their "preference for the literate professions and office jobs" precluding "any occupation involving manual labor."[128] Lack of social and political contact with the cultivators naturally placed the *bhadralok* at a great disadvantage in their campaign to mobilize rural support. To make matters worse, in East Bengal, where "Muslim communal consciousness was aroused by partition, Hindu *bhadralok,* in the absence of cross-cutting agrarian ties, were easily isolated from the Muslim peasantry."[129]

McLane in this article became the first to see the Swadeshi period, or at least its origins, not so much from the vantage point of Calcutta politics as from that of the mofussil. His dismal portrait of the Calcutta *bhadralok* turning in desperation to rural Bengal reminds us not only of Broomfield's work but of Blair Kling's as well. Lack of Bengali entrepreneurship and quite the reverse phenomenon among non-Bengalis had led by 1905 to "Bengali loss of control" and their own realization that they were "already irrelevant for much of Calcutta's life."[130] Said McLane: "Bengalis were in Calcutta but they were not where the power and money were."[131]

McLane argued that Bengalis felt themselves emasculated by the British and seized upon the partition of Bengal in 1905 to crystallize their anger and frustration against the foreign overlord. Undergoing a renewed crisis of identity, the *bhadralok* began to rediscover "symbols and institutions associated with rural life."[132] In the remainder of the article, McLane gave a detailed history of the *bhadralok* failure to "establish enduring links with the peasants."[133] Muslim hostility, *goonda* activity, and police brutality were among the chief obstacles to fulfilling that end. In a larger sense, "the 1905–1907 period was a phase in the prolonged, painful, and unresolved dilemma which rural India presents for the educated classes."[134] And, as McLane also concluded, the collapse of the movement was part of the overall collapse of the Swadeshi movement, "leaving the Hindu *bhadralok* more bitter, frustrated, divided, and threatened than they had been before 1905."[135]

In the same year of 1969 Rachel Van M. Baumer, in a special edition of *Books Abroad* devoted to Indian literature, wrote an article entitled "Sankar: Twentieth-Century *Kathak*." The importance of the article for Bengal studies was that it attempted to bridge the widening gap between medieval and modern Bengali literature as interpreted by traditionalists and modernists, respectively. She reprimanded medievalists for treating the Bengali literary tradition before 1800 as "something completely frozen in a particular pattern."[136] As for the modernists, she wrote: "By contrast, the modern literature (after 1800) is often thought of as being completely innovative and devoted to experimentation, having very little in common with the earlier body of literature."[137]

By analyzing the earlier novels of Moni Shankar Mukherji, otherwise known as Sankar (born 1933), Baumer was able to demonstrate that literary conventions of the medieval period persist in modern writers who are most adept in their "mastery of accommodation of new and old in a simple, yet captivating style."[138] This ability to integrate new and alien forms into indigenous literary traditions was not simply restricted to Sankar and to nineteenth- and twentieth-century Bengali writers; according to Baumer, "innovation and change are, in fact, important elements in Bengali literature in all ages."[139]

To the superficial observer, therefore, Sankar's novels might seem highly Western, but on closer analysis they represent a twentieth-century version of the medieval *kathak* or storytelling tradition of Bengal. The significance of this approach and method cannot be minimized. For one thing, Baumer restored historical perspective to Bengali literature by demonstrating change as well as continuity of a given tradition. On the one hand, she has moved away from the one-dimensional view of the anglophiles who judged all modern Bengali literature from the vantage point of British influence; on the other hand, she has moved away from the one-dimensional view of the medievalists who have tended to judge Bengali literature as cultural purists denying the relevance of growth by synthesis. It should come as no surprise, therefore, that in Sankar's work the problem of identity should be paramount. When the intelligentsia seek to modernize their culture's traditions, literary or otherwise, some sort of identity crisis seems inevitable.

In 1969–1970, Stephen Hay's monograph on Tagore was published as *Asian Ideas of East and West.* Hay's interests had changed considerably over the years: from Bengal to Gujarat, from Rammohun and Rabindranath to Gandhi, and from social thought to an examination of the individual psyche. Though the book did constitute a comparative study or cross-cultural history of Tagore and his critics in Japan, China, and India, Hay carefully refrained from any elaborate methodological schemes taken from history or the social sciences. Hay's basic framework still remained Asian intellectual response to Western influences, although he had tried to probe deeper into the relevant Asian cultures per se. This set of perspectives on the Asian intelligentsia established Hay as a historian of ideas. As he put it, "I have tried to reconstruct what I have variously called their intellectual landscape, their thought-world, or the structure, spectrum, movement, currents, or universe of their ideas."[140]

But aside from intellectual history, Hay found another perspective even more important: "to see each individual thinker as a study in himself, as an independent agent with a unique life history and world view."[141] To achieve this, he had tried "to plumb the depths of each man's psyche—correlating the historical and contemporary development of his family, region, and country in the political and the cultural realms, on the one hand, and his own psychological development and impact on his society and culture on the other."[142] Hay made it clear that he had turned away sharply from "simplistic theorizing about historical 'forces,' or 'movements' such as 'nationalism.' "[143] There was a danger in the overuse of such concepts:

They can conceal the incalculable diversity of human experience behind a facade of plausible half-truths, and by conveying a brilliant illusion of certainty can discourage that tentative but persistent groping for more reliable generalizations about the real world which is the heart and soul of scientific work. . . . To this end I ask that my readers approach with caution the concept of "revitalization" of cultural traditions on which I have placed some emphasis. The phenomenon to which it refers is not the operation of some abstract and impersonal "historical force" but the free activity of unique human beings living in specific environments and personal circumstances.[144]

In considering that Hay chose to write on more than eighty Chinese, Japanese, and Indian intellectuals, depicting each as an individual, it is understandable why he has underscored his justification for what may be called the psycho-history of ideas. Moreover this was no mere intellectual history of Tagore, or of Bengal, or of India, but of East Asia as well. The method for writing this kind of comparative intellectual history was to replace the usual focal point of Western impact with Tagore's own ideology, to which Asian intellectuals responded. By so doing, Asian intellectuals expressed their attitudes, values, and ideas on their own traditions, on Asian unity, and on the positive and negative features of Western intrusion.

It was perhaps unfortunate that in the only monograph done by an American on Tagore to date, so little emphasis was placed on Rabindranath's immediate Bengali environment, either as shaping the young man as a prophet or as interacting with the poet as a mature man. Though Hay became the third American writing on a Bengal theme to win the Watumull Prize, his works have not so much illumined aspects of Bengali society as they have dealt with individual personalities and their work. In his first chapter, "The Making of a Modern Prophet," Hay simply reviewed those features of the Bengal renaissance which seem to have shaped Tagore's ideas of East and West. It undoubtedly served as a good survey of background material on Tagore for understanding what followed in the 1920s—at least from Hay's point of view of what was most relevant about Tagore's ideology in that decade. But it ignored the ambivalence between nationalism and universalism in the quest for identity, a vital part of the Brahmo ideological legacy which Tagore imbibed through his family. It is curious that in a book on psycho-history Hay should have ignored Rabindranath's identity crisis: he said little or nothing about the Swadeshi phase in the poet's life when he sought to resolve his nationalist-universalist ambivalence with the writing of his best novel, *Gora*.

Instead, Hay chose to explore in great detail and from every perspective what he believed to have been Tagore's core concept in his thought on

East and West. The West represented materialism while India or the East (they were apparently synonymous in Tagore's mind, according to Hay) "was distinguished by spiritual profundity."[145] Hay found this notion to have been important among the Bengal intelligentsia, and retraced its development from Rammohun through Keshub to Vivekananda, Aurobindo, and Rabindranath. Indeed, of all the ideas selected, reinterpreted, and synthesized from both Indian and Western sources throughout the renaissance period, Hay argued that this one was most significant. Nevertheless, even when articulated by Tagore, it was rejected in Bengal:

> But the synthesis he proposed between Indian or Eastern spirituality and Western material civilization was criticized increasingly in the twentieth century by younger men, at first because their nationalist bias demanded political equality with the British, and later because their secular world view denied validity to the realm of the spiritual.[146]

In 1970, Barrie Morrison's work on ancient Bengali history was published as *Political Centers and Culture Regions in Early Bengal*. Morrison's was a highly specialized and technical work, the achievement of a pioneer archaeologist who is exuberant about listing and organizing all available data but who is modest about hypotheses and generalizations. His main discovery, as already pointed out in discussing his article for *Bengal Regional Identity*, was in determining the four subregions of ancient Bengal. In the book he not only filled in the details but lucidly described how he went about dating and locating the inscriptions and their appearance and organization. As a historian-archaeologist, Morrison confirmed the general chronological scheme for pre-Muslim Bengali history from an analysis of seventy-one engraved copper plates and one engraved stone slab. Thus there was Bengal under the Guptas (A.D. 400–600), when the territory was tightly organized under a larger empire and transfer procedures were similar in Bengal to those elsewhere in the empire. Between the sixth and eighth centuries Bengal "was fragmented into local rulers and dynasties."[147] In the ninth century Pala influences were distinct, whereas in the twelfth century the Senas displaced the Palas. By the thirteenth century the Muslims predominated and the "older Hindu and Buddhist dynasties were destroyed or disappeared."[148]

A third significant scholarly effort to appear in 1970 was an article in the *Journal of Asian Studies* by Philip Calkins: "The Formation of a Regionally Oriented Ruling Group in Bengal, 1700–1740." Calkins was dealing with an important though relatively ignored period when the all-India Mogul empire was beginning to disintegrate into regional kingdoms. The article was a well-constructed history of the Bengali elite between Aurangzebe's death and the rise of an independent Bengal under Alivardi

Khan. Calkins asked whether the decay of Mogul India meant also—as often implied—a decay in the provinces. His own research indicated that although "some sort of decay is evident in the political life of the provincial governments . . . in Bengal high standards of administrative efficiency were maintained."[149]

For Bengal specialists the article's worth lies in Calkins' discussion of the changing elite structure during the period under consideration. In the seventeenth century the Mogul system was still highly centralized and viable, with the result that however much power the indigenous landlords may have had locally in their position as zemindars, the government officials or *mansabdar* controlled the zemindars. But in the eighteenth century the *mansabdari* position weakened, primarily because they had much less support from the center. Calkins demonstrated how the need for more revenue for the center led to detailed surveys of existing holdings and a squeeze on zemindars "to bring payments up to the required level or lose the zemindari to the government or to money lenders."[150]

By 1727 the fifteen largest zemindars were responsible for almost half the revenue of the province. Gradually banking houses such as the Jagat Seths came into power who not only supported the governor but earned considerable interest on loans to zemindars who could not pay their revenue. In the 1730s the power of the governor declined while that of the large zemindars and bankers increased. It was their combined power which brought Alivardi Khan to the governorship in 1739. A year later Bengal was virtually independent from the center. One of Calkins' important conclusions was that this coalition of interests "continued to govern Bengal until the military intervention of the British began to destroy the system."[151]

In 1971, Marcus Franda published his second monograph, *Radical Politics in West Bengal*, which constituted the first effort by an American specialist of the delta region to go beyond the era of nationalist politics under Congress leadership to the rise of communism. Because the communist movement in Bengal had achieved great power and influence, the subject was naturally vital and meaningful for understanding contemporary events. A topic like this one could be treated in some wider context (such as international diplomacy). Or the subject could be treated by a Bengal specialist as a means for understanding modern Bengal rather than using Bengal to understand modern communism.

Franda's work, though it could be used for the latter purpose, was clearly designed to accomplish the former. For one thing, as with his first book, Franda was dealing with regionalism; it was Bengali communism that he concerned himself with almost exclusively and it was about Bengali communism that his conclusions were framed. In fact one of his important questions was this: Why have Bengalis been so active in the communist movement while other Indians have for the most part sought alternative outlets for political expression and participation?"[152] Moreover, Franda brought to the book his eleven years of accumulated knowledge of Bengal and the scholarly work of other Bengal specialists which combined to give the monograph cultural authenticity and scholarly stature similar in its contribution to Bengal studies to the MIT Studies on Communism, Revisionism, and Revolution.

From the very start, under "Party Leadership: Sources of Elite Recruitment," Franda placed the radical left in Bengal in the social context of the *bhadralok* and in the cultural context of the Bengal renaissance. The elite from which "the Bengali Communist and Marxist Left parties have drawn their leadership (and much of their following) is the Bengali *bhadralok*, an elite that is unique to the Bengali-speaking area."[153] In the nineteenth century this elite "experienced a cultural renaissance . . . that placed Bengal firmly in the forefront of almost all Indian associational life."[154] In the manner of Broomfield, Franda has characterized this grouping as a "privileged minority most often drawn from the three highest castes . . . very well educated, very proud of their language, their literacy, and their history."[155]

Franda seemed too much a specialist of Bengal to hypothesize that the Bengali communist movement was simply an adjunct of the Moscow and Peking variety, but he was too much a political scientist to view the movement as simply a manifestation of a unique and closed cultural system with no essential relationship to foreign sources. Thus Franda continued the Bengal studies modernist technique of framing problems around the theme of culture contact and acculturation. His communist leaders, leaders in contact with Russian and Chinese communists, seem to be an extension of the *bhadralok* function of a century ago of using Englishmen as "windows to the West."

For example, there was a direct relationship between the origins of the communist movement in Bengal in 1921 and the Soviet Comintern. The generation of nationalists who joined the communist movement from the 1930s were encouraged to do so "by older members who had been in contact with international communism since 1921."[156] External considerations that centered about Russia's struggle for survival against Nazi Germany prompted Communist Party of India members of join "with the British government in support of the Allied war effort."[157]

In more recent times, the major factional split within the Communist Party of India, which brought into being the Communist Party Marxist in April 1964, was in large part occasioned by Bengali response to the growing Sino-Soviet ideological rift and to the Chinese invasion of India in

1962. The creation of a third communist party in Bengal, the Communist Party Marxist-Leninist in April 1969, though occasioned by an internal event known as the Naxalbari movement, was nevertheless based also on an ideological response to Mao's indictment of the Communist Party Marxist for abandoning guerrilla-style revolutionary struggle in favor of participation in the electoral process.

Franda maintained a good balance in his analysis of the interaction between the "internal" pressures of Bengali society, culture, and history and the "external" pressures of foreign ideological, political, and military considerations and events. For Franda, as evidenced in his final chapter, "Communism in a Bengali Environment," the indigenous environment was not merely caste, kin, and the pool of religious symbols but also the historical situation of twentieth-century Bengal itself. Like Kling, Broomfield, McLane, and others, Franda saw contemporary Bengal as an essentially tragic place broken by a long series of catastrophes. Thus Franda saw partitions, refugees, famines, communal riots, and general political and economic decline as very real cultural or environmental factors. In fact they constituted the most pressing "internal" source of Bengali communism:

> The sources of Bengali communism are primarily regional, being intimately related to the decline of Bengal in this century and to the Bengali search for a new regional identity and regional political power. The ability of the Bengali revolutionaries to adapt communism and Marxism to their own regional traditions and perceived political needs explains their high level of involvement with communist and Marxist ideas, despite the absence of such involvement in most parts of India.[158]

EPILOGUE

After less than a decade of scholarship, it is too early to draw conclusions about Bengal studies in the United States. If one judges from the richness and variety of fields pursued by the Bengal specialists, the clarity in defining the issues between them, and the quality of their scholarship, then support for promoting area studies in South Asia has served a positive purpose. It is evident in this review that neither regional parochialism nor academic gamesmanship resulted from the area studies emphasis in the United States during the 1960s.

And there is every indication that the 1970s will see even greater development in Bengal studies—either along lines set by Dimock, Hay, and Weiner or along new lines of investigation. Of great importance to this development are the younger scholars who are attacking old problems with a new vigor and reinterpreting them according to fresh perspectives.

Recent dissertations and papers at seminars and conferences suggest both a continuity of themes and a change in which entirely different lines of inquiry are being followed. Religious modernism in the context of Bengali renaissance and nationalism, for example, is currently being researched by Alexander Lipski (neo-Vaiṣṇava movement), David Kopf (Brahmo Samaj), and Barbara Southard (Ramakrishna Mission). Also related to this "subculture" within Bengal studies is the dissertation by Geraldine Forbes on the positivist movement in Bengal. Rachel Van M. Baumer's close analysis of Vidyasagar's innovations in Bengali language and literature should prove significant from the vantage point of literary modernization. The Bengal uniquists are presently at work applying the concepts of Lévi-Strauss to the region, and one looks for imaginative results in the 1970s—particularly from such anthropologists as Ralph Nicholas, Ronald Inden, and Akosh Oster. One new area which has been relatively neglected is that of the Bengali Muslim. The creation of Bangladesh has radically changed that situation, and one can now look forward to studies dealing more with East than West Bengal and more with Bengali Islam than with Bengali Hinduism.

NOTES

1. The title representing this kind of literature is from V. Mehta, "City of Dreadful Night," *New Yorker*, XXXXVI (21 March 1970), pp. 47–112.
2. J. Lelyveld, "Can India Survive Calcutta?" *New York Times Magazine* (13 October 1968), pp. 56–84.
3. E. Dimock, "Preface," in *Bengal: Literature and History* (East Lansing: Michigan State University, 1967), pp. 2–3.
4. Ibid., p. 3.
5. Ibid.
6. Ibid.
7. Ibid., p. 4.
8. D. Kopf, "Preface," in *Bengal: Regional Identity* (East Lansing: Michigan State University, 1969), p. i.
9. E. Dimock, *The Thief of Love* (Chicago: University of Chicago Press, 1963), p. ix.
10. Ibid.
11. Ibid., p. x.
12. Ibid., p. 2.
13. Ibid.
14. Ibid., p. 5.
15. S. Hay, "Western and Indigenous Elements in Modern Indian Thought: The Case of Rammohun Roy," in *Changing Japanese Attitudes Toward Modernization* (Princeton: Princeton University Press, 1965), p. 311.
16. Ibid., p. 313.
17. Ibid.
18. Ibid.
19. Ibid.

20.   Ibid., pp. 313–314.
21.   Ibid., p. 314.
22.   Ibid., p. 325.
23.   Ibid., p. 328.
24.   E. Dimock, *The Place of the Hidden Moon* (Chicago: University of Chicago Press, 1966), pp. 2–3.
25.   Ibid., p. 3.
26.   Ibid., p. 4.
27.   Ibid., p. 5.
28.   Ibid., p. 2.
29.   Ibid., p. 16.
30.   B. Kling, *The Blue Mutiny* (Philadelphia: University of Pennsylvania Press, Press), p. 220.
31.   Ibid., p. 222.
32.   R. Inden, "The Hindu Chiefdom in Middle Bengali Literature," in *Bengal: Literature and History* (East Lansing: Michigan State University, 1967), p. 22.
33.   Ibid., p. 25.
34.   Ibid., p. 41.
35.   Ibid.
36.   Ibid.
37.   Ibid., p. 42.
38.   Ibid.
39.   D. Kopf, "The Dimensions of Literature as an Analytical Tool for the Study of Bengal," ibid., p. 107.
40.   Ibid., pp. 116–117.
41.   W. Gunderson, "Modernization and Cultural Change: The Self-Image and World-View of the Bengal Intelligentsia as Found in the Writings of the Mid-Nineteenth Century, 1830–1870," ibid., p. 127.
42.   Ibid.
43.   Ibid., p. 128.
44.   Ibid., p. 133.
45.   Ibid., p. 135.
46.   Ibid., pp. 149–150.
47.   R. Van M. Baumer, "Communal Attitudes in the Nineteenth and Twentieth Centuries," ibid., p. 96.
48.   Ibid.
49.   Ibid., p. 98.
50.   Ibid., p. 101.
51.   J. Broomfield, *Elite Conflict in a Plural Society* (Berkeley: University of California Press, 1968), pp. 5–6.
52.   R. Nicholas, "Structures of Politics in the Villages of Southern Asia," in *Structure and Change in Indian Society*, eds. M. Singer and B. Cohn (Chicago: Aldine Press, 1968), p. 243.
53.   Ibid., p. 245.
54.   Ibid., p. 248.
55.   Ibid.
56.   Ibid.
57.   Ibid.
58.   Ibid., p. 280.
59.   M. Franda, *West Bengal and the Federalizing Process in India* (Princeton:

Princeton University Press, 1968), p. 10.

60.   Ibid., p. 18.

61.   Ibid., p. 222.

62.   Ibid., p. 223.

63.   D. Kopf, *British Orientalism and the Bengal Renaissance* (Berkeley: University of California Press, 1969), p. 275.

64.   B. Morrison, "Region and Subregion in Pre-Muslim Bengal," in *Bengal: Regional Identity*, p. 4.

65.   Ibid., p. 5.

66.   Ibid., p. 13.

67.   Ibid.

68.   Ibid.

69.   Ibid.

70.   Ibid.

71.   Ibid., p. 14.

72.   E. Dimock, "Muslim Vaisnava Poets of Bengal," ibid., p. 24.

73.   Ibid., p. 25.

74.   Ibid., p. 30.

75.   Ibid.

76.   R. Nicholas, "Vaisnavism and Islam in Rural Bengal," ibid., p. 33.

77.   Ibid., p. 36.

78.   Ibid., p. 40.

79.   Ibid., p. 41.

80.   Ibid.

81.   Ibid., p. 45.

82.   Ibid., p. 40.

83.   Ibid., p. 45.

84.   Ibid.

85.   Ibid.

86.   R. Van M. Baumer, "Bankimcandra's View of the Role of Bengal in Indian Civilization," ibid., p. 62.

87.   Ibid.

88.   Ibid., p. 64.

89.   Ibid., p. 65.

90.   Ibid.

91.   Ibid., p. 70.

92.   B. Kling, "Entrepreneurship and Regional Identity in Bengal," ibid., p. 75.

93.   Ibid.

94.   Ibid.

95.   Ibid.

96.   Ibid., p. 76.

97.   Ibid.

98.   Ibid., p. 78.

99.   Ibid.

100.   Ibid., p. 81.

101.   L. Gordon, "Bengal's Gandhi: A Study in Modern Indian Regionalism, Politics, and Thought," ibid., p. 87.

102.   Ibid., p. 95.

103.   Ibid., p. 105.

104.   Ibid., p. 106.

105.   Ibid., p. 90.
106.   Ibid., pp. 114–115.
107.   R. Park, "Preface," in *Urban Bengal* (East Lansing: Michigan State University Press, 1969), p. i.
108.   E. Dimock and R. Inden, "The City in Pre-British Bengal," ibid., p. 6.
109.   Ibid.
110.   Ibid.
111.   Ibid.
112.   Ibid., p. 14.
113.   P. Calkins, "The Role of Murshidabad as a Regional and Subregional Center in Bengal," ibid., p. 19.
114.   Ibid., p. 21.
115.   Ibid., p. 22.
116.   Ibid., p. 23.
117.   Ibid., p. 24.
118.   Ibid., p. 27.
119.   D. Kopf, "The Urbanized Intelligentsia of Calcutta and Their Asian Counterparts in the Nineteenth Century," ibid., p. 32.
120.   Ibid., p. 32.
121.   Ibid.
122.   Ibid.
123.   Ibid.
124.   Ibid., p. 42.
125.   J. McLane, "Calcutta and the Mofussilization of Bengali Politics," ibid., p. 63.
126.   Ibid.
127.   Ibid., p. 64.
128.   Ibid.
129.   Ibid.
130.   Ibid., p. 66.
131.   Ibid.
132.   Ibid.
133.   Ibid., p. 81.
134.   Ibid., p. 80.
135.   Ibid., p. 81.
136.   R. Van M. Baumer, "Sankar: Twentieth-Century Kathak," *Books Abroad*, XXXXVI (Autumn 1969), p. 487.
137.   Ibid.
138.   Ibid., p. 489.
139.   Ibid., p. 487.
140.   S. Hay, *Asian Ideas of East and West* (Cambridge: Harvard University Press, 1969), p. vii.
141.   Ibid., pp. vii–viii.
142.   Ibid., p. viii.
143.   Ibid.
144.   Ibid.
145.   Ibid., p. 21.
146.   Ibid., p. 263.
147.   B. Morrison, *Political Centers and Culture Regions in Early Bengal* (Tucson: University of Arizona Press, 1970), p. 15.

148.   Ibid., p. 16.
149.   P. Calkins, "The Formation of a Regionally Oriented Ruling Group in Bengal, 1700–1740," *Journal of Asian Studies*, XXIX (August 1970), p. 799.
150.   Ibid., p. 803.
151.   Ibid., p. 806.
152.   M. R. Franda, *Radical Politics in West Bengal* (Cambridge: M.I.T. Press, 1971), p. 3.
153.   Ibid., p. 7.
154.   Ibid.
155.   Ibid.
156.   Ibid., p. 20.
157.   Ibid., p. 29.
158.   Ibid., pp. 268–269.

Index

Adi Brahmo Samaj. *See* Brahmo Samaj
Adi Brahmos. *See* Brahmo Samaj
Adi Samaj. *See* Brahmo Samaj
anglicization, 47, 100, 111, 157–161, 164–165, 173–174, 229
anti-Brahmo movement, 68–69
anti-Hindu criticism, 109–111. *See also* Young Bengal
ashrāf, 8–10
Badruddin Tyabju, 155
banian, 28, 29
Bankimacandra Chatterji, 91–93, 95, 96, 121; attitude toward Hindus and British, 121–122; definition of dharma, 93–94; and Kali, 124–125; and Krishna, 123–124; reinterpretation of Vaisnavism, 125; and religion as a key, 122–123; theme of Hindu nationalism, 91–92
Basu, Rajnarian, 50–53, 56, 62, 65, 66
Baumer, Rachel van M., 82–98, 100, 202, 212–213, 222–223, 231–232
Bengal, history of, 7–8, 26–29, 178–180; colonial status of, 33. *See also* East Bengal; West Bengal
Bengal Congress of 1918, 133, 138
Bengal Congress movement, 151–153
Bengal Hindu Sabha, 140
Bengal Legislative Council, 134
Bengal Provincial Congress Committee, 138–139
Bengal Studies, 202
Bengali Hindu upper castes, 15, 17, 60, 119, 136, 173, 195; disunity of, 140; traditional morality of, 21–23, 209, 211, 213. *See also* Bengal Hindu Sabha
Bengali merchant class, 27–28, 38–39
Bengali nationalism, 27, 45, 46, 57, 67, 210, 223; divisive effect of Brahmo intellectuals, 53; flourished, 141; unification destroyed, 142
Bengali renaissance, 43, 51, 56, 65, 109, 121, 174, 211, 217–218, 236

bhadralok, 27, 148–150, 162, 173–174, 206, 213–214, 215, 222, 230–231, 236; defined, 143–144; dominance of, 150
Brahmans, 6, 121
Brahmo Samaj, 44, 47, 89–90, 113, 115, 137, 164, 166; Adi Brahmo Samaj, 56–58, 60, 63, 65, 67, 116–117, 121; Adi Brahmos, 56, 58, 60, 61, 65, 67, 70; and split with Keshubites, 62, 72; attacked, 117; emulation-solidarity conflict of, 114–115; offering a reformed Vedantism, 47–50; Sadharan Brahmo Samaj, 64, 90, 126, 168; and social reforms, 53–54, 65, 90–91, 117, 166; and the Tagore family, 47; Tattvabodhini Sabha, 47, 75n, 115
Brahmos, as distinct legal entity (not reformed Hindus), 63, 117, 163–164; emulation-solidarity conflict of, 116, 117; first church of, 59–60; as Hindus, 20, 62–63, 115, 163–164; marriages of, 61–62, 163–164, 170; unity split, 53–54, 56–57; weaknesses of, 50–51; Western influence of, 18, 20, 47, 51–52, 53, 61, 115, 118, 165–166
bhakti, 124–125; Bankimcandra's view of, 95; and priti, 94–95
British, attitude toward Westernized Bengalis, 118–119, 120–121; in Bengal, 7, 134–135, 208; commercial activity in Bengal, 27–29, 35; discrimination against Hindu nationalists, 136, 153; and Indian cooperation, 26–27, 28, 29, 34, 104–105, 224; influence of, 22–23, 85–86, 152–153; Orientalists, 44, 46, 100, 106, 108–110, 114, 210, 218–219; rule of preferred by Indians, 34, 160–161
British governors general, 31–32, 109, 181
British Indian Association, 134, 135, 166–167
Broomfield, John, 132–146, 202, 213
Calcutta, as acculturation center, 44, 99,

243

Orders for Asian Studies at Hawaii publications should be directed to The University Press of Hawaii, 2840 Kolowalu Street, Honolulu, Hawaii 96822. Present standing orders will continue to be filled without special notification.

Asian Studies at Hawaii

No. 1 *Bibliography of English Language Sources on Human Ecology, Eastern Malaysia and Brunei.* Compiled by Conrad P. Cotter with the assistance of Shiro Saito. Two parts. September 1965. (Available only from Paragon Book Gallery, New York.)

No. 2 *Economic Factors in Southeast Asian Social Change.* Robert Van Niel, editor. May 1968. Out of print.

No. 3 *East Asian Occasional Papers (1).* Harry J. Lamley, editor. May 1969.

No. 4 *East Asian Occasional Papers (2).* Harry J. Lamley, editor. July 1970.

No. 5 *A Survey of Historical Source Materials in Java and Manila.* Robert Van Niel. February 1971.

No. 6 *Educational Theory in the People's Republic of China: The Report of Ch'ien Chung-Jui.* Translation by John N. Hawkins. May 1971. Out of print.

No. 7 *Hai Jui Dismissed from Office.* Wu Han. Translation by C. C. Huang. June 1972.

No. 8 *Aspects of Vietnamese History.* Edited by Walter F. Vella. March 1973.

No. 9 *Southeast Asian Literatures in Translation: A Preliminary Bibliography.* Philip N. Jenner. March 1973.

No. 10 *Textiles of the Indonesian Archipelago.* Garrett and Bronwen Solyom. October 1973.

No. 11 *British Policy and the Nationalist Movement in Burma, 1917–1937.* Albert D. Moscotti. February 1974.